I0064002

PREACTIVE LEADERSHIP

Also by Owen Allen

Weatherization Production Control

Personal Profile Labs

Management Power the Specific Action Way

Personality Power the Specific Action Way

Master of Personal Excellence Program

The Specific Action Management System

The Specific Action Personality System

PREACTIVE LEADERSHIP

*Three Actions that Can Double Your Leadership
Ability in One Week—Whether You're Leading a
Corporation, Civic Club, Church, Government
Agency, Family, or Yourself*

OWEN ALLEN

MANAGEMENT HOUSE BOOKS
Denver, Colorado

MANAGEMENT HOUSE BOOKS
Denver, Colorado

PREACTIVE LEADERSHIP

Copyright © 2012 by J. Owen Allen, Ph.D.

All rights reserved. Except as permitted under the U.S. Copyright Act of 1976, no portion of this book may be reproduced, stored in a database or retrieval system, distributed, or transmitted in any form or by any means— electronic, mechanical, photocopy, recording, scanning, or other—except for brief quotations in critical reviews or articles, without the prior written permission of the publisher.

Management House Books is an imprint of Specific Action Corporation, publisher, PO Box 19125, Greensboro, NC 27419-9125. Published by arrangement with Lightning Tree Creative Media, Denver, CO 80237.

For information on custom editions, special sales, corporation purchases, or bulk purchases for educational, business, fund-raising, or sales promotions purposes, email info@managementhousebooks.com.

SAN 687-4894

ISBN 978-0-932569-03-5

Book design by Lightning Tree Creative Media

Printed in the United States of America

For Joanna

A thousand poets dreamed a thousand dreams,
and then you were born, my love.

Contents

Part III   The Three Ineffective-Inefficient Situations

Part IV   Leadership Strategy and Tactics

Appendix

Author's Note

It's a definite pleasure to be able to write a personal note for a book that was first written 40 years ago. The first version of this book was written in 1971, and early versions of it were read by thousands of leaders in the United States, Canada, Mexico, and several European and Asian countries.

Earlier versions of this book were used as texts in the countless seminars I taught worldwide, and writing this author's note reminds me of many unforgettable people, exotic places, and strange happenings. I remember the time I taught a four-day seminar to only three participants because the other twenty attendees cancelled. I remember the time I taught a seminar in Alabama in August with no air conditioning. I also remember the time en route to a seminar in New York when I slipped on the ice and fell down a flight of stairs with my luggage on top of me. And I still smile about the time I left my keys at the hotel and had to get my notes out of my briefcase by breaking it open in the seminar room while the participants watched and laughed.

Teaching leadership seminars has its mental challenges, too. Such as the time I was bumped off of a night flight, and had to teach in Hilton Head, South Carolina the next morning with only thirty minutes of sleep, and the night in rural Pennsylvania when I was so tired from teaching all week that I forgot to claim my luggage at the airport, and had to drive back in the wee hours of the morning to retrieve it.

But above all, I remember my seminar participants. I remember their changed careers, their promotions, and their excitement as they realized that efficient leadership really is possible. I remember the client company that did a survey and discovered that each of my seminars saved them an average of $50,000. I remember the trainee I met in an airport five years after his seminar who could still quote the cases and jokes I used in his session, and I remember the young assistant supervisor who walked out of my seminar one afternoon, went back to his assembly line, used techniques he'd just learned, solved a trouble that had haunted his plant for four years—and got promoted—all in 15 minutes.

But looking back over the early editions of this book, what I mostly feel is gratitude. I feel gratitude for the hundreds of training directors in the dozens of Fortune 500 companies who hired me; and for the thousands of executives, managers, and supervisors who sat, worked, and laughed as I showed them the secrets of effective leadership.

I want to acknowledge Larry Earwood, Tom Ryberg, Roland McAbee, Lee Spratt, Larry Neely, Lewis Morris, Andy Symmes, Lee Wilsman, Justice Tucker, Rose Lanning, Dave Adams, Sid Sidland, Hank Metzger, Rock Batey, Rod O'Conner, Jim Ervin, Tony DelSignorie, John Cinelli, Jay Wenberg, Dave Hirst, and the dozens of other executives—too many to name here—who have scheduled participants for my seminars all these many years.

But now it's *your* turn to join the long line of men and women who've opened the covers of this book to improve their jobs, careers, and lives. Let's get your adventure started.

J. Owen Allen, Ph.D.
Palm Beach, Florida
Jude 24

Introduction

et's start your adventure with this statement: *Preactive* leadership is easy. It's fun. It pays well. And the icing on the cake is that you don't have to be highly educated, highly intelligent, highly connected, or even highly aggressive to be a *Preactive* leader. (You *can* be those things—if they happen to be you—but you don't *have* to be those things.) The leadership techniques in this book are simple. Most of them are common sense. Anyone can learn them. Anyone can use them. And anyone can get promotions with them.

In my author's note, I mentioned a young assistant supervisor who solved a four year old trouble on his assembly line and got promoted in 15 minutes. He was about 20 years of age and had a high school education. He was a new assistant supervisor on one of the assembly lines in a northeastern U.S. plant, and the only reason he was in my seminar was that he was a substitute for a more senior manager who was ill.

I noticed the young man because he was so shy. He said little and kept his eyes lowered. But I could tell he was listening because he often picked up his pen and made notes on his pad. My training contract with that plant was completed that particular afternoon, and as I dismissed the employees for the last time, I saw the young man jump to his feet, gather his belongings, and hurry from the room. I assumed he was anxious to get back to work and thought little of it. I began packing my briefcase, while answering final questions and shaking hands with well-wishers.

About 15 minutes passed, and as I was turning off the lights in the training room, I saw the young assistant supervisor striding back toward me with a big smile on his face. Walking beside him was his superior (who had also been a participant in the seminar). The superior was wearing a big grin, too. The two walked up to me, and the young man said shyly, "Well, I did it."

I looked at him in surprise and said, "Did what?"

He answered, "What you said in class."

His superior interrupted and blurted out, "He went back to his assembly line, and used cause-finding on a repeater we've had for four years! Nobody else in the plant could do it. Not even the engineers. I promoted him on the spot. Meet the new *supervisor* of assembly line four!"

I looked at the young man and said, "That's wonderful! But exactly what did you do?"

"Oh," he answered, "only what you said in class. I had a Current Trouble on my line that was a repeater. I found the critical change, found and verified the True Cause, took the best Correcting Action, and then told my boss what I'd done." (You'll learn the meanings of all these new terms in future pages.)

The superior beamed and nodded in agreement. We did more handshaking and backslapping, and they returned to work. I drove my rental car back to the airport, and flew on to my next seminar. Since my contract with that plant was fulfilled that day, I never went back. But I'll always remember the shy young assistant supervisor who got promoted in 15 minutes.

Now—what's the lesson in this story? Let's talk about how you can be rewarded, too.

The Rewards of Preactive Leadership

This book shows you how to be a *Preactive* leader, regardless of who you are or what you do. It shows you how you can double your leadership ability in only one week, whether you're leading a corporation, civic club, church, government agency, family, or yourself. How's that possible? It's possible because the practical, hands-on techniques in this book work, and they work equally well in every field of human endeavor. That's why the young assistant supervisor in our story was able to do what he did. (By the way, the only reason I remember the young assistant supervisor so clearly is that his story was dramatic. But the techniques he used *aren't* dramatic. I've seen seminar graduates use them on the job hundreds of times.)

Now, how can this book help you?

A lot of flowery answers come to mind—empowerment, self-actualization, life enrichment, satisfaction, personal fulfillment, helping others, and similar terms. But one of the leadership principles you'll learn in this book is to always keep things *simple*. So let's keep our discussion of these techniques simple.

If you use the techniques in this book, you'll be rewarded. Great contributions in the efficiency and effectiveness of projects earn great rewards, and great rewards take many forms. They can come in the shape of bonuses, promotions, pay raises, bigger titles, bigger offices, and more responsibility. Or they can come in the shape of less stress, deeper personal satisfaction, more peace of mind, better relationships, and sounder sleep at night. But one thing is certain. You *will* be rewarded if you use the techniques of *Preactive* leadership in your personal life, on your job, and in your family.

Let's say that another way.

I try to be practical, and I try to keep my teaching practical. The word *practical* means capable of being put into effect. So here's the truth. Some leadership classes and leadership books aren't very practical. Yes, they're filled with colorful stories, illustrations, cartoons, discussions, checklists, homework questions, charts, and graphs. Yes, they're filled with tales of famous people doing famous things in famous places. And don't misunderstand me, audiences and readers can be entertained and even draw some interesting conclusions from such classes and books.

But to be deathbed honest, how *practical* are those lessons? How often do the graduates of those seminars—and the readers of those books—go back to their private lives and use the lessons to increase effectiveness, efficiency, and quality in their jobs, relationships, and families? Not too often. But that's what being *practical* requires. So, the purpose of this book is to show you how to be a more practical leader in your own life; and thus now to get more personal rewards from being a more practical leader. Okay, but how do we start being practical? That question leads us to the theme of the book.

Our Theme

In the simplest terms, to be a *Preactive* leader, all you need to do is focus on *Preaction* in your job and life—instead of *Reaction*. The word "Preaction" is a word I coined many years ago. It's still not in any formal dictionary that I know of. What does it mean? We'll define it more fully in coming chapters but, briefly, "Preaction" means *to accomplish as much as possible in your life and on your job without seeing any trouble in your tasks.*

Think about that a second.

In fact, I often say the motto of *Preactive* leadership is: *Lead in the absence of trouble.* (Not in the presence of trouble.) The prefix "pre" refers to something that comes *before* something else. So "Preaction" refers to action taken *before* you see trouble in your work or life. A *Preactive* leader doesn't react to trouble. He or she preacts to trouble.

That last sentence sounds a little odd the first time you read it, I know, but it makes perfect sense when you think about it. Let's say it another way. Since *Preactive* leadership prevents trouble in tasks, it makes you more effective and efficient as a parent, plumber, pilot, priest, or whatever your role in life happens to be.

> ## Preaction
> *To accomplish as much as possible in your life and on your job without seeing any trouble in your tasks.*

But let's slow down here to define the words "effective" and "efficient." *Effectiveness* is the degree to which you *achieve* your goals. It's the degree to which you accomplish the desired end-results in your life and tasks. But since *trouble* keeps us from reaching goals, trouble makes us ineffective, and that's why we want to prevent it.

Efficiency is different. It's the degree to which you **avoid** waste. It's the degree to which you pursue your life and tasks without wasted time, money, or materials. But since *trouble* makes us wasteful, trouble makes us inefficient, and that's the second reason we want to prevent it. Preventing trouble makes us more effective and more efficient, and that's why *Preactive* leadership is all about preventing trouble.

Now, what's the big message in these ideas? As you become a more *Preactive* leader, you become more and more effective and efficient. You reach goals easier, faster, and with less waste. So here's the big principle. In this book, we're going to use the term "*Preactive*" as a synonym for being both effective and efficient. We're going to treat all three words ("*Preactive*," effective, and efficient) as interchangeable terms. We're going to say that:

Preactive leadership is effective and efficient,
and effectiveness and efficiency are Preactive leadership.

But the reverse is also true. We're going to use the term "Reactive" in this book as a synonym for being ineffective and inefficient. More on that later. But if you see these simple ideas, you're already starting to think *Preactively*, and you're ready to talk about the six *situations*.

The Six Situations

Where does *Preactivity* start? If we're going to be practical, exactly how do we start becoming *Preactive* leaders? The answer is deceptively simple. *Preactive* leadership is based on four simple ideas:

1. There are six *situations* that happen in everyone's life and job.
2. There are six *actions* that everyone takes on these six situations.
3. Three of the situations are effective and efficient and should be *encouraged.*
4. Three of the situations are ineffective and inefficient and should be *avoided.*

That's all there is to it. You're going to learn in these chapters how to recognize the three effective and efficient situations in your life and job and how to focus on them. This means that the simple secret to being a *Preactive* leader is to:

Seek the three effective situations in your life and work.
Avoid the three ineffective situations in your life and work.

That's *Preactive* leadership. That's how you can double your leadership ability in one week, whether you're leading a corporation, civic club, church, government agency, family, or yourself as an individual.

Now, we've used the word "leader" several times in these pages. So what *is* a leader? We'll find out in Chapter 1.

PART I

THE STRUCTURE
OF LEADERSHIP

CHAPTER 1

WHAT IS A LEADER?

How do we define that mysterious thing called "leadership"? How do we define that mysterious person we call a "leader"? One of the most important tasks any leader is to accurately *define* his or her terms.

Clear definitions are vital in leadership, and one of the purposes of this book is to define all the major leadership terms for you. So let's start by defining two words that we've been using for several pages now.

1. What is a *leader*?

2. What is *leadership*?

For years, I've asked managers in dozens of corporate, government, non-profit, and civic club seminars: "What is a leader?" They always answer the same way. A leader is someone who plans, organizes, directs, and controls. A leader is someone who coordinates, motivates, delegates, gets results, inspires others, and energizes groups.

All that's true.

But it's also simply repeating the same principle over and over in different words. To see the principle behind all of these words, let's look for the common denominator in them. What *one* idea ties all these thoughts together? What one term expresses all of these activities at once?

Here's the answer. The one term that ties all these thoughts together is the word *action*. So this means that:

    1. A leader is an *action-taker*.

    2. Leadership is *action*.

If you think about it, planning, organizing, directing, controlling, delegating, coordinating, inspiring, energizing, etc., all have one thing in common—they're *actions* that we take. *Action* is the root principle of leadership.

But let's dig deeper.

Management textbooks usually define leadership as *influencing others*. That's true. I teach that myself. But how does influence work? The word *influence* means to sway, change, or affect the behavior of others. But, how do we do that? We do it by

> ### Leadership
> *1. A leader is an action-taker.*
> *2. Leadership is action.*

the *actions* we take in their presence. We do it by our behavior while they're watching us.

If we take effective and efficient actions in the presence of others (and teach them to take effective and efficient actions, too), we change their behavior in positive ways. Conversely, if we take ineffective and inefficient actions in the presence of others (and teach them to take ineffective and inefficient actions, too), we change their behavior in negative ways.

Sadly, both forms of influencing others are *valid* leadership. Changing people in either a *positive* or a *negative* way is still leadership. Many textbooks don't admit that. They don't admit there's as much negative leadership in the world as positive leadership.

To summarize, we influence other people by how we *act* in their presence. Call it influencing others with our personalities, conduct, actions, or stage presence, leadership is behavior in the presence of other people that changes them either positively or negatively. And with that background, we're ready to define the *root principle* of leadership.

The Root Principle of Leadership

*Leadership is taking action in the presence of others
that influences them enough to create a positive
(or negative) change in their behavior.*

But now we need to define the word *action*:

> *Action is anything you do, at some time,*
> *in some place, to some extent.*

Regardless of your lifestyle, if you're *doing* things with, by, for, or through others, you're a leader. Whether your job title is president, supervisor, or janitor—whether you're a teacher, banker, writer, airline pilot, or sales associate—if you're doing things in the presence of others, you're *leading* them to some greater or lesser extent.

A big mistake we make right here is to be status-conscious when we define the term "leadership." It's common for people to think of presidents as leaders—but janitors aren't. Board members are leaders—but book-keepers aren't. Teachers are leaders—but tree trimmers aren't.

That idea is false. If we delete *status* from our mental hard drives, the only difference between a president and a janitor (or between a board member, bookkeeper, teacher, or tree trimmer), is the *content* of the things they're taking action on. A president might be acting on a merger. A bookkeeper might be acting on a budget. A janitor might be acting

---

Leader

An action-taker. Any person who takes actions (behaves) in the presence of other people, and influences them enough to cause a positive change in their behavior.

on a broom. But presidents, book-keepers, and janitors are all acting in the presence of others—so they're all leaders. The only difference is the *content* of their activities.

> **Action**
>
> *Action is*
> *anything you do,*
> *at some time,*
> *in some place,*
> *to some extent.*

This is important to know because regardless of whether you're a plant manager, stock broker, mechanic, kindergarten teacher, airline pilot, plumber, electrician, mother, or father, you're a leader—and that means the *Preactive* leadership techniques in this book apply to you.

That's why the young assistant supervisor in our Introduction story was able to do what he did on his assembly line. Despite his entry-level position, his youth, his lack of education, and his lack of assembly line experience, he was able to use leadership techniques that the engineers couldn't use. He was able to take actions he learned in the seminar—and the engineers couldn't take those actions because they hadn't attended the seminar.

To summarize what we've said: Leadership boils down to action-taking in your life and work, and to making certain that the *actions* you take are *effective* and *efficient* ones. We're going to see diagrams, definitions, and instructions for how to take effective and efficient actions in later pages. But before we do, let's make one more point. All the actions that good leaders take must obey one very special law.

The Law of Bestness

As a leader, your goal is not merely to take any old action you want to take. Your goal is to take the *best* action you can take in every situation that you face. I call that the Law of Bestness. ("Bestness" is another word I coined many years ago that isn't in any formal dictionary that I know about.)

The word *best* comes from a root that means the most suitable, useful, and desirable. So, your goal is to take the most suitable, useful, and desirable action you can in every situation you face. Have you ever thought about your life and job that way?

There's an old saying that we should never give up best for good. We should never settle for good actions when we can take the best actions. Let's link this law to your paycheck. For many years, I've asked seminar participants to tell me—*in ten words or less*—why their organization pays them. (I also ask them if they'd be willing to bet their next paycheck that their answer is correct.) Many can't. Or won't. Would you?

Once again, the answer is simple. Using the Law of Bestness we've just discussed, here's why

> **Law of Bestness**
> *The word best means "the most suitable, useful, and desirable." The Law of Bestness states that leaders should take the one best action in every situation they face.*

all leaders are paid. They're paid:

To always take the one best action in every situation.

That's ten words. Count 'em. Then think about what those ten words mean. Aren't those ten words more logical than simply saying a leader is paid to do a good job, or to reach goals, or to help others, or to make a profit?

Now, notice that we're also using the word "situation" again in this definition. *Situations* are the keys to *Preactive* leadership, so let's focus on them now.

What is a Situation?

Regardless of our job titles, we're taking actions every day on situations. Situations are the triggers of our actions. Said another way, our actions are responses to our daily situations. That means we can't understand actions until we understand the situations that are triggering them. Now, obeying our earlier rule that leaders must accurately define their terms, let's pause here to define the word situation.

The word *situation* comes from a root meaning a location, or a place. Thus, most simply, a situation is a person or thing located in a certain place at a certain time. But since we're studying action-taking in this book, let's put an action spin on the definition.

The Definition of a Situation

A situation is anything requiring you to take some action,
at some time, in some place, to some extent.

A few paragraphs back, we said that *Preactive* leadership is based on six effective and efficient situations that you respond to during the day with actions—and we said this book is going to diagram and describe those six situations. But a new principle we need to learn right here is that all actions *take their identities* from the situations to which they're responding. That is, the only difference between one action and another one is the identity of *situations* to which they responded. That's why situations are so important in this book. *That's* why we're basing the whole technique of *Preactive* leadership on the identification of situations—or "sits," as I sometimes call them for short.

> ### Situation or Sit
> *Anything requiring*
> *you to take*
> *some action,*
> *at some time,*
> *in some place,*
> *to some extent.*

The second principle to see here is that effective leaders always take the *best* action in every situation, regardless of whether that situation is effective or ineffective. In other words, even if a situation is an inefficient one, a good leader takes the best action possible on it.

However, this last sentence opens the door to a bigger question: How do we *know* which action is best in a situation? This entire book...the whole *Preactive* leadership process...and your life and career...hang on the answer to this question. And the answer is that the *Master Principle* is what tells us which action is best in any situation.

The Master Principle

How do we know which action is best in a situation? The answer to this question shapes every area of our lives, relationships, and jobs. The answer is what makes *Preactive* leadership possible. The answer is what's called the Master Principle of Satisfying Needs.

Satisfying the needs of situations is the secret of all successful action-taking, and it's also the secret of all successful leadership. Here's how we know which action is best in any situation we face:

The needs of situations define the best actions to
take in those situations.

The Master Principle of Satisfying Needs says that leaders don't take action by guesses, opinions, feelings, fears, or rumors. They take action by providing situations with what they need. Good leaders listen to what situations are "asking for," and then they give the situations what they "want."

That's just common sense when you think about it. And as we've said, leadership is simple once you understand it. Now, there's one final piece of the puzzle we need to talk about.

Anyone Can Learn Preactive Leadership

During my decades as an international trainer and consultant for Fortune 500 companies, local, state, and federal government agencies, civic clubs, non-profits, and citizen's groups, I've discovered that effective leadership isn't an art. It isn't a science, opinion, instinct, or even years of experience. At least, it's not totally those things.

Instead, leadership is a set of *learnable techniques* that anyone can learn in one week or less. Think about what that can mean in your own life, career, and relationships. How do I know this is true? I know it because for decades I've taught four-day and five-day seminars to all kinds of groups

> ### Master Principle
> *"The Master Principle of Satisfying Needs" is the key to successful Preactive leadership. This principle says that leaders should not act by guesses or opinions, but should act by supplying situations with what they need.*

worldwide, and I've seen hundreds of graduates start to use the techniques successfully by the end of their seminars.

In other words, after watching hundreds of seminar graduates start using the techniques in a four or five day timeframe, I've realized that good leadership can be learned by anyone and that anyone can start applying it within one week. Effective leadership isn't part of our DNA. It isn't an accident of birth reserved for the elite. It's available to all of us, here and now.

But there's a catch, and that catch is *practice*. You'll be successful in *Preactive* leadership in direct proportion to how much time you spend practicing it. I ask people to practice *Preactive* leadership the same way they'd practice a new hobby, such as playing the guitar, or a new sport, such as playing tennis. If you wanted to learn the guitar, you'd have to practice. You'd expect your instructor to tell you to practice. And you'd make the time to practice.

Yet, somehow it never occurs to us that leadership must be *practiced*, too. (When's the last time you sat down on your sofa and said to yourself, *Okay, I'm going to practice my Preactive leadership for the next twenty minutes.*)

There's an old saying that practice makes perfect. But it doesn't. Nothing does. However, practice *does* make us better, and that's what we want in *Preactive* leadership. Thus, your mission in this book is to *practice* the techniques as you learn them in the coming chapters. *Think* about the techniques often. Set aside time to *rehearse* the techniques both privately and in groups. Do these things, and you'll be a more *Preactive* leader in one week or less.

Summary of Chapter 1

1. A leader is a person who takes enough action in the presence of others to influence their behavior.

2. Leadership is taking action in the presence of others that influences them enough to create a positive (or negative) change in their behavior.

3. A *Preactive* leader is an action-taker who influences others in a *positive* way that increases the effectiveness and the efficiency of the people and things around him or her.

4. Action is anything you *do*, at some time, in some place, to some extent.

5. A situation is anything requiring you to take some *action*, at some time, in some place, to some extent.

6. Actions take their identities from the *situations* to which they're responding.

7. Leaders are paid to take the one *best* action in every situation they face.

8. The *needs* of situations define the best actions to take in those situations.

9. *Preactive* leadership is a learnable technique that anyone can learn, can practice, and can be rewarded for using.

Now we're ready to jump to our central issue. The major principle we need to look at next is this: All actions are preceded by a *decision*. You can't take an action without making a *decision* first. That means the quality of your actions comes directly from the quality of your decisions. In Chapter 2, we're going to learn how to make quality decisions.

CHOICE SITUATIONS AND DECISION-MAKING

L eadership just got a whole bunch easier because, in truth, there's really only *one* type of situation that each of us faces each day. That situation is the generic situation that we call the "Choice Situation." In the simplest terms, all of us are taking actions on Choice Situations all day long and that's the process that we call leadership.

However, here's the trick. These *generic Choice Situations* appear in our lives and on our jobs in six different shapes. That can be confusing. But to keep this simple and practical, we only need to remember that all six of these shapes are generic Choice Situations—no matter what else they might look like.

Said another way, the six situations only *look* different because they're wearing six different masks. They'll either be wearing the mask of one of the three effective and efficient situations, or they'll be wearing the mask of one of the three ineffective and inefficient situations. For example, one of the masks that Choice Situations can wear is the mask of a *Current Trouble* situation. That was the mask that confronted the young assistant supervisor who got promoted in 15 minutes in earlier pages.

But to repeat, behind these six masks, every situation we face is a Choice Situation. And that means that all of them require us to make a *decision* (or *series* of decisions) on them. Because of this, the name we give to *actions* taken on Choice Situations is "Decision Actions." And if we connect Decision Actions to Choice Situations in a linkage or connection, they're the process that textbooks call *decision-making*. For simplicity, we'll call it that, too.

Now, let's repeat the principle for good measure. Leadership is the process of taking best Decision Actions on Choice Situations, regardless of which mask they're wearing. That's good news because once you've learned to do that, you've learned leadership. It's that easy.

Building on this principle, now we're ready to flesh out our definition of leadership. In Chapter 1, we defined leadership as taking actions in the presence of others that influence them enough to create a positive (or negative) change in their behavior. That's still true. But now, using what we've learned in recent paragraphs, we can flesh out our definition.

The Complete Definition of Leadership

Leadership is taking best Decision Actions in Choice Situations to positively influence the behavior of others while directing and correcting tasks.

Note in this fuller definition that we've dismissed from discussion one previous principle, and we've added two new principles. First, we've dismissed the earlier principle of *negative* leadership. We're assuming from this point forward that you want to be a *positive* leader—that you want to change people's behavior in *positive* ways. So we won't continue discussing negative leadership.

Second, we added two new principles to our discussion. They are that the two basic purposes of leadership are to *direct* and *correct* tasks. In other words, the reason we *influence* other people is to help them either *direct* or *correct* tasks in a positive way.

To summarize, accurate decision-making (defined as best Decision Actions on Choice Situations) is effective leadership, and effective leadership is accurate decision-making. But now we need to think about how accurate decisions are made.

How to Make
Accurate Decisions

We've said that accurate leadership is decision-making that *directs* and *corrects* tasks in an accurate way. But precisely *how* do we make an accurate decision? Researchers have known for centuries that a decision is a *choice*. Decision-making is the process of *choosing* things, people, times, places, and amounts. And since we've agreed that leadership should be positive, we've added the Law of Bestness to our definition—accurate decisions are the *best* choices of things, people, times, places, and amounts. Thus:

1. A decision (in one word) is a *choice*.
2. A decision (in two words) is a *best* choice.
3. Decision-making (as a system) is the *process* of making best choices.

But, since choices are made by humans, decision-making has four built-in weaknesses that we should be honest enough to admit.

1. Decisions are *judgmental* choices formed by our personalities, cultures, education, training, experiences, instincts, and opinions.

2. That means decisions are never totally *factual*—they're judgmental choices made at one point in time and space using the facts available at that point in time and space.

3. That also means no decision is ever totally *right*. However, no decision is ever totally *wrong*, either. All decisions are a mixture of judgment and facts, and that's why we use the term *best* choice in this book. We don't use the terms "right" and "wrong" choices. All choices have some *disadvantages*—thus no choice could ever be totally right. But all choices also have some *advantages*—thus no choice could ever be totally wrong, either. Accurate decisions are the *best choices* possible using sound judgment and the available facts.

> **Leadership**
>
> *Taking best*
> *Decision Actions*
> *in Choice*
> *Situations to*
> *positively* **influence**
> *the behavior of*
> *others while*
> **directing** *and*
> **correcting** *tasks.*

4. Finally, no decision is ever made in *isolation*. All decisions are part of a linkage or chain of previous decisions that came from the *past*, and that will continue into the *future*. That is, all present decisions were shaped by past decisions. And all present decisions will shape future decisions. No decision is ever set in concrete because we live in a world of change. That means both the past and the future must be considered when making a *best decision*.

Now, these four built-in weaknesses make decision-making dicey at the best of times—and that's why we need an accurate decision-making process. We'll look at that accurate process next. But first, in Chapter 1, we learned that good leaders always define their terms. So let's obey that rule and define a *best decision*.

The Definition of a Best Decision

The **choice** *of an alternative thing, person, time, place, or amount that best satisfies the* **needs** *of a situation with the least risk of Future Trouble.*

Notice that there are five defining elements to a best decision.

1. A decision is a *choice*.
2. It's the choice of an *alternative* thing, person, time, place, or amount.
3. It's the *choice* of the *best* alternative.
4. That alternative is best because it satisfies the *needs* of the situation best.
5. That alternative is also best because it has the least risk of *Future Trouble*.

Now let's blend these five elements into a complete decision-making process. Here's the eight-step process for best *choices*.

The Eight Steps in a Best Choice

Using everything we've learned, let's list the eight linked and interactive steps in the decision-making process.

1. Recognize that a Choice Situation exists.

2. Write a clear choice statement.

3. List what the situation needs.

4. List at least three alternatives that might satisfy the needs.

5. Measure the alternatives against the needs and make a tentative choice.

6. List the Future Troubles that might occur if the tentative choice is used.

7. If there are *no* overwhelming Future Troubles, the tentative choice is the final choice.

8. If there *are* overwhelming Future Troubles, the Future Troubles of the second-best alternative are listed, and if they are less than those in the tentative choice, the second-best alternative is the final choice.

Those eight steps are the entire process for an accurate decision. It's true that some books add extra steps—such as getting coworkers to agree with a decision, implementing a decision, and following-up on a decision, etc. But those aren't part of the *choice* process. They're part of the communicating, implementing, and monitoring process, so we don't include them in this book.

> ### Best Decision
> *The **choice** of an alternative thing, person, time, place, or amount that best satisfies the **needs** of a situation with the least risk of Future Trouble.*

Now, these eight steps are very important, so let's discuss each of them more fully. Note carefully that each step in the process is interactively linked to the steps both above and below it and that each step has to accurately reflect its place in the process.

The Eight Steps of Decision-Making Fully Explained

Step 1. *Recognize that a Choice Situation exists.* Choice Situations can be large or small, urgent or non-urgent, simple or complicated. Often, they're just part of our daily routine. They are brought to our attention by coworkers, friends, or family members. Synonyms for the word *decision* are often used in statements such as: We need to *improve* our communications… let's find a *way* to reduce our costs…the vice president wants us to *recommend* a new location, etc. The italicized words in each of these sentences is a synonym for choice—each of these sentences is asking us to make a decision.

Step 2. *Develop a clear action statement.* This next step is linked to Step 1 but is often overlooked. A choice statement can be expressed mentally, verbally, in longhand, by email, hand-held PC, or by any other method. Choice statements begin with the phrase, "I (or we) want to choose the best _____ _____." Then the blank is filled in with *what* is being chosen, *who* is effected, the *deadline*, the *place* of implementation, and the *amount* being chosen. All fuzzy words are clarified, and all five of the factual categories (*what, who, when, where,* and *amount*) are included. (We'll discuss fuzzy words and the five factual categories in detail later.)

For example, let's pretend that you work in an office, and that your job is to issue new policies by email to the department heads in your plant each month. But, these department heads have been forgetful and haven't been reading and implementing the new policies in your emails. You need to *correct* their forgetfulness, so for Step 2 in your decision-making, you might write, *I want to choose the best Correcting Action to keep all the Gaston Plant Department Heads from forgetting to read and implement my monthly policy emails.*

Step 3. *List the needs of the situation.* This step is the next link in the process and can be called needs assessment, standards writing, setting policies, and other such terms. The point is, before listing the alternatives for your choice, you must first list the *needs* that those alternatives are intended to satisfy. This can be done mentally, verbally, in longhand, by email, by hand-held PC, or by any other method. You should list the things the situation needs to *have* and also the things the situation wants to *avoid*. A list of needs can be simple or complicated, long or short. Special techniques can be used, such as dividing the needs into "absolutes" and "desirables," rank ordering them by importance, or assigning numeric weights to them. But to illustrate in our simple email case here, the needs for the choice statement presented in Step 2 might look like this (we'll abbreviate the Gaston Department Heads as "GDHs" for brevity):

☐ I need my monthly policy emails to be as *authoritative* as possible with all the GDHs.

☐ I need to prove as much as possible that all the GDHs have *received* my monthly emails.

☐ I need to prove as much as possible that all the GDHs have *read* my monthly policy emails.

☐ I need to prove as much as possible that all the GDHs have *implemented* our new monthly polices.

☐ I need to correct as much as possible the *forgetting* of my monthly emails by all of the GDHs.

Now, since this illustration is a simple one, we've only listed five needs. Real situations should never have less than three or four needs and can have as many as 20 or 30 needs (as you'll see in later chapters). The number of needs comes directly from the complexity of the situation. Note that each need is spelled out in the five factual categories (*what, who, when, where, amount*).

Step 4. *List alternatives that might satisfy the needs.* As the next link in the process, you make a list of a minimum of three alternatives that might satisfy the needs listed in Step 3. Alternatives can be called options, courses of action, solutions, possibilities, and other such synonyms. For example, in a hiring decision, the alternatives would be the *candidates* you are going to interview. In an automobile purchasing decision, the alternatives would be the *cars* you are going to test drive. But it's important to have a *minimum* of three alternatives because it limits your creativity to think of decisions as only *Yes-No* or *Do-Don't* choices. *Yes-No* or *Do-Don't* choices are called binary decisions, and they restrict the field of alternatives in an illogical way. For example, a person might say, "I don't know whether to cook carrots for dinner tonight." But that's a *Yes-No* decision. The choice isn't that simple. There are other alternatives, such as cooking carrots for lunch, cooking some other vegetable for dinner, having pizza delivered, eating dinner out at a restaurant that night, etc. The point is, the alternatives for what a person is going to eat for dinner aren't limited to a simple *Yes-No* answer on carrots. To break binary decisions, we develop more alternatives by creative techniques such as brainstorming. Or by creating combination and compromise alternatives. Or by asking experts for advice. Or by doing Internet research. Or by using techniques such as the *Delay-for-30-Days-to-Think-it-Over* trick, or the *Do-Nothing* trick. Using these techniques, it's easy to develop three alternatives for any decision. The rule is:

The accuracy of a decision increases in direct proportion to the number of alternatives considered. Now, continuing with our case, some alternatives that might satisfy the needs we've listed in Step 3 for this case could include:

A) Follow-up by *phone* each month to ask if the GDHs have received, read, and implemented my policy emails.

B) Set up *folders* in my email program to store read receipts and replies from the GDHs and monitor these folders, sending mid-month follow-up emails marked High Importance and using the read receipt option each time I send one.

C) Follow-up by *letter* each month to ask if the GDHs have received, read, and implemented my policy emails.

D) Ask the GDHs in *person* at the monthly staff meeting if they have received, read, and implemented my policy emails.

Step 5. *Measure the alternatives against the needs and make a tentative choice.* This step is linked to Step 4, and this is only a tentative choice at this point in the process. The final choice comes in a later step. Measuring the alternatives against the needs can be done mentally, verbally, in longhand, by email, by handheld PC, or on paper with a mathematical method. For example, a Microsoft Excel spreadsheet with a numeric process can be used to display scores for the alternatives. (We'll study this technique later.) But to keep this case simple, we'll only discuss it mentally and verbally. Thus, if we *mentally* measure the four alternatives (Step 4) against the five needs (Step

3), the tentative choice becomes clear after some thought. Our situation needs a strong alternative that proves the GDHs have received, read, and implemented our new policy emails, and that includes good recordkeeping, and keeps a good paper trail proving that the GDHs have implemented the policies, documenting the dates and times they were notified, etc. Thus, Alternative B (the mid-month email follow-up plan) becomes our tentative choice. The other alternatives (a monthly letter, a monthly phone call, or chatting at monthly staff meetings) don't offer the same level of recordkeeping, verification, follow-up, and enforcement that the email plan offers.

Step 6. *List Future Troubles that might occur.* Step 6 is a negative step linked to Step 5 to serve as a threat assessment. This is necessary because if the Future Troubles threatening a tentative choice outweigh that choice's positive values, it can't be used. Studies show that as much as 40 percent of all tentative choices have future negatives that outweigh their positives. This means that Step 6 is just as important as the other steps and can't be skipped. (However, it is skipped in many classes and books.) To proceed with Step 6, we ask "If I implement this tentative choice, what could go wrong?" (That is, what mistakes, misunderstandings, delays, or waste could occur if the tentative choice is used?) If no overwhelming Future Troubles leap to mind, it's usually safe to implement the tentative choice as the final choice. But if serious Future Troubles are probable, we skip Step 7 (the next step), and jump to Step 8. However, in this simple email case, there *aren't* any overwhelming Future Troubles threatening Alternative B. So we continue to Step 7.

Step 7. *If no overwhelming Future Troubles are threatening, the tentative choice is final.* At this point, we accept the mid-monthly follow-up email plan as the final choice. We can tell the world that we have made the best choice and that our decision is final.

Step 8. *However, if there **are** overwhelming Future Troubles threatening the tentative choice, then optional Step 8 must be used.* Step 8 is an optional step linked back to Step 4 and is only used when Step 5 (the tentative choice) has been over-

---

8 Steps of Decision Making

1. *Recognize that a Choice Situation exists.*
2. *Write a clear action statement.*
3. *List the needs of the situation.*
4. *List alternatives that might satisfy the needs.*
5. *Measure the alternatives against the needs and make a tentative choice.*
6. *List the Future Troubles in the tentative choice.*
7. *If no overwhelming Future Troubles are threatening, the tentative choice is final.*
8. *Optional: If there are overwhelming Future Troubles, go back to the second-best alternative in Step 4.*

whelmed by threatening future negatives. When that happens, we go back to the *second-best* alternative in Step 4, and evaluate *its* Future Troubles. If *it* has less Future Troubles than the tentative choice, *it* becomes our final choice instead of the tentative choice. But that didn't happen here in our GDHs email case, so our case ended at Step 7.

And there you have it: a full discussion of the eight steps in decision-making. The steps may seem complicated at first, but after you think about them for a few days, you realize that they're practical, logical, and airtight. Best of all, once you've tried them a few times, they become second nature. Before continuing, let's pause to highlight the three basic *formats* we can use in decision-making.

The Three Formats for Decision-Making

Depending on the complexity of the choice, we can make decisions by either an *intangible* process, a *tangible* process, or a *combination* of the two. Simple decisions can be made intangibly, simply by thinking about them and talking about them with other people. I call that the *Mental-Verbal Format* for decision-making. Complex decisions can be made tangibly by writing them out on paper or using other visual aids such as Excel spread sheets. I call that the *Hard-Copy Format* for decision-making. Decisions of medium complexity can be made by a combination format called the *Simple-Pattern Format.* (We'll study examples of both formats in later chapters.) Let's repeat the principle. The three formats for decision-making are:

1. *The Mental-Verbal Format*—making the choice by thinking and talking about it.
2. *The Hard-Copy Format*—making the choice with writing and other visual aids.
3. *The Simple-Pattern Format*—making the choice by a combination of thinking, talking, and writing.

Thus, a simple decision (a simple situation with only a few facts) can be made correctly and logically just by talking about it. But a complex decision (a complex situation with many facts) should be made in writing with visual aids. And a decision of medium complexity (a situation with an average number of facts) can be made by a combination of talking and writing. To prove how easy the eight steps of decision-making really are, we'll do a fun practice case in the next chapter, and we'll do it with the *Mental-Verbal Format* simply by talking about it with other people.

Summary of Chapter 2

1. There's only *one* generic situation in life's activities and that's the generic Choice Situation.

2. All situations are Choice Situations, but the six situations masquerade as either one of the three effective and effi-

cient situations or as one of the three ineffective and inefficient situations.

3. Choice Situations and the Decision Actions we take on them form the process we call decision-making.

4. Leadership is taking *best* Decision Actions in Choice Situations to *positively* influence the behavior of others while *directing* and *correcting* tasks.

5. A decision (in one word) is a *choice*.

6. A decision (in two words) is a *best choice*.

7. Decision-Making (as a system) is the *process* of making best choices.

8. Fully defined, a best decision is the choice of an alternative thing, person, time, place, or amount that best satisfies the needs of a situation with the least risk of Future Trouble.

9. Decisions can be made in three different formats: the *Mental-Verbal Format* where the choice is made only by talking and thinking about it; the *Hard-Copy Format* where the choice is made by writing it out on paper with visual aids such as numeric spreadsheets, charts, tables, and graphs; and, the *Simple-Process Format* where the choice is made both by talking and writing about it.

Next, we're going to practice what we've learned about the *Mental-Verbal Format* with the fun practice case of the New Car Puzzle.

CHAPTER 3

THE CASE OF
THE NEW CAR PUZZLE

The Formats for
Accurate Decision-Making

Decision-making is going on all day, every day, all around us. It's the most frequent thing that people do—and the most important thing that people do—in all cultures, all over the globe, in corporations, civic clubs, churches, government agencies, and families.

Some years ago, the lyrics of a popular song said, "Love makes the world go round." But it doesn't. *Decision-making* makes the world go round.

Each of us makes choices all day long, and then we take action on those choices, minute by minute, hour by hour. We choose where to go, and what to eat, wear, do, and say. Our decision-making is continuous from the moment we wake up, until the moment we go to sleep. Decision-making is the fabric of our lives and makes us what we are. To paraphrase an ancient saying, *As we decide, so we become.*

But let's keep this simple. Let's talk about a family that wants to buy a car. Let's call this the case of the New Car Puzzle. Let's use it to review the eight steps of decision-making we learned in Chapter 2, and to practice *Mental-Verbal Format* decision-making for the first time. True to the eight steps, let's start by recognizing a choice situation.

Step 1: The Situation

One sunny afternoon, you're trimming the shrubbery along your back yard fence, when Jack McIntire, a neighbor whose yard adjoins yours, walks toward you across his lawn. "Hey," he calls. "We're in a pickle and need your help. We've got to buy a new car this week, and we've got a real puzzler."

"Oh," you answer. "Sorry about that. But what's so puzzling about a new car?"

Jack gives you a serious look and says, "Well, our whole family has been looking at cars for a week. We've test-driven half a dozen, and we've narrowed it down to four cars we like. All four of them seem to fit our general needs. They all have nice colors, seats for four people, leather and wood interiors, navigation, and all the other gadgets we want."

"Great," you add. "So what's the puzzle?"

"The puzzle," Jack laughs, "is that I like one car. My wife, Jan, likes another. Our teenage son, Mark, likes another. And Meg, our pre-teen daughter, likes the fourth. We've looked at the brochures for hours, and we can't decide which car to buy."

"Ouch. I see the puzzle. But what can I do?"

"Well, remember last week when you told me about the book called *Preactive Leadership* that teaches accurate decision-making?"

"Yes, I remember."

"That's how you can help. We've agreed that if you'll guide us through the eight steps of decision-making you were telling me about, we'll buy the car the process picks. Jan and the children are reading car brochures on the patio right now. Can you stop trimming long enough to help us?"

"I'll do what I can," you laugh, putting down your clippers. "In fact, you've already taken Step 1."

"We have?" Jack asks in surprise.

"Sure. Step 1 is recognizing that you have a Choice Situation and that you've got to make a best choice on it. You've already done that. So I'll be happy to help."

Step 2: The Action Statement

You join the McIntire family on the patio. They're leafing through four colorful brochures on the wrought-iron table and offer you one to read. You politely refuse. "No thank you," you smile, "as I told Jack, you guys are trying to make an accurate decision, and there's a certain sequence of steps that we can't break in doing that. You took Step 1 when you realized that you have a Choice Situation.

"Now it's time for Step 2, a clear action statement. After that, we'll go to Step 3 and discuss your needs. It's only after we've completed those first three steps in that sequence that we can discuss alternatives by looking at brochures. If we break our sequence by looking at alternatives first, our final choice might be biased."

The family members glance knowingly at one another. Jack McIntire winks at the children and chuckles. "See, I told you he'd know what to do."

"Okay," you continue, "let's try this for a clear action statement. *We, the McIntire family, want to choose the best new car for our family today here on the patio.*

The McIntire's son, Mark, glances at you. "That was Step 2?"

"Yes, Mark. That's what's called a clear action statement. Until you understand the *what-who-when-where-amount* factual categories of an action, you can't make an accurate decision on it. Do all of you agree with the statement?"

The family nods in agreement.

"Okay, then, let's move on."

Step 3: The Needs

"Step 3," you say to the family, "is the most important one. Notice that we're moving slowly and carefully here. We don't want to get out of sequence, and we don't want to rush. In Step 3, we've got to talk honestly about your *needs* for a new car. You've already narrowed your choice down to four cars that satisfy your general needs—color, seating, leather, wood, navigation, and the other frills. What you must do now is think about your *deeper* needs. What are some of the more serious factors, economies, and considerations you need in a car? And while you're at it, think about the *importance* of each of those deeper needs relative to one another."

The family sits silently, looking confused.

Then Jack sits up and says, "Wait, I see what you mean. For one thing, our car payment can't be over $600 a month, and we need to stay as far below that figure as we can. I think low monthly payment is our most important need."

Jan speaks next. "Jack's right, and another serious need we have is miles-per-gallon. I think a high MPG is our second most important need."

"Excellent," Jack agrees, "and don't forget our discussion of warranties. We need the best warranty we can get. I think that comes in after low monthly payment and gas mileage. Do we all agree?"

The family nods.

"Keep going," you urge. "What are some other serious needs that you have?"

"I think I know what's next," Mark says, holding up his hand as if he was in the classroom. "I think soft ride is next. When we test-drove the cars, some had a soft, luxury feel, and others had a hard, SUV feel. I think we should have a soft, luxury ride, don't you?"

Everyone accepts Mark's idea.

Meg speaks for the first time. "Look, we've talked about monthly payment, good mileage, factory warranty, and soft ride, in that order. Right? But I think cool design is next. Some of these cars are dorky, and I don't want to be embarrassed each time you drop me off at school. Can I have cool design next?" Everyone laughs and agrees.

The family lapses into thoughtful silence. Finally, Jack speaks. "The only other thing I can think of," he says, "is that we need a car with low maintenance. We're all so busy that we don't want a car with a lot of service, or one that won't start when we need it the most. I don't think maintenance is very important, though, because we'll be under warranty with any of these cars, and they're all new. So this is probably the least important standard, don't you think?"

The family agrees.

Mark summarizes, "Okay, Dad, we've ended up with six needs. In order of priority, we need lowest monthly payment, best gas mileage, longest warranty, softest ride, coolest design, and lowest maintenance. Am I right?"

Everyone nods. Jack glances at you. "Okay," he says, "we've got our needs, and we've ranked them by importance. What's Step 4?"

Step 4: The Alternatives

You reach for a pad and pen on the table. "Step 4 is to think of at least three alternatives that might satisfy your needs. You never try to make a decision with only one two alternatives. You always need a minimum of *three* or more, and you never discuss the alternatives until you've taken the first three steps in sequence. Technically, you guys shouldn't have looked at car brochures and test-driven cars until you'd taken the first three steps.

"But now you have your alternatives. You have the facts on these four cars from your test-drives and the brochures. Now, since we're doing this decision by what's called the *Mental-Verbal Format*, we'll just talk about the cars conversationally as you choose. But let's cheat a little for some practice. If you'll tell me about the cars, I'll jot the facts down on this pad. Who wants to start?"

The family starts to leaf through the brochures on the table, calling out facts, figures, and impressions. When they're finished, you show them what you've written on the pad.

1. *Alternative One.* The *Bison A300.* Payment $595 a month. 37 mpg. 40,000 mile warranty. Good soft ride. Fair design. A lot of maintenance required.

2. *Alternative Two.* The *Leno XK2.* Payment $550 a month. 22 mpg. 50,000 mile warranty. Fairly soft ride. Good design. Medium maintenance required.

3. *Alternative Three.* The *Mala B5.* Payment $400 a month. 18 mpg. 100,000 mile warranty. Bad ride. Weak design. Medium maintenance required.

4. *Alternative Four.* The *Riva Z400.* Payment $395 a month. 38 mpg. 45,000 mile warranty. Very soft ride. Very good design. Lowest maintenance required.

You put the pad on the table. "Excellent," you say. "I think you've got enough facts to go to Step 5."

Step 5: *The Tentative Choice*

"Okay guys," you continue, "your tentative decision is going to be the alternative car that satisfies your needs the best. In this step, you're going to make a *tentative* choice. You're going to mentally compare your four cars to your six prioritized needs, and you're going to pick the car that seems to satisfy those needs the best at this point in the process."

"But," Mark interrupts, "why are you calling this the 'tentative choice'? Aren't we ready to pick our final car?"

"Good question, Mark, but we actually have three more

steps. We're learning how to make a best decision here, something that many people never do. The process has eight steps that can't be skipped or taken out of sequence."

"Oh, I see."

"Great, so let's review the prioritized needs we listed. In order of importance, they are lowest monthly payment, most gas mileage, longest warranty, softest ride, coolest design, and least maintenance. Right?

"Now, as you keep these needs in mind, I'm going to pass the pad around, and let each of you read the facts we listed about the cars. In your minds, compare the *facts* to the *needs* you set earlier, and decide which car you think satisfies your needs the most.

"Next, tear off a little piece of paper from the back of the pad, and write down the car of your choice. But don't tell anybody. Keep your car a secret until I call on you. Okay, here's the pad. Someone take it, read the facts and needs, tear off a piece of paper for your car, and pass the pad to the next person."

One by one, the McIntire family takes the pad, reads it, tears off a slip of paper, writes something on it, and passes the pad on. Everyone laughs and jokes as the pad moves around the circle. After a few minutes, everyone is finished. Meg hands the pad back to you.

"Okay, folks, this is the moment of truth. When I call your name, read aloud what you've written on your piece of paper. Let's start with Jack."

Jack unfolds his paper. "Well, I picked the *Riva Z400*."

"Jan?"

Jan laughs. "I picked the *Riva Z400*, too."

The family starts to giggle and nudge one another.

"Mark?"

"The *Riva*."

"Meg?"

"The *Riva*."

"Outstanding, a home run," you laugh. "All of you picked the *Riva*."

Everyone is smiling and talking at once.

"Hold it, folks," you say. "Let's finish the decision before we celebrate. The *Riva* is only your *tentative* choice and most of the time the tentative choice will be your final choice. But we still have a few more steps to go before we know for sure."

Step 6: The Future Troubles

"Guys," you say, "your next step is to discuss the tentative choice you just made—the *Riva* car—to see if it has any over-whelming Future Troubles threatening it. If it does, you can't buy it, even though it was your tentative choice. But if it doesn't have any overwhelming Future Troubles threatening it, it's your final choice, and you'll buy a *Riva*.

"In this step, you ask yourselves this question: 'If we buy the *Riva*, what could go wrong with it? What mistakes, trou-bles, or hidden expenses does the *Riva* have?'

"So what do you think, McIntires? Does anyone see overwhelming Future Troubles threatening the *Riva*—troubles so serious they'd keep you from buying it?"

The family sits quietly.

Finally, Jack speaks. "No, I don't think the *Riva* has any more potential troubles than any of the other cars. All of them are new. All of them are under warranty. All of them were made by reputable manufacturers and are sold by reputable dealers. All of them are on this year's 'Top Ten Cars' list in the consumer magazines. So I don't think we should be afraid of the *Riva*."

The rest of the family grins.

"Okay then," you respond, "since you agree that the *Riva* has no serious troubles in its future, let's move on to Step 7."

Step 7: *The Final Choice*

"In the previous step," you say to the family, "you agreed that the Riva car has no serious troubles in its future. So in this step, you simply *agree* now as a family that the *Riva Z400* is your final choice, and that tomorrow you're going to buy one. Your best judgment is that the *Riva* car satisfies your family's needs best, and it's the one you're going to get. Case closed."

"But," Mark says, holds up his hand again, "You said earlier that decision-making has eight steps. What's the *eighth* step?"

You chuckle. "Mark, you're sharp. Even though we didn't need it today, you are right. We ought to teach Step 8 to the family. It's an optional step, and we didn't need it today because there were no Future Troubles in your tentative choice.

"But now let's pretend that you *did* have troubles threatening the *Riva* car. Maybe it had an underpowered engine or something equally serious. Here's what we'd do."

Step 8: The Second-Best Alternative

"If your choice process ever hits a wall back in Step 6, the Future Troubles step," you say to the family, "and your tentative choice has overwhelming Future Troubles, you can't make your final decision in Step 7 the way we did today. Instead, you skip Step 7 and you jump down to Step 8, an *optional* step at the bottom of the process for such cases. Can anyone guess what we're going do in this step?"

Meg is the first to answer. "I think we'd go back to the other cars we studied and buy one of them, right?"

"Absolutely, Meg. It'd make no sense to ignore all the research and hard thinking you've already done on new cars. Why start from scratch and go visiting car dealerships again? Instead, you go back to the other cars you've analyzed, and you choose your *second-best* car. So, which of the other three cars on your list do you think is second-best?"

"Let me see the list again," says Jack. You hand him the pad. He studies it a moment. "Okay," Jack says, "I see a pattern. The *Bison* is clearly out. Our second-best car is either the *Leno* or the *Mala*. They're about tied in value. But the *Leno* has better gas mileage, a softer ride, and a better design than the *Mala*. I think the *Leno* is our second best car."

The other family members huddle over the pad a moment, and soon agree.

"Good thinking, guys," you say. "I agree that the *Leno* is second-best. So if the *Riva* really did have a factory defect, you'd eliminate it from consideration, and you'd buy the *Leno* instead. Case closed once again."

"But," Mark asks, "how often do people have to use this last optional step? How often do people go back to the second-best alternative?"

"Not very often, Mark. Studies show that in 60 to 70 percent of all decisions, the tentative choice is the final choice. So this optional Step 8 is only used 30 or 40 percent of the time. Still, this step is important. Because if we didn't have it (and many books and seminars *don't* teach it), people would always pick their tentative choice as the final decision—and 30 to 40 percent of the time they'd be choosing a *less than best alternative*."

"Whoa," Mark laughs. "I'm glad you came over today. We might have bought the wrong car."

"No, Mark, let's just say you might have bought *less than the best* car. The decision-making process is about *best* choices at one point in time under the available facts. It's not about 'right' and 'wrong' choices."

You stand up, stretch, and say, "Well, folks, this has been fun. As I told Jack last week, the book *Preactive Leadership* spells out in detail everything we've done here today."

Jack grins. "Well, I can tell you this, it certainly is an accurate process!"

"Yes, it is, Jack. And don't forget that accurate decision-making has emotional benefits, too. All of you are happy with the *Riva* car today because you all participated in the process. That's extremely important in decision-making, and I hope your family starts a new tradition today of always making group decisions."

The family smiles and laughs.

"Let me ask one last question," you say. "Why do you think the family's vote for the *Riva* car was *unanimous*? Why didn't at least one member of the family vote for another car?"

"I know," says Mark, holding up his hand. "It's because we used the eight-step process, and we discussed the steps as we went along with everyone agreeing on what we did."

"Exactly, Mark. Every decision, no matter how complex, only has *one* best answer at a point in time under the known facts. So, if you use the eight-step process you learned today, you'll always find that one *best* answer. Most importantly, the eight-step process creates peace and harmony in a group, just as you saw today."

You turn to walk away. "Good luck with your new *Riva*."

"We can't thank you enough," Jack says quietly. "You've taken a big load off our shoulders. We'll buy a *Riva* tomorrow, and we'll be pleased with it."

"It was my pleasure, folks. But if I don't get back to my hedge trimming, my wife is going to be doing some decision-making too, and I'll be sleeping in *my* car tonight.

A Review of the Mental-Verbal Format for Decision-Making

Now, if you're like many people, the *Mental-Verbal Format* for decision-making (the one we just used with the McIntire family) may have seemed a little hard to follow just by reading the dialog of the characters. So let pause a moment to spell out the format more clearly. This is our most simple format for decision-making, and the easiest to use. At its root, it's based on four simple questions that you ask yourself and/or other people when faced with a simple choice. Following are the four questions that make up the core of the *Mental-Verbal Format*.

The format opens when a simple situation occurs that requires the choice of a thing, person, time, place, or amount that best satisfies the situation's needs with the least risk of trouble. This is what we had in the case of the New Car Puzzle when the McIntire family was sitting on the patio. First, they mentally developed a clear action statement and then, boiled down to its core, they asked the following four questions in sequence.

1. *The Needs.* "What are this situation's most serious *needs*?"
2. *The Alternatives.* "Do we have three or more *alternatives*?"
3. *The Tentative Choice.* "Which alternative seems to *best* satisfy the needs?"
4. *The Future Troubles.* "If this tentative choice is implemented, what could go *wrong*?

Since no serious Future Troubles were probable with the McIntire family's tentative choice, the *Riva* car, their decision was complete. If serious Future Troubles had been probable with the *Riva*, the family would have returned to their second-best alternative, the *Leno* car, and if it had less Future Troubles than the *Riva*, it would have been their final choice instead of the *Riva*.

This easy four-question process can be used anytime, anywhere, by anybody, and it's our most frequent decision-making process because most of us make most of our decisions mentally. This simple process is the one you should practice the most, and should use the most at home and on the job.

Now, the McIntire's New Car Puzzle wasn't a complex case, and most people probably buy new cars using some type of *Mental-Verbal Format*—even if they don't realize they're doing it. But, as we said in Chapter 2, there are *three* different formats for decision-making that are used according to the complexity of the situation. So next, let's look at the *Hard-Copy Format*. It's for our most complex decisions when there are a lot of confusing facts to sort out. Of course, the New Car Puzzle wasn't that complex. But since we've already done it once and know all its facts, let's do the McIntire's car case again to illustrate how the *Hard-Copy Format* works.

A Hard-Copy Decision-Making Format for the New Car Puzzle

Figure 1 on page 74 is a spreadsheet showing how the McIntire family might have made their new car decision if they had used the *Hard-Copy Format*. Let's see how a spreadsheet format can make a complex decision more visible, understandable, and justifiable.

Hard-Copy Decisions: The Needs, Columns 1, 2, 3

Column 1 in Figure 1 lists the needs the McIntire family set during their conversation on the patio. Column 2 shows the priorities the family assigned to those six needs. Column 3 *quantifies* (puts a number on) the priorities. The family prioritized its needs by putting a numeric "weight" (value) on each need.

The easiest way to do this is count the number of needs (there are six in this case), and then number the needs *back-*

Figure 1: The New Car Puzzle

A Hard Copy Format Decision-Making Case

(The McIntire Family's New Car Decision Shown in a Hard-Copy Format Spreadsheet)

Action Statement: "We, the McIntire family, want to choose the best new car for our family today here on the patio."

Columns: 1	2	3	4	5	6	7	8	9	10	11	12	13	14	15
		WEIGHT OF	1st CAR'S FACTS:	NEED	SCORE	2nd CAR'S FACTS:	NEED	SCORE	3rd CAR'S FACTS:	NEED	SCORE	4th CAR'S FACTS:	NEED	SCORE
McINTIRE FAMILY'S	IMPORTANCE OF		"BISON			"LENO			"MALA			"RIVA		
# NEEDS	EACH NEED	EACH NEED	A300"	RANK	(3x5=)	XK2"	RANK	(3x8=)	B5"	RANK	(3x11=)	Z400"	RANK	(3x14=)
			(Notes)			(Notes)			(Notes)			(Notes)		
1 Lowest Payment	Most Important	Weight of 6	$595	1	6	$550	2	12	$400	3	18	$395	4	24
2 Best MPG	Next Most Import	Weight of 5	37	3	15	22	2	10	18	1	5	38	4	20
3 Longest Warranty	Next Most Import	Weight of 4	40,000	1	4	50,000	3	12	100,000	4	16	45,000	2	8
4 Softest Ride	Next Most Import	Weight of 3	Good	3	9	Fair	2	6	Bad	1	3	Very good	4	12
5 Coolest Design	Next Most Import	Weight of 2	Fair	2	4	Good	3	6	Weak	1	2	Very good	4	8
6 Least Maint.	Least Important	Weight of 1	A Lot	1	1	Medium	3	3	Medium	3	3	Lowest	4	4
TOTAL SCORES:			BISON		39	LENO		49	MALA		47	RIVA		76
FINAL RANK-ORDER OF CARS:					[4th]			[2nd]			[3rd]			[1st]

INSTRUCTIONS: Column 3. To create "weights," count needs in Column 1 (there are six in this case) and number them backwards by importance. Numbers become the "weights." Columns 5, 8, 11, 14. To create "ranks," count alternatives (there are four here), and number backwards by degree of need satisfaction. Numbers become the "ranks." Columns 6, 9, 12, 15. To create "scores," multiply "weights" (Column 3) times the "ranks" (Columns 5, 8, 11, 14). Answers are "scores" to be totaled at bottom.

Future Troubles: Since the Riva Z400, the first place car, had no known Future Troubles, it was verified as the final choice, and the McIntire family bought it.

wards, starting with the most important need and working down to least important, like this: 6, 5, 4, 3, 2, 1. Numbering them this way "rewards" the most important need with the highest value of 6, and "devalues" the least important need with the lowest value of 1.

Hard-Copy Decisions:
The Facts, Columns 4, 7, 10, 13

Columns 4, 7, 10, and 13 list the facts of each car the McIntires are studying, displaying the monthly payments, mileage, warranties, etc. These facts came from the McIntire's brochures, and the family wrote them on the scratch pad during the patio conversation.

Hard-Copy Decisions:
The Rankings, Columns 5, 6, 11, 14

Columns 5, 8, 11, and 14 are a *ranking* of the four cars against the family's six needs. This is done by comparing the *facts* of each car (columns 4, 7, 10, and 13) against the *needs* (column 1). The family did this mentally on the patio. But in the *Hard-Copy Format*, the degree to which each car meets each need is quantified with a numeric *rank*. Again, the easiest way to do this is to count the number of cars being studied (there are four), and then number them back against the needs from most satisfying to least satisfying like this: 4, 3, 2, 1. This "rewards" the best car with the highest rank of 4, and "devalues" the least satisfying car with the lowest rank of 1.

Hard-Copy Decisions:
The Scores, Columns 6, 9, 12, 15

Columns 6, 9, 12, and 15 create *scores* that show how well each alternative car satisfies the needs. The family did this mentally during their patio conversation. But here in the *Hard-Copy Format*, the degree to which each car meets each need is quantified with a numeric *score*. The easiest way to do this is by multiplying the *weight* of each need (column 3) times the *rank* of each car (columns 5, 8, 11, 14). The results of this multiplication "rewards" the best car with the highest score, and "devalues" the least satisfying car with the lowest score.

Hard-Copy Decisions:
The Totals, Columns 6, 9, 12, 15

Finally, to finish the *Hard-Copy Format*, each *vertical* column of "scores" for each car (columns 6, 9, 12, and 15) is totaled at the bottom of Figure 1. These totals reveal the final ranking of each car, showing the degree to which each satisfies the family's needs.

Okay, as a quick review of the *Hard-Copy Format* for decision-making, let's practice it once by walking through the first horizontal row of numbers in the McIntire case.

A Review of the First Row of Cells

A Review of the Needs. The first horizontal row of numbers in Figure 1 starts at column 1, cell 1. This cell represents the need for the "lowest possible payment." In column 2, cell 1, the family agreed that this was their "most important" need. Finally, in column 3, cell 1, the family quantified the value of this most important need with the highest "weight" of six.

A Review of the Facts. In columns 4, 7, 10, and 13, this first row of cells was filled in with the facts on each car. This row of cells shows the need for "lowest possible payment." So in column 4, cell 1, the *Bison's* monthly payment is $595, and the monthly payments of the other cars are filled in for columns 7, 10, and 13.

A Review of the Rankings. In the first row of "ranking" cells (columns 5, 8, 11, and 14), each car was ranked by measuring it back against the need for "lowest possible payment" (column 1, cell 1). To rank each car, the cars were numbered backward: 4, 3, 2, 1. Since the *Riva* car has the lowest monthly payment, it was "rewarded" with the highest rank of *four* (column 14, cell 1). The *Mala* had the next lowest payment, so it has a rank of *three* (column 11, cell 1). The *Leno* had the next lowest payment, so it has a rank of *two* (column 8, cell 1). And the *Bison* was the most expensive car, so it was "devalued" with the lowest rank of *one* (column 5, cell 1).

A Review of the Scoring. In the first row of "scoring" cells (columns 6, 9, 12, and 15), each car was scored by multiplying its *rank* times the *weight* of the need in column 1, cell 1. In the headline at the top of column 6, a small instruction appears like this: (3 x 5 =). That means to multiply column 3 times column 5 to get an answer for column 6, cell 1. The need for the lowest possible payment has a weight of *six* (column 3, cell 1), and the *Bison* car has a value ranking of *one* (column 5, cell 1). So to get the answer for column 6, cell 1, *six was multiplied times one*, and the answer was "6." The same process continued (see instructions at the top of each column) across the first row of cells, filling in the "scores," until the first row of figures was completed.

A Review of the Totals. After all columns and cells have been filled in, the *vertical* scores for each car are totaled (columns 6, 9, 12, and 15), and placed in the boxes toward the bottom of Figure 1. Because the *largest* score wins, the format reveals the following rank-order of the cars, from best to worst: *Riva, Leno, Mala, Bison.*

A Review of the Future Troubles. There were no serious Future Troubles threatening the *Riva* car, so columns and figures aren't included for the *optional* Step 8. If there *had* been serious

Future Troubles threatening the *Riva,* and it had been necessary to consider the second-best car, this could have been done with notes at the bottom of the Figure 1, or with a separate sheet of paper, using the same processes and techniques.

In summary, you can create your own spreadsheet similar to Figure 1 in your own favorite spreadsheet program, and use it as a template for your own decisions—both personally and on the job. *Hard-Copy Formats* are especially useful for justifying decisions to superiors, for creating harmony in groups, and for long-term recordkeeping. (Even years later, you can show someone exactly why an important decision was made.)

Okay, let's recap all that we've said thus far. Here in Chapter 3, the first thing we did was illustrate a *Mental-Verbal Format* decision-making case with the New Car Puzzle case. That was the verbal story of the McIntires on the patio trying to choose a new car.

The second thing we did was illustrate a *Hard-Copy Format* decision-making case with the same McIntire story, but this time we displayed the case on a spreadsheet and showed the McIntire's story with visual rankings and scores.

Now, let's close Chapter 3 with our third format. It's called the *Simple-Pattern Format* for decision-making. It combines the best features of both of our previous formats. The *Simple-Pattern Format* is a template you can use for any decision of medium complexity (personal, career, family, civic club, or hobby group); that is, one that's too complex for the *Mental-Verbal Format,* but too simple for the *Hard-Copy Format.*

The *Simple-Pattern Format* obeys the same eight steps we used in the previous two formats, but it can be used over the phone, in conferences, by email, by PDAs, and in letters, reports, and memos. It's truly an all-purpose format.

The Simple-Pattern Format for Decision-Making

1. *Recognize a Choice Situation.* Recognize a situation requiring the choice of a thing, person, time, place, or amount that best satisfies its needs with the least risk of trouble.

2. *Develop a Clear Action Statement.* With all fuzzy words and the *what-who-when-where-amount* facual categories clarified, write a clear action statement starting with "*I (or we) want to choose the best* _____." (Write *what* is being chosen, *who* is effected, the *deadline*, the *place* of implementation, and the *amount* being chosen.)

3. *Develop the Needs.* With all fuzzy words and the *what-who-when-where-amount* factual categories clarified, list a minimum of four things the situation needs. Rank the needs by importance, giving the highest number (4) to the most important need, and the lowest number (1) to the least important need. "Needs" are things the situation is "asking for," such as *most* quality, production, morale, experience, and profit, etc.; and *least* cost, waste, maintenance, storage, damage, and raw materials, etc.

❏ We need _____

_____.

❏ We need _____

_____.

❏ We need _____

_____.

❏ We need _____

_____.

4. *Develop the Alternatives.* With all fuzzy words and the *what-who-when-where-amount* factual categories clarified, list a minimum of three alternatives that might satisfy the situation's needs. "Alternatives" are possible methods, ideas, people, options, places, amounts, times, plans, products, etc., that might satisfy the situation's needs. List all of the relevant facts about each alternative.

a) _____

_____.

b) _____

_____.

c) _____

_____.

5. *Make a Tentative Choice.* Compare the alternatives (Step 4) to the needs (Step 3) and make a tentative choice by asking which of the alternatives seems to *best* satisfy the situation's most important needs.

The tentative choice is _____

_____.

6. *Consider Future Troubles.* List the serious probable Future Troubles (if any) in the tentative choice if it is implemented. "Future Troubles" are serious probable mistakes, accidents, waste, bad quality, failures, misunderstandings, delays, and low morale, etc. _____

_____.

7. *Make a Final Choice.* If the tentative choice has no serious probable Future Troubles, it is the *final choice*. But if the tentative choice *does* have serious probable Future Troubles, continue to optional Step 8 of the format.

8. *Optional—Evaluate the Second Best Alternative.* To use this optional step, return to the remaining alternatives (Step 4), compare them to the needs again (Step 3), and choose the *second* best alternative in the format.

The second best alternative is _____

_____.

List the serious probable Future Troubles (if any) in the second best alternative. _____

_____.

If the second best alternative has fewer serious probable Future Troubles than the tentative choice, the second best alternative becomes the *final choice*. In the rare event that both the first and second alternatives have serious probable Future Troubles, a list of better alternatives should be developed before a choice can be made.

Summary of Chapter 3

Let's ask an interesting question. Why did we put so much emphasis in Chapter 3 on decision-making? Why did we show three different templates for making decisions? The answer is simple. Decision-making is one of the biggest keys to *Preactive* leadership, and when you master the technique of best choices, you've essentially mastered *Preactive* leadership.

That means Chapter 3 is probably the most important chapter in this book and the one you should review, study, and rehearse the most often. So discuss it with your family, friends, and coworkers. Practice its techniques. The very first week that you do, you'll find your decision-making ability has at least doubled.

Next, Chapter 4 is about another major key to *Preactive* leadership. It's about identifying the situations you're facing in your life, family, and work.

CHAPTER 4

HOW TO IDENTIFY SITUATIONS

In previous chapters, we learned several important principles. First, we learned that the biggest key to effective and efficient leadership is to focus first and foremost on the *Preactive* situations in our work—in other words, to always try to take all of our actions *before* trouble starts in our tasks (not after) and to take actions that prevent trouble from ever starting.

Second, we learned that all of the situations in our life and work are generic *Choice Situations*. They look different from one other because they occur in six different shapes, as if they were wearing six different masks. But regardless of which mask a situation is wearing, it's our duty to take the *best* action possible on it.

Then, we learned that three of the situations people face in life and on the job mask as Effective-Efficient situations and that we must emphasize them to be *Preactive* leaders. The other three situations mask as Ineffective-Inefficient situations, and if we focus on them, we're being *Reactive* leaders.

Finally, we said the key to being a *Preactive* leader is to identify the three Effective-Efficient situations when we see them—and then act on them—while trying to avoid being forced to act on any of the Ineffective-Inefficient situations. What these principles mean is that before we can read the coming chapters that diagram, define, and describe the six situations, we must first learn how to "identify" situations and how to write "clear statements" about them. But to do that, we must overcome the two big *communication traps* that make identifying situations difficult.

Two Communication Traps

In Chapters 2 and 3, we talked about writing clear action statements in decision-making. Those lessons were important and necessary. But now we need to talk about the other half of the leadership equation—how to write clear *situation* statements. Think about it. How can we make accurate choices on inaccurate situations? How can we satisfy the needs of situations if we didn't know what those needs are?

So, the first step in identifying situations is to learn to describe them clearly, both verbally and in writing. Learning that will also polish our skill at writing and speaking clear action statements as we practiced them in Chapters 2 and 3. So now, let's conquer *fuzzy words* and *smokescreen statements*.

Fuzzy Words and Smokescreen Statements

The quickest way to *identify* a situation is to disarm the two communication traps that make them hard to identify. These traps actually blend together as one big trap, but let's disarm them separately. The two traps are "fuzzy words" and "smokescreen statements." Let's start with an example of fuzzy words.

Imagine that you work in a factory. Your superior comes to your office door one bright and sunny Monday morning, and says cheerily, "Hey, we need to increase shipping capacity this week, and I'd like you to take care of it."

Your superior has just given you a *situation* that he or she wants you to act on. (We could also call it an assignment, job, project, task, and similar words.) But you *can't* identify it or act on it because of the way your superior presented it to you. Your superior presented the assignment to you in fuzzy words—and they make a situation unidentifiable.

In previous chapters we talked about the importance of clear action statements—but now we can see that it's even *more* important to have clear *situation* statements. This is true because action statements are based on *situation* statements. That is, action statements are "mirrors" of the situation statements they're acting on. So, if the situation statement is fuzzy, the action statement will also be fuzzy, and the final decision will be fuzzy, too.

Think about that before reading on. The entire linkage starts with a clear situation statement. This cause-and-effect linkage means that leaders have three big tasks.

1. To develop clear verbal and written *situation statements*.

2. To develop clear *action statements* that "mirror" the situation statements.

3. To take the *best* action possible on the action statements.

Note carefully the sequence of these steps. This sequence can't be broken. Also note that the first link in the sequence is *clear* situation statements. They're the gateway. They're where *Preactive* leadership begins. So now let's take a hard look at *fuzzy words* in situation statements.

Fuzzy Words

Returning to our factory story in the chapter, let's look at the mistakes the superior made as he or she stood at your office door. What fuzzy words did the superior use? The superior said, "Hey, we need to increase shipping capacity this week, and I'd like you to take care of it."

That's a verbal situation statement. But do you see the fuzzy words in it? There are several. But, the two most dangerous ones are the phrase, "shipping capacity." What does your superior mean by that? What is there about the "shipping capacity" of the factory that your superior wants you to increase? For example, does your superior want you to increase the number of *trucks* delivering your products? Or the number of *products* being manufactured? Or the number of *employees* working in the shipping department? Or the speed of the *conveyor belts* on the shipping dock?

You don't know *what* your superior wants you to do because the phrase "shipping capacity" is *fuzzy*. Until you clarify it, you can't logically take any action at all—unless you're willing to *assume* what the superior wants, and assumptions are deadly in leadership. For years, I've asked seminar participants this humorous question, "Where do *assumptions* get you in business?" And when they look blank, I answer: "Out of business!"

So let's not make any assumptions about the superior's situation. Instead, let's dig out the needs in the assignment, starting with the definition of a fuzzy word.

What Is a Fuzzy Word?

I often say in seminars that the most important leader-ship book ever written is the one book that many leaders read the *least*. Can you guess what that book is? It's the *dictionary*. As we said in Chapter 1, effective leaders always define their words. We'll say it over and over, "Words *matter*."

If you're like most people, you live in a world filled with "buzz words." Everybody's saying them. Everybody's hearing them. Everybody's writing them. But nobody knows what they mean. So let's cut through the fog with a definition.

The Definition of a Fuzzy Word

*A fuzzy word is any fact, word, or phrase in a situation statement or action statement that could refer to two or more **situations**, or that could imply two or more **actions**.*

We could call them blanket words, cluster words, abstractions, or corporate jargon, but I like to call them *fuzzy words* because people laugh when they hear the phrase and then remember it.

In our factory story, the phrase "shipping capacity" in the superior's situation statement is a classic fuzzy phrase. It could refer to two or more *situations* in the factory, and it could also refer to two or more *actions* in the factory. Thus, when your superior says he or she wants you to increase "shipping capacity" in the factory, you have no idea what situation or action he or she is referring to.

Do you see how *deceptive*

> **Fuzzy Word**
>
> *Any fact, word, or phrase in a situation statement or action statement that could refer to two or more **situations**, or that could imply two or more **actions**.*

fuzzy words are in leadership? Every day, all around us, we hear friends, family members, and coworkers saying things like, "*Fix* this for me…take *care* of that by Friday…*improve* this by the end of the month…do *better* on that before the vice-president gets here…increase the *quality* of this by the next quarter…take *more* time on that next year," and so on ad infinitum.

But the *italicized* word in each of these situation statements is fuzzy. It represents a fuzzy situation and a fuzzy action. So at the risk of being repetitive, let's be repetitive. Fuzzy words are dangerous because they make us guess what situation a speaker or writer has in mind, and what action the speaker or writer wants us to take.

In short, fuzzy words *conceal the identities of situations and actions*. To see this better, let's look at the principle in reverse. Politicians and advertising agencies sometimes purposely use fuzzy words to keep others from knowing what situations and actions they're referring to—and thus they avoid responsibility for the actions they end up taking.

Politicians often get elected by saying they're for "reform" —but without defining the fuzzy word "reform." That leaves them free to pass whatever laws they want to pass, and call it "reform."

Likewise, ad agencies often sell products by saying the products are "new"—but without defining the fuzzy word "new." That leaves them free to sell whatever products they want to sell, and call them "new."

So fuzzy words work splendidly when we don't *want* to be understood. They don't work well at all when we *do* want to be understood. The lesson is obvious. We can't use fuzzy words and phrases as *Preactive* leaders. So here's how to *clarify* fuzzy words.

How to Clarify Fuzzy Words

What should you do when faced with a fuzzy word? If you're speaking or writing the fuzzy word yourself, it's *your* responsibility to clarify it. For example, in my own writing, I put quotation marks around fuzzy words (as I've been doing in this chapter), and then I *clarify* the fuzzy word in parentheses following it. For example, if I was writing a report with the following ideas in it, here's what I would write: "We need to decrease 'rejects' (the number of defects per thousand pieces) by ten percent on assembly line four in the Gaston plant by December 31st."

You should do the same thing in your own speaking and writing. On the other hand, if someone else uses a fuzzy word on *you* and doesn't clarify it, it's your responsibility to help them clarify it. Here's how to do that.

Two Questions that Clarify Fuzzy Words

In our factory story, your superior came to your office and said, "Hey, we need to increase shipping capacity this week, and I'd like you to take care of it." We realize that the phrase "shipping capacity" in the superior's statement is fuzzy, and we know the superior didn't clarify it. So it becomes your responsibility to do so. To clarify the fuzzy phrase, you can ask one (or both) of the two fuzzy word clarification questions.

1. "What do you mean by...(*put the fuzzy word or phrase here*)?"
2. "What would you like me to do to...(*put the fuzzy word or phrase here*)?"

For example, if you used the first question, you might say to the superior, "Sure, I'll be glad to take care of that. And to help me get started, what do you mean by '*shipping capacity*'?"

In response, the superior might say, "Well, we need to be ready for the big advertising push we're planning next week, and I'm afraid the shipping department won't have enough storage space for the extra products we'll be producing."

Presto! You've *clarified* the fuzzy phrase "shipping capacity." The situation your superior is worried about is a potential lack of *storage space* in the shipping department. Moreover, the action your superior wants you to take is to *increase* storage space in that department.

As a second example, if you wanted to use the second clarification question, you might say to your superior, "Sure, I'll be glad to take care of that. And to help me get started, what would you like me to do to increase '*shipping capacity*'?" At which the superior would give the same answer. So when faced with fuzzy words, all we do is ask one (or both) of our special clarification questions and repeat as needed until all fuzziness is gone.

Notice it's often helpful to *reword* the questions in various ways, as long as you don't change the intent of them. For instance, you might have said to your superior, "Sure, I'll be glad to take care of that for you. But by '*shipping capacity*,' do you mean you want me to increase the speed of the conveyor belts?" At which the superior might have replied, "Well, no, I wasn't thinking about the conveyor belts. I was thinking about a potential lack of *storage space* in the shipping department." See how it works?

Finally, note that it's often helpful to embed the clarification questions in otherwise innocent sentences to soften their bluntness. I often embed my clarification questions in sentences such as, "Sure, I'll be glad to take care of that. And to help me get started...." This keeps superiors and coworkers from thinking I'm being disrespectful.

Now, it may surprise you after all this to know that some leaders are *reluctant* to ask the clarification questions. And you can guess why. They have too much pride. Or they're afraid to look uninformed. Or they want to look in control. But these reasons are false and create inefficiency. Failing to ask the fuzzy word clarification questions leaves us, our superiors, our coworkers, and our families all floundering in a fog of fuzzy situations and fuzzy actions.

Example: You give the keys to the family car to your teenager on Saturday evening, and say, "Now, Matt, I want you home *early* tonight."

To which Matt responds, "Okay, okay! Can I just go now?"

Guess what time Matt will get home?

Not early. Because "early" is a fuzzy word, and it leaves Matt free to interpret what time "early" means. It also leaves you helpless to enforce the time you thought Matt should be home that evening. That's what fuzziness does to us. So at home or on the job, any time we face a situation requiring us— or someone else—to take an action, we need to clarify the fuzzy words in the situation. We must be confident enough to ask the fuzzy word clarification questions of superiors, coworkers, family members, and friends.

If we don't, it's going to be very difficult to be *Preactive* leaders. Next, let's look at the second communication trap that makes the identification of situations difficult. It's called *smokescreen statements*.

What Is a
Smokescreen Statement?

Let's return to our factory story because it's typical of how we speak and write to one another. In the story, your superior stood at the door of your office and said, "Hey, we need to increase shipping capacity this week, and I'd like you to take care of it."

We agreed you couldn't take action at that point because of the fuzzy phrase "shipping capacity." But we used the fuzzy word clarification questions and discovered that "shipping capacity" meant the superior was worried over a potential lack of storage space for extra products the following week.

So we have a clue to the *identity* of the superior's situation—but only *one* clue. We still don't understand the superior's situation. Why not? Because it's still in a condition that textbooks call vague, abbreviated, or undeveloped.

The term I use for this is that the superior's situation statement is a "smokescreen statement." I use that term because when seminar participants hear it, they chuckle and then they remember about smokescreen statements.

In Chapter 1, we defined a "situation" as anything requiring you to take some *action*, at some time, in some place, to some extent. Thus, if your superior wants to be crystal clear about what action he or she wants you to take, the superior must tell you *five* important things about the situation. We call these important facts the *five factual categories*. Let's look at them.

1. What
2. Who
3. When
4. Where
5. Amount (How Much, How Many)

Note that these are the same *what-who-when-where-amount* factual categories that you saw in Chapters 2 and 3 while learning to write clear action statements. I tell seminar participants that they can remember these categories by thinking, *Four Ws, and an A.* Also note that the *amount* category can be answered two different ways. If you're dealing with an intangible subject (such as human motivation), you express the amount as *how much*. If you're dealing with a tangible subject (such as automobile parts), you express the amount as *how many*.

The rule with situation statements is this: To be "clear," they must have at least *one* clear fact in *each* of these five categories. Statements can have *several* facts per category, but they must have at least *one*. Thus, a clear situation statement must tell us five things: *What* needs to be done. *Who* needs to do it. *When* it needs to be done. *Where* it needs to be done. *How Much/How Many* of it needs to be done. With that, let's define a *smokescreen statement*.

The Definition of a
Smokescreen Statement

A smokescreen statement is any situation statement or choice statement that has a fuzzy fact, or a missing fact, in any of its five **what-who-when-where-amount** *factual categories.*

It's important to remember that both situation statements and action statements can be smokescreens, and that both must be clear before you can take a best action. Also remember that for any statement to be clear, each of its fuzzy words *and* each of its five factual categories must be fully clarified. Finally, notice that the "facts" in a smokescreen statement can be either *fuzzy* or *missing*.

Now, here's a principle that we haven't mentioned yet. Smokescreen statements always have duplicated fuzziness in them. That is, the unclear *facts* in smokescreen statements are usually also the fuzzy words in them. Again, the *same* words in statements are usually both fuzzy and unclear. To understand this principle, let's look again at the assignment the superior gave you in our factory story. The superior said, "Hey, we need to increase shipping capacity this week, and I'd like you to take care of it."

But now let's pause and break down the superior's statement to observe how the unclear facts in the statement's factual categories are also the statement's fuzzy words.

1. First, notice that two of the statement's required five factual categories were expressed in fuzzy or unclear words: The *what* category was expressed with the fuzzy phrase "shipping capacity," and the *when* category was expressed with the unclear phrase "this week."

2. Second, notice that the statement's *amount* category was expressed with the single fuzzy word "increase."

3. Third, note that the statement's *where* category was missing completely.

4. So *only* one of the statement's five factual categories was present and clear: The *who* category was clear—*you* were the person being asked to take action.

To summarize, four of the five factual categories in the superior's statement were either fuzzy, unclear, or missing. Said another way, *80% of the facts* in the superior's statement were either fuzzy, unclear, or missing. Imagine what that would mean for a subordinate trying to take a best action on the superior's situation.

> ## Smokescreen
> ## Statement
> *Any situation statement or choice statement that has a*
> *fuzzy fact, or a missing fact, in any of its five*
> **what-who-when-where-amount**
> *factual categories.*

It's sad, but true, that smokescreen statements are the *typical* way we communicate with one another at home and on the job. We communicate through fuzzy words, unclear facts, and missing facts. Is it any wonder that there's so much ineffectiveness, inefficiency, stress, pain, and confusion in our lives? So let's do something about it. Here's how to *clarify* smokescreen statements.

How to Clarify
Smokescreen Statements

What should you do when you encounter smokescreen statements? If you're speaking or writing the statements yourself, you're obligated to clarify them for your reader or listener *yourself*. However, if someone else is presenting the smokescreens statement to you, and expecting you to act on it, it's your responsibility to help him or her clarify them.

The clarification of smokescreen statements is done the same way we clarified fuzzy words earlier—by *asking questions*. (Someone once said that the most powerful leadership technique of all is "the right question at the right time.") But this time we're going to ask five special *factual clarification questions*.

Five Questions that Clarify Smokescreen Statements

In our factory story, the superior said, "Hey, we need to increase shipping capacity this week, and I'd like you to take care of it." Then, by asking the two fuzzy word clarification questions, you discovered that the superior's fuzzy phrase "shipping capacity" meant the superior was worried about a potential lack of *storage space* for extra products the coming week. But that's all you know at this point. The superior's statement is *still* too clouded for you to act. You still need more information. To get it, you use the five factual categories we've been discussing, and you convert them into five questions.

1. "What?"
2. "Who?"
3. "When?"
4. "Where?"
5. "Amount?" ("How Much?" / "How Many?")

In earlier paragraphs, we already answered questions 1 and 2. Storage space is *what* you're supposed to increase, and you're the *who* being asked to do the increasing.

But you don't have answers to the remaining three categories—the *when*, *where*, and *amount*. Thus, in a conversational manner, you ask the superior the clarification questions for these fuzzy, unclear, and missing categories. You embed the questions in conversational sentences, so you don't seem disrespectful, and you might say, "Sure, I can increase our storage space. And since we need it increased *this week,* would you like me to do it by 5:00 pm Friday?"

At which the superior might answer, "No, I was actually thinking it needs to be done by 4:00 pm Thursday."

You reply, "Okay, and have you thought about *where* it should be increased? Like maybe in the production department?"

"No, I was thinking the increase needs to be done in the shipping department."

"Great idea. And *how much* increase do you think we need? Maybe 20 percent?"

"That's a good guess, but I think we should have at least 30 percent."

"Okay, 30 percent it is. I'll get started on this immediately."

And, presto, without being disrespectful, you've checked off the remaining factual categories in a relaxed, conversational way and developed a clarified situation statement that you can take action on.

Okay, adding these clarifications to your superior's original statement, here's how the superior's statement might look if he or she spoke it again, "Hey, I need you to increase storage space 30 percent in the shipping department by 4:00 pm this Thursday afternoon."

Note that it's acceptable to change the *order* of the categories in a statement, as long as you don't skip a category or leave one fuzzy, unclear, or missing. In this example, you realigned the categories like this: *who-what-amount-where-when.* The important thing is that all five categories are clarified.

Now let's make a special point. Let's take the *clarified* statement we just created, and let's compare it to your superior's original smokescreen statement at your office door. Then let's ask an important question about that comparison.

1. Here's the smokescreen statement as your superior originally voiced that Monday morning: "Hey, we need to increase shipping capacity this week, and I'd like you to take care of it."

2. Here's the clarified situation statement we've worked on: "Hey, I need you to increase floor space 30 percent in the shipping department by 4:00 pm this Thursday afternoon."

Comparing these two versions, here's the important question. *Which* one of these two statements would be the safest for you to act on? Better yet, which one of these two statements would give you the best chance at effective action? Better yet, which one of these two statements would give you the best chance for future promotions, pay raises, recognition, and other career rewards? Doesn't the clarified version win hands down?

If you see this powerful lesson, it means that one of the first steps you can take toward doubling your leadership ability in one week is to start clarifying your situation and action statements the way we've done it here. But let's drill even deeper. A common question I hear in seminars is "Why don't we include the *how* and the *why* factual categories in statements?"

What Happened to the How and Why?

In 1902, the English poet Rudyard J. Kipling wrote a poem entitled *The Elephant's Child*. In that poem, he penned one of his most famous lines, "I keep six honest serving-men (they taught me all I knew); their names are What and Why and When, and How and Where and Who."

This Kipling poem is the source of the motto "Five Ws, and an H" that journalism students memorize in college (who, what, where, when, why, and how). And perhaps, due to Kipling's poem and this journalistic motto, people often ask why we don't use the *how* and *why* categories in situation and action statements. The answer is that we *can* use them if they're necessary for a best action, but if they're not necessary, we leave them as options at the discretion of leaders. Here's why. In this book, we're learning how to write clear situation and action statements, not how to write poems and news stories.

In leadership, it's not necessary for busy leaders to explain to coworkers and subordinates *why* something needs to be done. (Although that's often helpful for good communications.) Nor is it necessary for leaders to explain to coworkers and subordinates *how* something needs to be done. (Coworkers and subordinates usually know how to do their jobs, and are being paid to know how.) Thus, unless the *why* and *how* categories are required for a best action, these categories are optional in the field of leadership.

It's also interesting to notice that Kipling didn't include the *amount* category in his poem, and neither do the journalism schools. Kipling apparently felt the *amount* category isn't necessary in poems; and the journalism schools apparently feel it's not necessary in news stories, either. But it *is* necessary in leadership.

Now, let's do some fine-tuning. How do we know when a statement is *really* clear?

When is "Clear" Really Clear?

Another thing people often ask is how they can know when a statement is *really* "clear." How can they know when all the fuzzy, unclear, and missing facts are *totally* clarified in a statement? Here's the answer. Statements are totally clear when *anyone* hearing them can understand them—even employees from other departments, trainees, outsiders, or anyone else. Let's return to our factory story to see how that works.

The word *clear* means without confusion and unmistakable in the mind. So, when the superior asked you to "increase" storage space for extra products "next week," the statement was still confusing. It was still mistakable in your mind. You didn't know *how much* the storage space was to be increased, you didn't know *when* next week it was to be increased, and you didn't know *where* it was to be increased. So you asked the *amount*, *when*, and *where* factual clarification questions and found that storage space was to be increased 30 percent by 4:00 pm this Thursday in the shipping department.

Now—the lesson is that *anyone* can understand the words "30 percent," "4:00 pm this Thursday," and "shipping department." Even employees from other departments, trainees, outsiders, or anybody else can understand them. True, outsiders may not have the skills to *act* on the words without help. But they can *understand* what the words in the situation statement are saying. This means that a statement is "clear" when anyone who hears it or reads it can *understand* it, even if they don't have the skills to take a best action on it.

Finally, there's one last principle in clarifying statements that we need to know. It's this. Sometimes the five clarification questions must be *repeated* several times before a statement is totally clear.

Repeating Until a Statement is Clear

Sometimes the clarification questions we're learning must be *repeated* several times before a fact in a statement becomes totally clear. That applies to both fuzzy words and smokescreen statements, and applies to both situation statements and action statements.

For example, in our factory story, imagine that you are trying to clarify the *when* factual category in your superior's original smokescreen statement. You'll recall that the superior stood in your office door and said you should increase storage space *this week*. But the phrase "this week" is still unclear. It's still confusing and mistakable in your mind.

So you ask the superior the *when* clarification question, "*When* this week?"

The superior smiles pleasantly and says, "Oh, later this week."

The superior has answered your question. But the *when* category is still unclear because what does "later this week" mean?

So to escape the trap, you repeat the *when* clarification question over and over until the category is at last clear. Sometimes a question must be repeated two or three times before the category is finally clear. Let's demonstrate that by returning to the superior standing in your office door, and let's pick up the thread of the conversation again. This time, you're going to repeat the *when* clarification question until the superior's statement is totally clear.

Your superior has just said, "We need to increase storage space *this week.*"

You have just said, "*When* this week?" (You have asked *when* the first time.)

"Oh, later this week," the superior has answered with a pleasant smile.

But now you continue by asking again, "*When* later this week?" (You're asking *when* a second time.)

"Oh, Thursday would be okay," the superior replies.

"*When* Thursday?" you ask. (You're asking *when* a third time.)

"Well, Thursday afternoon would be good," says the superior.

"*When* Thursday afternoon?" you ask. (You're asking *when* a fourth time.)

"Well, let's do it by 4:00 pm, because I'm leaving town then."

And, zap! The superior's unclear phrase "this week" suddenly becomes *Thursday afternoon at 4:00 pm.*

But you had to ask the *when* clarification question four times to get the phrase clear. Yes, this example was silly. I purposefully made the superior much harder to work with than he or she would have been in real life. But, I wanted you to see the full questioning process as it sometimes needs to be applied. In a real life conversation, it usually only takes two, or at most three, repeats of a question to get a category clear. Okay, a final thought about clarifying questions.

What If You
Don't Know the Answer?

Sometimes, in situations involving planning, forecasting, and other futuristic activities, you won't have clear facts for the *amount* and *when* categories, and you won't be able to get them. With situations that extend into the future, we often can't predict *how much* of the task can be accomplished, or *when* it can be completed.

In such cases, it's acceptable to use the well-known abbreviations "amap" (as much as possible), and "asap" (as soon as possible), in statements. This proves to your readers and listeners that you didn't forget these categories—you just didn't have any facts for them.

For example, if had we been using this technique in our factory story, the superior's situation statement might have sounded like this, "Hey, I need you to increase floor space *amap* in the shipping department *asap*." Of course, we can't get lazy and use these abbreviations in every statement we develop, but they're acceptable when we have no option.

And there you have it. Now you know how to write crystal clear situation and action statements. Next, let's see why clear statements are so important and why they're worth the hard work to develop them.

Putting the Icing on the Cake

It turns out that leadership is a two-step process, like putting the icing on a cake. In this analogy, the "cake" (which we bake first) is a clear *situation* statement for a task. The "icing" (which we cook second) is a clear *action* statement for the decision and action on the situation. And, like icing on a cake, action statements must fit perfectly on top of situation statements.

This means that situation statements (the cake in leadership) are the *foundations* for action statements (the icing in leadership). Said another way, the facts of action statements must be perfect "mirrors" of the facts in situation statements. Let's say that yet another way. The *what-who-when-where-amount* facts of action statements must perfectly match the *what-who-when-where-amount* facts of situation statements. When you think about it, that's the only way we can obey the *Master Principle of Satisfying Needs* that we discussed in Chapter 1.

In summary, since we now see the difference between clear and unclear statements, and between action statements and situation statements, we're ready to start *identifying* situations, starting with the superior's situation in our factory story.

How to Identify Situations

At last, we're ready to *identify* the superior's situation in our factory story. Of course, this step will also reveal the identity of the action we're going to take on the situation. To review a moment, our most recent version of the superior's situation statement now reads, "I need you to increase storage space 30 percent in the shipping department by 4:00 pm this Thursday afternoon."

That's our cake. It'll be the foundation for the decision and the action we're going to take. But now we need the icing for the top of the cake: We need a action statement that mirrors the facts of the situation. Thus, our action statement might read like this, "I want to choose the best way to increase storage space 30 percent in the shipping department by 4:00 o'clock this Thursday afternoon."

Neat and tidy, don't you think? Our cake is complete. We have a strong and clear action statement fitted securely on top of the superior's strong and clear situation statement. We know exactly what the superior's situation needs, and exactly what kind of decision we're going to make to satisfy those needs.

But let's pause a moment to be certain we understand the difference between a situation statement (a cake), and an action statement (the icing). How do we know which is which?

Situation Statements vs. Action Statements

The best way to tell the difference between situation statements and action statements is to remember two rules.

1. Situation statements describe the needs of the task to be performed. They're normally assigned to us by other people. Thus, they usually open with words like, "*We need to....*" Or "*I want you to....*"

2. Action statements describe the *action* we're going to taken on the situation. They're normally developed by us, or by our team of coworkers, in response to previous assignments. Thus, they usually open with the words we learned in Chapters 2 and 3, "*I (or we) want to choose the best* _____ _____.*"*

With this background, it's time to identify the superior's situation in our factory story. Now that we know how to clarify situation and action statements, we can safely *identify* them.

The Identity
of the Superior's Situation

The word *identity* means the characteristics of something that make it recognizable. For example, the characteristics of our faces make us recognizable to friends. So, the purpose of the clarification questions for fuzzy words and smokescreen statements in this chapter is to reveal the *characteristics* of situations so we can safely identify them.

So, what is the identity of the superior's situation in our factory story? And what's the identity of the action we're going to take on that situation? We already know the superior's situation is a generic Choice Situation requiring us to take a best Decision Action. But the specific question is: Which of the six "masks" is the superior's situation wearing?

For that matter, what *are* the six masks that situations wear? We're going to look at them briefly in the following Identification Tables, and then we're going discuss each one of the six different situations fully in following chapters.

The Identification Tables

The two Identification Tables on the following pages describe the characteristics of the six situations as they occur in our homes and workplaces. Each of the descriptions in these tables includes the name of the situation, the name of the action

IDENTIFICATION TABLE 1

The Three Effective-Efficient Situations

Directing Tasks Before Trouble Starts with Preactive, Offensive-Minded Strategies and Tactics

Name of Situation	In Chapter	Description Of Situation	Existence In Time	Name of Action	Leadership Technique
1. Normal Work (NW)	5	A routine, repetitive task being performed within set, clear, and agreed on standards	Present	Working Actions (WAs)	Work-Accuracy *I want to choose the best (WAs to meet all the standards in this NW sit).*
2. Work Improvement (WI)	6	A standard in a task that can be improved	Present	Improving Action (IA)	Standards-Betterment *I want to choose the best (IA to make this standard better in this NW sit).*
3. Likely Cause (LC)	7	A weakness that will probably cause performance to break a task standard in an unwanted way	Present but will cause trouble in the future	Blocking Action (BA)	Trouble-Prevention *I want to choose the best (BA to prevent this LC from hatching in the work standards in this NW sit).*

IDENTIFICATION TABLE 2

The Three Ineffective-Inefficient Situations

Correcting Tasks After Trouble Starts with Reactive, Defensive-Minded Strategies and Tactics

Name of Situation	In Chapter	Description Of Situation	Existence In Time	Name of Action	Leadership Technique
1. Current Trouble (CT)	8	A performance that is breaking a task standard in an unwanted way	Present but originated in the past	Suppressing Action (SA)	Trouble-Control *I want to choose the best (SA to suppress this CT in the work on this NW sit).*
2. True Cause (TC)	9	The reason that a performance is breaking a task standard in an unwanted way	Present but originated in the past	Correcting Action (CA)	Cause-Removal *I want to choose the best (CA to remove this TC from the work on this NW sit).*
3. Future Trouble (FT)	10	A performance that could break a task standard in an unwanted way at a future time	Will originate and exist in the future	Preparing Action (PA)	Trouble-Readiness *I want to choose the best (PA to wait to suppress this FT if it happens in this NW sit).*

to be taken in that situation, and the name of the leadership technique being used.

Study these tables carefully because we're going to use them to identify the superior's situation in our factory story. They're the focal point of this entire book and we'll refer to them repeatedly in the following chapters.

How to Use the Identification Tables

Let's find out which of the six identities in the Identification Tables fits the superior's situation in our factory story. You'll recall that the most recent version of the superior's situation statement reads, "We need to increase storage space 30 percent in the shipping department by 4:00 pm this Thursday afternoon." Looking at the tables, which of the six descriptions in the tables fits this statement? There are two techniques for using the tables. Let's look at them now.

Two Techniques for Using the Identification Tables

Once you have a situation statement fully clarified, and there are no fuzzy, unclear, or missing facts in it, there are two ways to use the Identification Tables to identify the clarified statement. Here they are.

1. A process of elimination.

2. A past-present-future test.

Either one (or both) of these approaches can be used to "unmask" a generic Choice Situation and reveal its identity. The techniques can be used together, or separately, in any sequence. Naturally, your skill at identification will increase with practice and experience. So use these tables on the job and practice them often. Let's now identify the superior's situation. Follow our thought process on the tables as we go.

1. I usually begin with a process of elimination starting at Table 1, Row 1 with the *Normal Work* situation. In this case, the superior's situation—as he or she assigned it to you at your office door—is a special, one-of-a-kind project. It *isn't* a regular, routine, repetitive, everyday task for you. It's a unique task your superior is assigning to you as a one-shot deal. Thus, the superior's situation *isn't* a Normal Work situation for you, and that eliminates Table 1, Row 1.

2. Next, let's check Table 1, Row 2, the *Work Improvement* situation. Your superior isn't asking you to improve a standard in one of your tasks to make your work exceed a customer's expectations in a surprising new way, so the superior's situation *isn't* a Work Improvement situation, and that eliminates Table 1, Row 2.

Let's pause here and turn back to Table 2 for a moment. (You can already see that the superior's situation is going to be a match with Table 1, Row 3.) We'll return to this row in a few seconds.

3. Next, let's check Table 2, Row 1 the *Current Trouble* situation. Your superior isn't asking you to fight the damage of an existing trouble that's occurring in the factory at the moment, so the superior's situation *isn't* a Current Trouble situation, and that eliminates Table 2, Row 1.

4. Next is Table 2, Row 2, the *True Cause* situation. But since there's no trouble occurring in the factory at this time, your superior isn't asking you to find, verify, and remove the True Cause of an existing trouble, and the superior's situation *isn't* a True Cause situation. That eliminates Table 2, Row 2.

5. Finally, let's check Table 2, Row 3, the *Future Trouble* situation. Now the superior *is,* in fact, worried about a potential trouble that might occur next week in the shipping department—the superior is afraid there won't be enough storage space in the shipping department to handle extra products starting next week. So, at first glance, the assignment the superior giving you *looks* like a Future Trouble situation. But the fact that locks down the identification is *when* the superior wants you to take action. Does the superior want action now, this week? Or later, next week?

6. Here's where we apply our second technique for identifying situations. Let's now use a past-present-future test. The question is: *When* is the superior asking you to take action on the assignment—*before* the lack of storage space occurs in the shipping department—or *after* the lack of storage space occurs?

Let's ask that a different way. Is your superior asking you to take action in the *present* (this week)? Or is your superior asking you to take action in the *future* (next week)? Obviously, your superior is asking you to take action *now* (in the *present*) to prevent a lack of storage space next week (in the future).

Looking at Table 2, Row 3, you superior *isn't* asking you to use the *Trouble-Readiness* technique and to take a Preparing Action that will wait to suppress the shortage of space next week after it occurs. Instead, you superior is asking you to use the Trouble-Prevention technique and to take a Blocking Action to *prevent* next week's trouble from ever happening in the first place.

7. Thus, the superior's situation *isn't* a Future Trouble situation, and that eliminates Table 2, Row 3. Instead, the superior's assignment given at your office door is a *Likely Cause* situation as described in Table 1, Row 3—the only situation we haven't eliminated. The superior is asking you to take a best Blocking Action now, in the *present*, to prevent trouble in the *future*. Case closed.

Using our two techniques (a process of elimination and a past-present-future test), we eliminated five of the six situations on the tables, and identified the superior's situation as a Likely Cause situation.

As a matter of fact, if your superior had been trained in *Preactive* leadership, he or she might have voiced your assignment something like this, "Hey, we need to increase storage space 30 percent in the shipping department by 4:00 pm this Thursday afternoon *to prevent a lack of storage space for extra products next week.*"

Now, your final steps in the factory story will be to write a clear *action statement* for the action you're going to take, to then make a *final decision* on exactly what you're going to do, and then to implement your final action.

Your Action Statement,
Final Decision, and Action

We've learned in this chapter that leadership is like baking and icing a cake. The cake is a clear situation statement. The icing is a clear *action statement* that mirrors the facts of the clear situation statement. But we don't have the icing in this case yet. So let's cook it now. We've identified the superior's situation as a Likely Cause situation requiring you to choose and implement a best Blocking Action.

Thus, your clear action statement might say something like this, "I want to choose the best Blocking Action to increase storage space by 30 percent in the shipping department by 4:00 pm this Thursday afternoon to prevent a lack of storage space next week."

Next, there's nothing to do but make the final decision and implement the final action. You learned how to make best decisions in Chapters 2 and 3. You start with a list of needs (in this case, things like "least disruption of work," "most employee safety," "fastest action," "cheapest action," etc.).

You continue by listing three or more alternatives (in this case, things like "knock down some partitions in the shipping department," "buy a new shelving system for the shipping department," "add more shelves to the old shelving system in the shipping department," "rent space in the warehouse next door," etc.).

Then you measure your alternatives against your needs and make a tentative choice. Let's pretend your tentative choice is "Add more shelves to the old shelving system in the shipping department."

After that, you check your tentative choice for overwhelming Future Troubles. To keep this case simple, let's pretend there aren't any. So your final decision is: *add more shelves to the old shelving system in the shipping department.*

At this point, nothing is left to do but stroll down to the shipping department and implement your new Blocking Action—to the applause, whistles, and cheers of your coworkers. End of story.

Jokes aside, do you see the power of writing clear situation statements, identifying them, writing clear action statements, making best choices, and implementing best actions? *That's* what we call *Preactive* leadership.

Remember, these are the exact techniques that the young assistant supervisor used in the Introduction of this book to get a promotion in 15 minutes. And—if the young assistant supervisor could do it then—you can do it now.

Finally, as we close this chapter, let's not overlook the *big strategic principle* hidden in our factory story.

Offensive-Mindedness

Before closing, we should realize that something profound just happened in our factory story that's not obvious on its surface. The factory story illustrates the theme of this book. It illustrates how *Preactive*, *directive*, and *offensive-minded* leadership must be habits in the workplace.

Let's say that a different way. Our story about the superior coming to your office on a Monday morning and giving you a *Preactive* assignment shows—despite the fuzzy way the superior gave you the assignment—that he or she is an *offensive-minded* leader, and that's a very good thing.

Procrastination being so prevalent, leaders in other factories might have taken the easy way out when faced with a potential lack of storage space in the shipping department, and might have said to themselves, "Well, I'll just cross that bridge when I get to it. I can find more space somewhere in the building if I need to. Right now, I don't have time to worry about it. I've got to get on with the job at hand."

Does that sound familiar? That's the sound of *defensive-minded* leadership on a roll. The point is that it takes courage, assertiveness, and alertness to be a *Preactive* leader. The only things needed to be a *Reactive* leader are timidity, passiveness, and absent-mindedness. We're going to go much deeper into exactly how to use *Preactive* strategies and tactics in your life and career in Chapters 11 and 12. But right now let's close this chapter.

Summary of Chapter 4

1. The only way to be a *Preactive* leader is to learn to *identify* situations. But there are two communication weaknesses that make identifying situations difficult. They are fuzzy words and smokescreen statements.

2. A "fuzzy word" is any fact, word, or phrase in a situation statement or choice statement that could refer to two or more situations or that could imply two or more actions.

3. The two fuzzy word clarification questions are: "What do you mean by... *(put the fuzzy word or phrase here)*?" Or, "What would you like me to do to... *(put the fuzzy word or phrase here)*?"

4. A "smokescreen statement" is any situation statement or choice statement that has a fuzzy fact, or a missing fact, in any of its five *what-who-when-where-amount* factual categories.

5. The five factual clarification questions are: *"What?" "Who?" "When?" "Where?" "Amount?"*

6. The best way to remember the difference between a situation statement and an action statement is that a situation statement describes the *task*, and is normally assigned to you by other people. So it usually starts with words like, "*We need to....*" Or, "*I want you to....*" On the other hand, an action statement describes the action you're going to take on the task and is normally developed by you. So it usually starts with the decision-making phrase you learned in Chapters 2 and 3, "*I (or we) want to choose the best....*"

7. The two Identification Tables for situations and actions are on pages 114-115, and we identified the superior's situation statement in our factory story as a *Likely Cause* situation requiring a best *Blocking Action* to prevent a lack of storage space in the shipping department from ever occurring next week.

8. This chapter ended with the writing of a clear action statement to "mirror" the facts of the superior's situation, and by walking through the decision to and implementation of the best Blocking Action to prevent the superior's Likely Cause situation from happening.

9. Last of all, we recognized that the factory story shows the theme of this book in a real-life way. All of us need to develop the habit of being strategically and tactically *Preactive*, *directive*, and *offensive-minded* in our lives and on our jobs.

In Chapter 5, we're going to learn all about the keystone situation that serves as the platform for all human activity. It's called the Normal Work situation.

PART II

THE THREE EFFECTIVE-EFFICIENT SITUATIONS

CHAPTER 5

NORMAL WORK SITUATIONS

The First
Effective-Efficient Situation
(See Table 1, Row 1, Page 114)

Description: A Routine, Repetitive, Task Being Performed Within Set, Clear, and Agreed On Standards

Existence in Time: The Present

Name of Actions: Working Actions

Leadership Technique: Work-Accuracy

Leadership Type: *Directing* Tasks with *Preactive* Strategies and Tactics

Action Statement

Template: *I want to choose the best (Working Actions to meet all the standards in this Normal Work situation).*

With Chapter 5, we begin our detailed discussions of the six situations or the six "masks," that generic Choice Situations can wear. The first of these masks is the Normal Work situation. It's the most common, basic, and frequent situation in our lives and jobs, and that's why we're taking it first. Normal Work situations are the foundations of all leadership, work, and life, so they're extremely important, and are described in Table 1, Row 1, on page 114.

Normal Work situations are the reason we do what we do. They're the reason we get out of bed in the morning. They're the reason organizations hire us, and the reason organizations pay us. They're the basic, sequential, routine units of all work. So it's logical to start our reading of our chapters on the six leadership situations with the *Normal Work* situation and with the actions we take on them, which we call *Working Actions*.

This chapter is also about our first leadership technique, *Work-Accuracy*, and we have a sample, or template for a typical action statement in this chapter that reads, *I want to choose the best (Working Actions to meet all the standards in this Normal Work situation).*

In the previous chapter you learned how to write clear situation and action statements, so you know how to flesh out this template with appropriate facts. For example, you might write, *I want to choose the best Working Actions to meet all of our communications standards as I write the Jackson Report in my office by its deadline of 12:00 noon, Friday, April 7th.*

Also notice that Normal Work situations are in the group of three Effective-Efficient situations in the tables on pages 114-115. This means Normal Work situations are one of the three situations we use to *direct* tasks toward goals with *Preactive* and *offensive-minded* type of leadership.

Now, before continuing, here's a tip. I write and speak a lot about situations, so I've developed my own shorthand for them. When I refer to Normal Work situations, I call them "*NW*" sits, and I refer to Working Actions as "*WAs*." These abbreviations are shown in the tables on pages 114-115, and you'll also see them in the diagrams in this book. Notice, too, that Working Actions are the *only* actions in the book that are always described in the *plural.* That's because we normally take *many* Working Actions on each Normal Work situation, as you'll soon see.

To continue, we were saying that Normal Work situations (NW sits) are the sequential units of *work* in our lives. That means they're also the rungs up the ladder of success as a leader. The other five situations we'll discuss in coming chapters are *connected* to NW sits and are *part* of them. Thus, once you master NW sits in this chapter, you've also begun to master the other five situations.

Now, as we begin talking about Normal Work situations, remember that you already know a lot about them. From Chapter 2, you know they're generic Choice Situations requiring you to take a best Decision Action to satisfy their needs. From Chapter 3, you know how to make a best decision on them. And from Chapter 4, you know how to clarify fuzzy words and smokescreen statements to identify Normal Work sits on your job.

So, as we start Chapter 5, you already have a large storehouse of knowledge about NW sits. But now let's start adding some fresh facts to your storehouse by breaking NW sits into two pieces, and looking at them one piece at a time. Let's begin with a definition of the word *normal*.

What is Normal?

The word *normal* comes from a root meaning a carpenter's square—a tool that measures how "square" things are. So the word literally means something that's perfectly square when measured with a precision tool. In other words, a *normal* situation is one that's regular, routine, correct, and is meeting all of its standards with no errors.

A Normal Work sit is a unit of work that's proceeding through time and space with *quality*. It has no defects. Everyone's happy with it. Superiors, coworkers, subordinates, and customers (or family members, friends, civic leaders, etc.) are pleased with it.

To apply the principle to your personal job—regardless of your title or pay scale—your Normal Work sits are the things you were hired to do with quality. (Always remember that quality is embedded in our definition of a Normal Work sit.) Thus, your work on your NW sits must always be regular, routine, and within standards. That's why the leadership technique in this chapter is called *Work-Accuracy*.

> ## Normal
>
> *A normal situation is one that's regular, routine, correct, and is meeting all of its standards with no errors.*

This chapter is about working on your job with quality. Let's think about it this way. If you're a writer, your NW sits are the books you're supposed to be writing with quality. If you're a pilot, your NW sits are the flights you're supposed to be flying with quality. If you're a house painter, your NW sits are the houses you're supposed to be painting with quality. NW sits are the work you were hired to do—and that you were hired to do with quality.

However, now we should pause and think about the word "quality" a moment. Have you ever thought about your life and job as being defined by the quality of your actions? Have you ever thought about your leadership in your job, family, civic duties, or church as being characterized by the quality of your accomplishments?

The word *quality* means conformance to standards, and the word *accuracy* means exact conformance to standards. That's what our actions in Normal Work sits are supposed to be doing—*conforming exactly* to the standards set for them by the family, club, non-profit, corporation, or individual for whom the work is being done.

Okay, now that we've seen what the word *normal* means in "Normal Work," let's look at the second half of the phrase, and see what the word *work* means.

What is Work?

The word *work* means to apply physical and mental effort to something. So "work" can refer to anything that people apply themselves to—from artists painting pictures, to authors writing books, to carpenters building houses. Work can refer to a person's career, job, trade, profession, or livelihood. More broadly, it can refer to any duty, task, assignment, project, performance, or chore we undertake. To make this clearer, here are some synonyms for the word work.

Common Synonyms for the Word Work

Task	Project
Job	Contract
Program	Operation
Assignment	Undertaking
Duty	Performance
Chore	Mission
Appointment	Errand
Activity	Exercise

There are probably a dozen more synonyms for *work*, but you get the idea. Work is any activity for which we assume responsibility, and during which we exert mental and physical effort. Adding all these thoughts together, Normal Work sits, as we're learning them, include any and all the tasks you undertake in your personal life, family life, and work life. The definition of a NW sit applies to everything we see people doing—whether they're students, parents, civic leaders, politicians, military officers, police officers, or corporate executives.

Against that broad background, let's define a Normal Work situation. In Chapter 1, we defined a *situation* as anything requiring you to take some action, at some time, in some place, to some extent. So using all that we've learned about situations, actions, standards, and decision-making, here's our full definition of a *Normal Work* situation.

The Definition of a Normal Work Situation

*Any regular situation (task, assignment) you undertake with clear and agreed on **standards** that requires you to choose Working Actions that best **satisfy** those standards with the least risk of Future Trouble.*

Before continuing, let's stop to highlight a key word in this definition. We mentioned this word in previous chapters, but now it needs to be emphasized. I've said in seminars for many years that this is *the most important word in leadership*. It's the word "standards." Let's define it.

What is a Standard?

The word *standards* is a fascinating word. It's from a root meaning to stand fast, in the sense of standing fast in battle. So the word literally means a standing place or a place to make a last stand. In today's language, standards are terms, numbers, and ideas that describe what you "stand for" in a task, project, or product.

Said another way, standards are terms you use to describe how you intend to meet the needs of your customers. Standards describe what you *should* do (and *should not* do) in a task. Another way to define the word standards is to look at its synonyms. Here are just a few.

Common Synonyms for the Word Standards

Needs	Controls
Policies	Rules
Procedures	Protocols
Guidelines	Goals
Objectives	Specifications
Blueprints	Criteria
Principles	Laws
Patterns	Beliefs
Morals	Doctrines
Statutes	Benchmarks
Values	Ethics
Styles	Assumptions

All of these words mean the same thing. They tell the world what you, your family, your friends, and your coworkers "stand for" when you're performing your tasks. They tell others how you measure your activities. In the briefest terms, standards are *measuring words*. They measure the extent to which your actions are satisfying the needs of your projects.

It's important here to recognize that the synonym "needs" (the first word in our list of synonyms) is probably the most *common* of the 200 or more synonyms for standards—and that's why we use it in our definition.

> ## *Normal Work Situation*
>
> *Any regular situation (task, assignment) you undertake with clear and agreed on **standards** that requires you to choose Working Actions that best **satisfy** those standards with the least risk of Future Trouble.*

In Chapter 1, we discussed the *Master Principle of Satisfying Needs*. Now we see that principle being applied here. The ruling principle in leadership is that our actions must exactly conform to the standards (needs) of our situations. When a Normal Work sit has "clear and agreed on standards," it has clear and agreed on measures to prove the degree to which our actions *are* (or *are not*) satisfying it. Using all these ideas, here's our full definition of a standard.

The Definition
of a Standard

*Any **word**, **phrase**, or **number** that describes what a situation
needs and that measures the degree to which actions
taken in that situation **satisfy** those needs.*

Thus, the purpose of clear and agreed on standards in a Normal Work sit is to be able to measure which of our Working Actions *are* (or are *not*) satisfying it. If we read that principle backwards, we *can't* take accurate Working Actions in a NW situation *unless* we have previously set, clear, and agreed on standards to measure those actions.

That said, we're ready to define "Working Actions." In Chapter 1, we defined *action* as anything you do, at some time, in some place, to some extent. So let's build on that definition to create a full description of *Working Actions*.

The Definition
of Working Actions

*Any **actions** you choose and implement in Normal
Work situations to best satisfy their clear and
agreed on standards and to move them toward
their goals with the least risk of Future Trouble.*

Okay, with these definitions in place, let's define the leadership technique of *Work-Accuracy*.

The Definition of the Technique of Work-Accuracy

*Choosing and implementing the **best** Working Actions to satisfy the clear and agreed on **standards** of Normal Work situations and to move them toward their goals with the least risk of Future Trouble.*

Stated in one sentence: Work-Accuracy is setting clear and agreed on standards for tasks and choosing best actions to satisfy those standards.

Now, in the Introduction, we said we wanted to keep leadership *simple* and *practical*. So let's do that here. We've been saying that NW sits are the platforms of all work. Let's now see a practical picture of what that platform looks like. Let's imagine that working on Normal Work sits with Working Actions is like building a brick walkway.

Standard
*Any **word**, **phrase**, or **number** that describes what a situation **needs** and that measures the degree to which actionstaken in that situation **satisfy** those needs.*

The Brick Walkway

Imagine that as a teenager you worked as a brick mason during the summers. You've only had bricklaying as a hobby since then, but your friends and neighbors know you once prac-ticed the trade. So one morning in early September, while you're at the mailbox getting your mail, your next-door neighbor, Terry Johnson, steps up to you and says, "Hey, don't you work as a brick mason sometimes?"

You reply, "Yes, but only as a hobby, once or twice a year. Why?"

"Well, I need a brick walkway in my front yard to increase the value of my property, and I'm wondering if you'd like to do the job for me."

> ### Working Actions
>
> *Any **actions** you choose and implement in Normal Work situations to best satisfy their clear and agreed on standards and to move them toward their goals with the least risk of Future Trouble.*

It happens that you need some extra spending money for next year's vacation, so you reply, "I might be interested. What do you have in mind?"

"Well, I need a brick walkway six feet wide and 100 feet long in the middle of my front yard, starting at the city sidewalk and running up to my front steps. I'll furnish the tools and supplies. I have mortar, shovels, hammers, wood, tape, and everything else you'll need in my garage, and I'll order the MW Grade bricks from the building supply store as you need them."

"Oh, you're planning to use Moderate Weather Grade bricks?"

"Yes, so all you'll have to do is the actual bricklaying. What do ya' say?"

> **Technique of Work Accuracy**
>
> *Choosing and implementing the **best** Working Actions*
> *to satisfy the clear and agreed on **standards** of Normal Work situations and to move them toward their goals with the least risk of Future Trouble.*

"I'm not sure. How soon would you want it finished?"

"No rush. Start when you can. Finish when you can. I'd just like to have it completed no later than November 1st, so that it's finished before cold weather sets in."

"Okay," you reply, "since I can have until November 1st to finish, I'll do it. I can use some extra spending money for next year's vacation. I can work an average of an hour a day, depending on rain, but I can't work more than two hours a day, even on weekends. Is that okay?"

"Sure, that's fine. In fact, that's better for us because we don't like too many distractions for our yard games, and when we cook out, and so forth. To have someone digging in the front yard when friends arrive for a BBQ gets old fast. So let's agree that you'll average a minimum of one hour of work a day and a maximum of two hours of work a day. Also, we'd like the bricks to lay flat on the ground, and we'd like to have quarter-inch spaces between them."

"None of that's any trouble. What's the job worth to you?"

"I don't know, but if I furnish the tools and supplies, would you be willing to lay the bricks for, say $900?"

"Sure, I can do it for that. Lend me a spare key to your garage so I can get your tools when I need them, and I'll start this coming weekend."

"Great! We have a deal," Terry says, shaking your hand before walking away.

Okay—what just happened at your mailbox?

What just happened was that Terry Johnson assigned you a Normal Work situation. Terry asked you to accept a common, garden-variety NW sit. If Terry had written a clear situation statement for the assignment, he might have written, "We need a brick walkway six feet wide and 100 feet long to be laid in the middle of our front yard by November 1st."

And if you had written a clear action statement to mirror the facts of Terry's situation statement, and if you had used the template provided at the beginning of the chapter, you might have written, "I want to choose the best Working Actions to lay a brick walkway six feet wide and 100 feet long in the middle of the Johnson's front yard by November 1st with the least risk of Future Trouble."

Nothing is left for you to do now but lay the bricks—being careful to stay within the clear and agreed on standards you and Terry established to measure the accuracy of your work.

But wait. What has all this got to do with leadership? Before continuing our discussion of Terry Johnson's brick walkway, let's see how this walkway story is an illustration of the principles of leadership.

What Has a Brick Walkway Got to Do With Leadership?

Our analogy of a fictitious brick walkway for Terry Johnson can give you a mental picture of what a Normal Work sit looks like. Terry's walkway illustrates how a task is assigned and performed. The walkway is a model of how quality work is planned and executed.

In fact, your *own* job performance on your *present* job as you read these lines should be following the model of the brick walkway. Think about it this way. When your current organization hired you, your superiors gave you—or *should* have given you—a job description that was a "bundle" of Normal Work sits. (Unfortunately, many organizations *don't* do this.) We might even say that your job description was a bunch of "brick walkways" that your superiors wanted you to build to receive a paycheck.

Of course, the "walkways" of your job are different from Terry Johnson's brick walkway in amounts, materials, places, times, priorities, techniques, products, services, and clients. But, in principle, your "walkways" obey (or *should* obey) the model of Terry's walkway. To make the picture clearer, let's now see a symbolic diagram of it.

Figure 2 on page 144 represents your bricklaying assignment with Terry Johnson. It's a diagrammatic picture of Terry's situation and the bricklaying actions you're taking on that situation. Let's discuss Figure 2 in detail.

The zigzag arrow represents the many linked *Working Actions* (WAs) being taken to move the Normal Work situation (NW sit) toward its objective. The "peaks and valleys" in the arrow of the work represent the natural *sine waves* that all linkages of WAs develop as they move through time and space. These are caused by the natural rhythms of the workplace—such as interruptions for meetings and phone calls, and breaks for lunch, coffee, maintenance on machines, replenishing supplies, etc. As long as the sine wave remains within the maximum and minimum time standards set for it by the Johnson family, the bricklaying work is in conformance and is quality work. This diagram is a picture of the leadership technique of Work-Accuracy. Note that WAs are effective actions and that they are *Preactive* leadership: *Leading in the absence of trouble.*

FIGURE 2
The Brick Walkway as a Normal Work Situation with Working Actions

MAXIMUM TIME STANDARD: AVG. 2 HRS PER DAY

TIME IN HOURS

2.00

1.75

1.50

1.25

1.00

START AT CITY SIDE WALK

WAs

END AT HOUSE DOOR STEP

MINIMUM TIME STANDARD: AVG. 1 HR PER DAY

←——— DISTANCE IN BRICKLAYING ———→

WAs = Working Actions

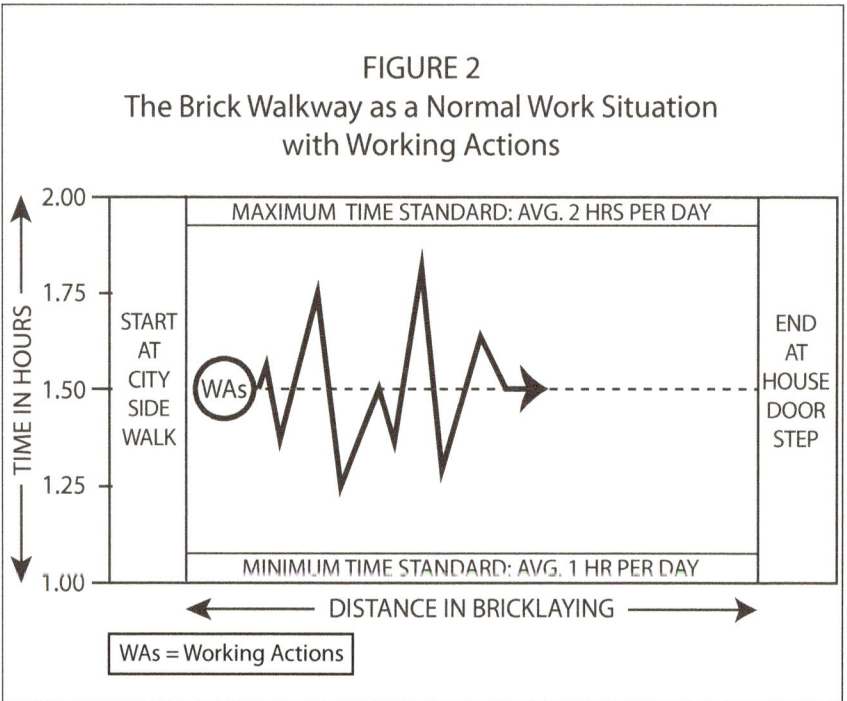

The Most Important Part of Any Task

Looking at Figure 2, let's first recognize its most important part. Let's also recognize that this part is often the most overlooked part. That part is the *standards* describing the situation's needs. (To keep Figure 2 simple and uncluttered, we're only showing the *time* standard in the drawing.) A few paragraphs back, we said that every Normal Work sit should have previously set, clear, and agreed on standards to measure the actions intended to satisfy it. So what standards did Terry Johnson set to measure your actions on his walkway? He gave you 13 measures for your job performance, and he tried to avoid fuzzy words and smokescreen statements as he gave them to you. Here are Terry's 13 standards.

1. The walkway needs to be in the middle of the family's front yard.
2. The walkway needs to extend from the city sidewalk to the front steps.
3. The walkway needs to be six feet wide.
4. The walkway needs to be 100 feet long.
5. The walkway needs to be worked on for a minimum average of one hour a day.
6. The walkway needs to be worked on for a maximum average of two hours a day.
7. The walkway needs for work to start this coming weekend at a time of your choosing.
8. The walkway needs to be completed by November 1st.
9. The walkway needs its bricks to lay completely flat on the ground.
10. The walkway needs its bricks to have quarter-inch spaces between them.
11. The walkway needs its bricks to be Moderate Weather (MW) Grade.
12. The walkway needs its bricks to be laid for a fee of $900.
13. The walkway needs the family's tools and supplies to be used for its work.

Note that these 13 standards are *quality tests* for your actions on the project. They're measures of your *Work-Accuracy*. You're being asked to conform to them. If you break even one of these standards, you're in non-conformance on the task. You aren't satisfying the Johnson's needs, and you aren't doing quality work for the family.

To repeat: The purpose of the 13 *standards* in this story is to define what the Johnson's situation needs, and to measure how well your actions satisfy those needs. Think about that a moment. Looked at in reverse, how could you start the Johnson's project without these clear standards? You *couldn't* logically start work without them.

But here's the pitfall. Clear and agreed on standards like these for the brick walkway are often overlooked in real life. In fact, the truth is that many corporate employees don't even have job descriptions–much less clear and agreed on standards for the tasks they're working on all day long. This failure by top management to provide employees with clear job descriptions is one of the biggest causes of stress, confusion, and inefficiency in the world of work. With that in mind, let's look more closely at Figure 2.

Many Small Actions
Make One Large Action

The first principle to notice in Figure 2 is the large "zig-zag" arrow down the middle of the diagram, moving from left to right. This arrow represents your daily *Working Actions* of bricklaying for the Johnsons (see WAs circle). Notice we're using the word actions in the *plural* form because it takes many *small* Working Actions to create one *large* Working Action. In this case, since your assignment with Terry is laying bricks, most of your small Working Actions will be the actual laying physical bricks, and your large Working Action will be the expanding *walkway* as you build it toward Terry's front steps.

Let's see this principle in some other applications. For example, if you're a news reporter, your "bricks" are the pages of news copy you write. If you're a sales associate, your "bricks" are the products you sell. If you're a teacher, your "bricks" are the subjects you teach.

However, in addition to laying physical *bricks* for Terry, you'll also be taking various *support* actions to assist your work. In this case, you might go to the hardware store to buy a new pair of gloves. Or you might stop work to clean some tools. Or you might use your tape rule to measure part of the lawn. But these support actions are simply additional small WAs that, along with the actual laying of bricks, move the task toward completion.

Think about it this way. A brick walkway isn't just one brick. It's hundreds of *small* bricks laid in conformance to the project's standards. Viewed from a distance, a brick walkway may look like one long brick. But as you get closer, you can see that it's really hundreds of small bricks laid in conformance to a mason's plan. That's true of all Normal Work sits, no matter what they are. Hundreds of *small* actions, taken over a period of days, weeks, months, and years, eventually accomplish one *large* action, and the task is complete.

The principle to remember is that all the small actions taken in a task *must also conform to the standards* set for the large action. For instance, in the analogy of the Johnson family's walkway, if you leave the jobsite to buy a new pair of gloves, that trip can't detract from your commitment to lay bricks for a minimum average of one hour a day. If you hit tough roots in the lawn and have trouble removing them, those roots can't detract from your commitment to lay the Johnson's bricks perfectly flat. All of your actions—small and large—must conform exactly to the standards set for the task.

Okay, but what do these principles mean to *you* today, on your *present* job? They mean that every phone call you make, every email you send, every staff meeting you attend, every report you write, and every spreadsheet you create, must exactly conform to the standards of the NW sits you're working on. As an example, let's imagine you work in the mailroom of an office building, and your job is to sort mail for 100 employees in the building. Your job description requires you to put the right mail in the right slots throughout the day, and to have all the mail sorted by 5:00 pm.

Thus, your main Working Actions are putting the correct envelops in the correct slots at the correct times. However, while you're doing that, you'll also be taking *support* WAs, too—such as phoning employees to verify names or addresses, looking up zip codes on your computer, and so forth.

But these support actions must also conform to the standards that were set for your overall task. That is, these support actions must assist you in sorting the correct mail in the correct slots at the correct times. Everything you do in the mailroom must conform to the standards your superiors set to measure the overall quality of your actions.

So, if you lock the mailroom door and start watching TV, or if you hide behind the mail bags and start texting friends, your actions would *not* conform to the standards set for your overall task, and you would *not* be doing quality work. Against that background, we're now ready to look at the second principle shown in Figure 2.

Working Actions Travel in Sine Waves

Another major principle is revealed by the zigzag arrow in Figure 2. The arrow also indicates your *progress* in laying bricks for the Johnsons. Notice that your progress moves forward in time and space by a series of steep "peaks and valleys." These are called *sine waves* as we said earlier. (*Sine* is pronounced like the word "sign" and means a curve.)

Sine waves are an important principle in work to understand, but they're often overlooked. The principle is this: Working Actions *never* travel in a straight line. In fact, it's *impossible* for work to travel in a straight line. People call this phenomenon the ping-pong effect or the hunting and seeking effect. What it means is that all work has a natural rhythm. Work ebbs and flows, and forms peaks and valleys, like the tides and mountain ranges.

This is important to know because if we're going to accurately measure the *quality* of the work on a task—and that's what we're talking about in this chapter—then our standards for that task must measure *both* the minimum work being done *and* the maximum work being done, and the standards must allow enough space between the two for the work to ebb and flow naturally.

But what causes sine waves? Why *can't* work travel in a straight line? Sine waves are caused by the normal rhythms of the workplace. It's easier to see that if we talk about standards in the *when* (time) factual category. You promised Terry Johnson that you'd work a minimum *average* of one hour a day. Notice you promised Terry an average. Not an absolute. You worded your standard that way because it's *impossible* for someone to work precisely one hour each day.

For example, on Monday, you have to stop because of rain, but you make up your lost time on Tuesday. On Wednesday, the supply store is late delivering your bricks, so you work more than two hours on Wednesday to make up your lost time. On Friday, you break a tool and leave the jobsite early to fix it, and so on. *That's* why work can only be measured in averages, not in absolutes.

All over America in factories, shops, fields, and offices, employees take coffee breaks, lunch breaks, bathroom breaks, supply breaks, breaks to get raw materials, and breaks to service equipment. These breaks are the natural rhythm of workplace. But they also interrupt the straight-line progress of work, and that creates natural sine waves in Working Actions.

What difference does that make? It makes a big difference because all tasks should have both high and low standards for the actions being taken, and enough space between the two for the natural sine wave of the work to operate. In Figure 2, these high and low standards are labeled on the diagram as the Maximum Time Standard: Average 2 Hours Per Day and the Minimum Time Standard: Average 1 Hour Per Day.

Now, the easiest way to set high and low standards for work is to check the historic high and low averages the work has recorded in the past, and then use those as the high and low standards for the work. Let's see an example of that.

The Case of the Mysterious Machine X

To better understand how sine waves operate, let's imagine that a certain *Machine X* in a certain factory has a recorded historic *low* average production of 60 units per day (when heavy raw material is being used), and a historic *high* average production of 120 units per day (when light raw material is being used).

Thus, Machine X's historic average production is 90 units a day—and top management knows this. Thus, when Machine X is needed on the assembly line, top management tells the supervisor of Machine X to bring it online, and to schedule it to produce 90 units per day. This can also be called Machine X's quota, piece rate, batch rate, and other such factory terms.

All that's good. Except for one thing. Machine X *never produces 90 units a day*. On Monday, it produces 91 units. On Tuesday, it produces 111 units. On Wednesday, it produces 62 units. On Thursday, it produces 113 units. And on Friday, it produces 73 units.

Machine X's operator, Andy, has a colored graph mounted over his machine showing its daily production, and this graph is a source of constant stress, confusion, and conflict between Andy and his supervisor, Adolph. Both Andy and Adolph are happy on the days Machine X produces *over* 90 units (as it did on Monday, Tuesday, and Thursday). On these *high* days, Adolph pats Andy on the back, and says, "Hey, Andy, I see you're over quota today. That's great! Keep up the good work!"

But, both Andy and Adolph are unhappy on the days Machine X produces *under* 90 units (as it did on Wednesday and Friday). On these *low* days, Adolph frowns, and says, "Hey, Andy, I see you're under quota today. What's wrong? Aren't you paying attention to your work? I want you back on quota by tomorrow, and I mean it!"

But here's the big lesson. All week long, Machine X *did produce normally at its average rate of 90 units a day.* What's wrong with Machine X? Nothing. What's wrong with Andy and Adolph? Nothing. The trouble in the story is that Andy and Adolph don't understand sine waves. The fluctuations that disturbed Andy and Adolph during the week were simply Machine X's normal hunting and seeking rhythm as its raw materials were changed, as Andy took coffee, lunch, and rest breaks, and as the maintenance crew serviced the machine.

The lesson is this: We can't accurately measure work on a task *without* including both high and low standards for the work, and without providing enough space between the two for the work to fluctuate in its normal sine wave. It's only when the sine wave of some work plunges below its *low* standard, or shoots above its *high* standard and stays outside the standard, that we have a valid trouble to correct. For example, if Machine

X had only produced 62 units for *several days* (if the average of its sine wave had been too *low*), or 113 units for *several days* (if the average of its sine wave had been too *high*), then Andy and Adolph would have had a reason to be concerned.

So the rule is: Never set just *one* standard for the Working Actions on a task. Always set two standards—a high (maximum or ceiling) standard, and a low (minimum or floor) standard. Then, as long as the Working Actions on the task bounce along inside these two standards—no matter how violently they bounce—everything's fine and dandy.

The truth is, there's far too much confusion, stress, and anger in workplaces because managers, supervisors, and employees don't understand sine waves, and don't realize that they should measure *average* work—not the temporary highs and lows of work. But now, let's make this personal.

How Clear are Your Standards?

For years, I've stood before seminar participants and suggested that they use the "KISS!" method of leadership (Keep It Simple, Stupid!). So let's keep this simple. Let's talk about *your* job—the one you hold as you're reading this book.

First question: Do you have a *written* job description?

Second question: If so, when was it last *updated*?

Third question: If you have one, and it's current, how *clear* is it?

Let's pretend you're sales manager for a certain large organization, and that the job description tucked away in your bottom desk drawer reads like this:

Job Title: Sales Manager

Reports to: Marketing Manager

Job Purpose: To supervise sales activities

Authority: As granted by the Marketing Manager

Responsibilities: 1. Supervise and coordinate company sales associates

2. Monitor and report company sales

3. Perform sales training

4. Coordinate success and growth of sales mission

5. (etc.)

You get the idea. But do you sense something *wrong* with this job description? You should see its flaws instantly from what you've learned in previous chapters. Notice the fuzzy words. Notice the smokescreen statements. Notice the lack of high, low, and average standards.

If we imagine that this fuzzy job description is *yours*, how would you know when your work was conforming to what your superiors wanted? How would you keep your superiors from evaluating your work based on opinions, guesses, and feelings? How would you keep them from evaluating your work based on misunderstandings and power plays? Let's ask a simple question: How could you be sure your superiors evaluated your work professionally? The answer is obvious. Using everything you've learned in previous chapters, you could "retool" your job description and renegotiate it with your superiors.

I call this the technique of *reconciling standards*. The word *reconciling* means to make compatible and to overcome distrust. So, you could clarify your job description with the techniques you've learned in these chapters. Then in a pleasant and relaxed way, you could meet with your superiors and reconcile the clarified job description with them.

Okay, but exactly how do you do that? Let's see a quick snapshot. Look at Responsibility #3 in the job description. It reads: "Perform sales training." Note that this is a smokescreen statement composed of three fuzzy words. Also note that there are no high, low, or average standards in the statement. All of this means that this so-called "responsibility" is a *land mine* waiting for you to step on it.

It would be impossible for you to do accurate work on such an unclear responsibility. But let's assume that, using what you've learned in these chapters, you sat down and clarified Responsibility #3 to read something like this: "I will present a minimum of one and a maximum of two training seminars on sales prospecting, sales presentations, and customer relations, once per calendar quarter (an average of six seminars a year) for all our sales associates in the Omaha training room on Saturdays from 9:00 am to 12:00 noon on dates to be set and agreed on with the Marketing Manager."

Now, let's ask the same question here that we've asked in similar illustrations previously. Which of these two responsibility statements would you rather base your next pay raise on? The original version that read, "Perform sales training"? Or the clarified version we just developed? Isn't it a no-brainer?

Notice you even provided for sine waves in your work by setting high, low, and average measures for the seminars you'll present each quarter. After all, some of your seminars might be cancelled by snowstorms or flu epidemics, and you don't want to be held accountable for forces beyond your control.

But wait. This kind of clarification is too time-consuming, isn't it? It's too hard to spell out responsibilities this way, isn't it? This whole thing is too much trouble, isn't it? Let's talk about "BSRIOFW."

BSRIOFW

For four decades, I've urged seminar groups to "Be Slow Right Instead of Fast Wrong." My abbreviation of that motto is BSRIOFW. But this motto is a bitter pill for some leaders to swallow. Many of us are impatient, even if we don't realize we're impatient. But the logic of the motto is inescapable. When is it ever "right" to be *wrong*—no matter how fast we do it? Likewise, when is it ever "wrong" to be *right*—no matter how slow we do it?

Of course, none of us wants to be slow, so what we really want is to be *fast right*. That's what this book is about. But let's face our challenge logically. If we invest more time on the front-end of tasks by defining fuzzy words, clarifying smoke-screen sentences, and setting high and low standards for our work, we'll automatically spend less time on the back-end of tasks reworking defects, repairing damage, fighting law suits, and soothing hurt feelings.

So if that's true—and I think it is—then which approach to leadership *really* is more efficient: being faster on the front-end and slower on the back-end? Or slower on the front-end and faster on the back-end?

That is, which approach is *really* more effective—investing the time needed on the front-end of tasks to *prevent* trouble in them? Or having your time taken from you on the back-end to *suppress* trouble in tasks? I think we can agree on the answer. Chances are, we'll earn more bonuses, rewards, promotions, and recognition by being careful, effective, and efficient on the front-end of tasks. We're going to discuss this principle in detail in later chapters and show how to implement it in your life and job.

Summary of Chapter 5

1. The Normal Work situation (NW sit) is the first of the three Effective-Efficient Situations we'll discuss in this book,

and is the first of the six "masks" that generic Choice Situations can wear.

2. The NW sit is the foundation of all leadership. It's the most important, basic, and frequent of all job situations. It's the first of the situations we'll learn in which we *direct* tasks with a *Preactive* and *offensive-minded* type of leadership.

3. The other five situations in this book (the other five "masks") are connected to the NW sit, and are part of it. Thus, once you've mastered the NW sit in Chapter 5, you've begun to master the other five situations, too.

4. The word *normal* means square or conforming to standards. That's also the definition of *quality*. The word *accurate* means exact conformance to standards. So the secret of accurate decision-making and quality work is having previously set, clear, and agreed on standards guiding your Working Actions and making sure your actions always satisfy these standards.

5. The word *work* means applying physical and mental effort to something. So work is any action, large or small, that we take on a task.

6. A Normal Work situation (NW sit) is any *regular* situation (task, assignment) you undertake with clear and agreed on standards that requires you to choose Working Actions that best satisfy those standards with the least risk of Future Trouble. NW sits can also be called tasks, jobs, projects, programs, contracts, assignments, and many other synonyms.

7. Working Actions (WAs) are any *actions* we choose and implement in Normal Work situations to best satisfy their clear and agreed on standards, and to move them toward their goals with the least risk of Future Trouble. Smaller WAs must conform to the standards set for the larger WAs and create larger WAs the way small bricks create a walkway.

8. The leadership technique of Work-Accuracy is choosing and implementing the best Working Actions to satisfy the clear and agreed on standards of Normal Work situations, and to move them toward their goals with the least risk of Future Trouble.

9. In one sentence, Work-Accuracy is setting clear and agreed on standards for tasks and choosing best actions to satisfy those standards.

10. A standard is any word, phrase, or number that describes what a situation needs and that measures the degree to which actions taken in that situation satisfy those needs. Clear standards are the most important parts of NW sits and are often the most overlooked part. Accurate and high-quality work is impossible without previously set, clear, and agreed on standards.

11. All Working Actions move forward in time and space toward their goals in sine waves. They fluctuate between high and low performance from the natural rhythms of the workplace. Much stress and confusion can be avoided by setting *high* (maximum) and *low* (minimum) standards for actions,

and then measuring the *average* of work instead of being upset by its highs and lows.

12. Figure 2 illustrates a Normal Work sit with its Working Actions.

13. Finally, it's better to Be Slow Right Instead of Fast Wrong (BSRIOFW). It's better to take the time on the front-end to be accurate and preventive, than it is to have the time taken from us on the back-end in rework, repair, and apologies.

And there you have it. Now you know how work is assigned and performed. You know all about Normal Work sits and the Working Actions we take on them. Regardless of whether you're employed by the military, a factory, bank, church, university, or farm, the principles are the same. The key to all work everywhere is accurate actions, and the key to accurate actions is to have previously set, clear, and agreed on *standards*.

Accurate work is simply meeting work standards, and that's just another way of talking about the Master Principle of Satisfying Needs we discussed in previous chapters. We'll return to this subject in later pages and talk in detail about how you can do your own job with accuracy.

Moving to Chapter 6 now, we're going to talk about the first of the situations that are *connected* to Normal Work sits. This first situation is one of the most glamorous situations in the workplace, and many best-selling books have been written about it. It's called the Work Improvement situation.

CHAPTER 6

WORK IMPROVEMENT SITUATIONS

The Second
Effective-Efficient Situation
(See Table 1, Row 2, Page 114)

Description: A Standard in a Task that can
Be Improved to Exceed Expectations

Existence in Time: The Present

Name of Action: Improving Action

Leadership Technique: Standards-Betterment

Leadership Type: *Directing* Tasks with
Preactive Strategies and Tactics

Action Statement

Template: *I want to choose the best (Improving Action to make this standard better in this Normal Work situation).*

In earlier chapters we learned that every situation in our lives and on our jobs is a generic Choice Situation that's requiring us to choose the best way to satisfy its needs. We learned that these Choice Situations occur in six different "shapes"—as if they were wearing six different "masks."

In the previous chapter, we discussed the first mask that generic Choice Situations can wear. It was the mask of a Normal Work situation, and it required us to pick a series of best Working Actions to work within its standards. We used the "brick walkway" analogy to illustrate how NW sits are structured, and we analyzed them symbolically with Figure 2. The big lesson we learned in the previous chapter is that accurate and high-quality work requires the setting and satisfying of clear and agreed on standards—and that's actually a springboard into this chapter's subject.

Here in Chapter 6, we're going to discuss the second "mask" that generic choice situations can wear. This situation connects to Normal Work situations, is a part of them, and is also one of the three Effective-Efficient situations we'll learn—so it's listed in Table 1, Row 2, page 114. We're now going to talk about the *Work Improvement* situation, and the actions we take in this situation, which are called *Improving Actions*.

Keep in mind that we talked at length in the previous chapter about the importance of *standards* in leadership. That's why this chapter is really an extension of the previous chapter. The purpose of Work Improvement situations is to create *better* standards in our work. The sample action statement or template in this chapter is, "I want to choose the best (Improving Action to make this standard better in this Normal Work situation)." For example, you might write, *I want to choose the best improved paint standard for all the gitwidgets being painted in the Gaston Plant by 5:00 pm this Friday.*

My shorthand abbreviation for Work Improvement situations is *WI* sits, and my abbreviation for Improving Actions is *IAs.* Now, let's open our discussion by coming in the back door. Let's talk about *expectations.*

What Do Other People Expect From You?

Have you ever wondered what your superiors, customers, coworkers, friends, and family members *expect* from you? The first thoughts that come to mind might be things like, "They expect me to be nice to them…to do an honest day's work…to keep my promises…to be loyal to them," etc.

All that's true. But we could also describe other people's expectations this way, "They expect me to meet the previously set, clear, and agreed on standards they have with me."

We've been talking about *standards* for many pages and about the importance of "exactly conforming" to them. We know, for example, that we're expected to obey the speed laws, pay our mortgages, be on time for appointments, keep certain job or family information confidential, and so on.

But here's a new thought. There's also something that people *don't* usually expect from us. They usually don't expect us to do *more* for them than they've asked us to do or *more* than we've agreed to do. Think about the times when you've exceeded standards that other people had for you—maybe the times you made a mortgage payment early, or arrived for an appointment early, or refused to reveal confidential information, and so on. How did people react? Probably with surprise, pleasure, and appreciation, didn't they?

That's the secret of the Work Improvement situation. That's the secret of the leadership technique of *Standards-Betterment*. The purpose of Standards-Betterment is to raise the standards of our products and services and to do it in a way that surprises and pleases the recipients. In other words, without being asked to do so, we replace a lesser or lower standard with a *better* or *higher* standard—and then we start meeting that better or higher standard. All without being asked. That surprises and pleases our recipients and makes them more loyal and appreciative than ever.

> # The Purpose of
> # Standards-Betterment
> *To **raise** the standards of our products and services
> and to do it in a way that surprises and pleases the
> recipients. Without being asked, we replace a lesser or
> lower standard with a **better** or **higher** standard.*

This process can be called upgrading, improving, innovating, enriching, raising the bar, and other such terms. I call it Standards-Betterment because that's what it is: A process of making standards better than the ones that were already expected and accepted by the recipients.

The word *better* means higher in quality, or to make more useful, suitable, and desirable. Interestingly, the word *better* comes from the same root as the word *best* that we discussed back in Chapter 1. So during Standards-Betterment, we're raising standards to make our work more useful, suitable, and desirable for its recipients—not for *us*. That's where the pleasure-power of WI sits lies.

Okay, but why does raising the standards for a product or service *surprise* people? The answer is simple. Improving Actions surprise people because—suddenly and without being asked—we start to do more for them than they expected. Think about the psychological impact of that. In other words, we set a *new normal* for our recipients, and they like it.

Setting New Normals

In the briefest terms, the purpose of the technique of Standards-Betterment is to "set new normals" for our tasks, services, and behaviors. We raise the standards for our tasks, products, and projects to new levels of quality and accuracy. Our actions begin to exceed anything we've ever done for recipients, so they appreciate it, and they become more loyal.

Years ago, Kenichi Yamamoto, the Japanese engineer and inventor who became president of Mazda motors, was the first person to teach the importance of "surprising and delighting" recipients. Many books and articles have been written about Yamamoto's idea since then. But twenty years have passed since he first taught the principle in Japan, and it's still slow to catch on in America.

For example, when was the last time you heard someone in your life or on your job say he or she wanted to "surprise and delight" a family member? Or a customer? Or a coworker? Or a superior? You probably haven't heard it very often, have you? However, surprising and delighting others is the essence of Improving Actions.

Now, to keep this chapter simple and practical, let's look at an easy example of a Work Improvement sit and the Improving Action that was taken in it. This story comes from a true incident. I call it *the case of the Colorful Assistant.*

The Case of the Colorful Assistant

Imagine you're on coffee break in the cafeteria of Apex Products where you're an employee. You overhear two employees talking at the next table. Sophia, administrative assistant to Jack Masters, the president, is talking to Emily, assistant to one of the vice presidents. Sophia is saying, "You know, I print a lot of sales reports for Mr. Masters, and they're all on plain, white paper. So I did something about it yesterday."

Emily responds, "Sure, all of use white paper all day. So what?"

"Well," says Sophia, "I noticed that Mr. Masters uses his *monthly* sales reports the most, but he always has trouble finding them on his desk because all his papers are white."

Emily laughs and says, "Sooo?"

"Sooo, here's what I did. Mr. Masters was happy with everything just as it was, but I decided to start printing his *monthly* sales reports on a new pale yellow paper that I found. That way, his monthly reports are more visible on his desk. I read in a magazine that black print on yellow paper is the easiest combination for people to read, so I'm helping Mr. Masters in two ways. I'm making his monthly reports easier to find, and I'm making them easier to read, too."

Emily smiles over the rim of her cup. "Why bother?"

"Oh, I don't know," replies Sophia. "I just keep thinking of ways to help Mr. Masters and make his job easier. He never asks me to change anything, and I don't think he expects me to. I just want to make his work easier."

Emily rolls her eyes over the rim of her cup, and the scene fades.

Now, what just happened in the Apex cafeteria?

What happened was this. Sophia, assistant to the president, found a Work Improvement sit in one of her tasks. Her task was to print sales reports, and the standard for that was to print them on *white paper*. Sophia had been meeting that standard for years, and all this was perfectly acceptable to Mr. Masters, her superior.

But Sophia realized that there was a Work Improvement sit connected to—and part of—her printing tasks. She realized that the *standard* for printing monthly sales reports on white paper could be made *better*. So she implemented an Improving Action to upgrade that standard. She changed the old standard to a new and better standard. She started printing the *monthly* sales reports on pale yellow paper, so they would be easier for her superior to find and read.

Now, let's pause here to be honest a minute. Many employees, like Sophia's friend Emily, would have left well enough alone. They wouldn't have invested the time to set a new standard for the reports. They would have taken the easy way out and continued doing what the president had always expected and accepted.

But not Sophia.

She researched colored papers and, without being asked, invested the time, energy, and brainpower to improve the president's reports in a creative new way. And what do you think the long-term result was of Sophia's Improving Action? That is, which of the two assistants do you think will probably stay the longest and earn the most at Apex Products? Sophia or Emily?

If we can agree that *Sophia* probably has the best chance of staying the longest and earning the most, then we're still following the theme of this book: that effective and efficient work always earns more rewards than ineffective and inefficient work. That said, let's define what we mean by a *Work Improvement* situation in this chapter.

The Definition of a Work Improvement Situation

*An existing **standard** in a Normal Work situation that's currently being met, but that can be raised, lowered, or changed in a way that **exceeds** the recipient's **expectations** in a surprising and pleasing new way, with the least risk of Future Trouble.*

Thus, a Work Improvement sit is a name for an old standard in a task that can be made *better*. It's a term for adding value to what the recipients for our work are receiving. The word value means to be worth something. So when we add *value* for a recipient, we're making whatever we're producing for that recipient *worth more* at no cost to him or her. That has great psychological power.

> ## *Work Improvement Situation*
>
> *An existing **standard** in a Normal Work situation that's currently being met but that can be raised, lowered, or changed in a way that **exceeds** the recipient's **expectations** in a surprising and pleasing new way with the least risk of Future Trouble.*

Let's see another example of a Work Improvement sit and an Improving Action. Let's return to our example of the "brick walkway" in Chapter 5. You'll recall that your neighbor, Terry Johnson, had hired you to build a brick walkway in his front yard. Here's part of the conversation you had with Terry back in Chapter 5.

You and Terry were standing at your mailbox, and Terry promised, "I'll furnish the tools and supplies. I have mortar, shovels, hammers, wood, tape, and everything else you'll need in my garage, and I'll order the MW Grade bricks from the building supply store as you need them."

You replied, "Oh, you're planning to use Moderate Weather Grade bricks?"

"Yes," Terry responded, "so all you need to do is the brick-laying. What do ya' say?"

As you recall, you accepted the job and started work the following weekend. But now let's *change* the story. Let's insert some *new dialog* that will illustrate how a Work Improvement situation and an Improving Action might apply to Terry's walkway.

Let's return now to Chapter 5 and pretend that the next day you phone Terry and say, "Terry, I've been thinking about your walkway, and I think I can make it even *better* for you."

"Well, maybe," Terry responds, "what do you mean by 'better'?"

"Look, you're planning to use MW, or Moderate Weather bricks, in the walkway, and I know you're happy with them. But I think the walkway would be safer for your family, and would last longer, if you used SW, or Severe Weather bricks. I have a connection at a building supply store where I buy supplies, and I can get you SW Grade bricks for the same price you're planning to pay for MW Grade bricks. If you want me to improve the grade of your bricks for you, I can place an order for them today."

"Wow," laughs Terry. "Great idea! If you can upgrade me from MW bricks to SW bricks at no extra cost, I'll do it! I really appreciate this."

"My pleasure," you reply. "I'll call the store and place the order right now."

Okay, what just happened?

This dialog shows how a Work Improvement sit can be developed and how an Improving Action can be taken on it. Let's summarize what occurred. As we know, a Work Improvement situation is an existing *standard* in a task that has already been accepted by a recipient and that we have already been meeting or have already agreed to meet. But the standard can be made *better* with an Improving Action that adds unexpected *value* to it. Thus, the four parts of our brick improvement story unfold like this.

1. The Normal Work sit is the *walkway* you're building for Terry.

2. The existing standard on the walkway is for *MW Grade* bricks, and Terry accepts and expects this grade to be used.

3. The Work Improvement sit is realizing that this existing standard can be made *better* by upgrading it to a new standard for *SW Grade* bricks, adding unexpected *value* for Terry at no cost or obligation to him.

4. The Improving Action is *ordering* the SW bricks and using them.

See how it goes? That's Standards-Betterment in a nutshell. The only thing that's required for an Improving Action is to identify an existing task *standard* that can be made better in a way that adds unexpected value for a recipient then start to meet that new standard. But, as Emily, the assistant at Apex Products, asked Sophia, "Why bother?"

What is the Motive?

Why *bother* with Improving Actions? What's the use? Aren't we busy, hassled, and confused enough already? Why pile on another task for us to think about? The answer may surprise you. Research shows that the motive behind Improving Actions is *respect and appreciation for the recipients of the product or service.*

Do you have those kinds of feelings for the recipients of *your* product or service—whether they're coworkers, customers, friends, or family members? If not, Improving Actions may prove difficult. Because IAs require a personal sacrifice of time, energy, effort, and expense without any promise of repayment. Said another way, IAs are *gifts*. They're surprise packages for recipients, no strings attached. They're a way of being nice to people. They're a type of organizational friendliness, business kindness, or corporate golden rule. Best of all, some of the world's most successful business leaders run their companies by this principle.

Of course, the tricky part with Improving Actions is that they're usually not listed in our job descriptions. Worse, since IAs are freebies to recipients, superiors and coworkers may not understand why we're "giving away the store." But our recipients will understand. And their enhanced loyalty will become more and more valuable over time.

But a word of caution. We can't be greedy with Improving Actions. We can't implement them with one hand behind our backs to receive a kickback. We could call it ethics, morals, integrity, or whatever word fits, but improvements should only be made with genuine appreciation for recipients.

Okay, now let's look at another example of a WI sit and an IA. But this time, let's include a diagram of what happens. Let's return to our example of building the brick walkway for Terry Johnson, but this time let's see a different standard being improved.

You'll recall from the original story that you had agreed with Terry that you'd work a minimum average of *one* hour a day on the walkway, and for the convenience of the family, you wouldn't work longer than a maximum average of *two* hours a day.

But let's pretend that, after working in the Johnson's yard a few days, and watching the family's habits (the way the children play games on the lawn, etc.), you decide that it'd be better for the family if you finished the walkway *earlier* than the agreed deadline of November 1st. You decide that Terry's existing standard of working a minimum average of one hour a day (60 minutes) can be upgraded and made *better*. You decide that if you increase your average work time to a new standard of a minimum average of *one and one-half hours* a day (90 minutes), you can finish the walkway several days early. So you implement your Improving Action, and you start working on this

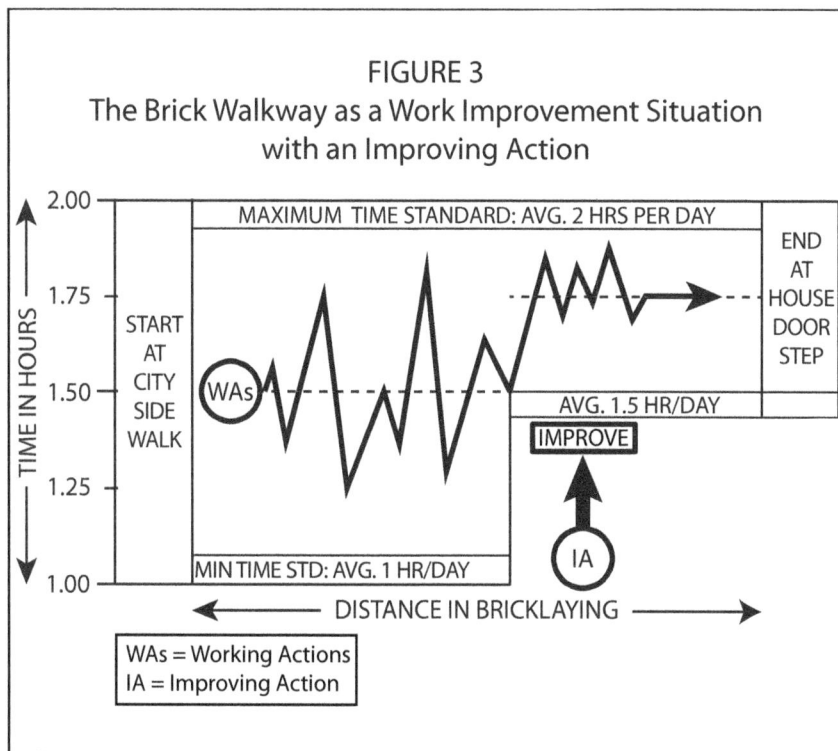

FIGURE 3
The Brick Walkway as a Work Improvement Situation
with an Improving Action

new schedule. Let's see what this Work Improvement sit and Improving Action would look like on the diagram we've been using.

Figure 3 shows the Improving Action you're taking on the existing standard in the *when* (time) category of the task. You've realized you can *increase* the old standard of working one hour a day to a *new* standard of working one and a half hours a day with the result that you can finish Terry's walkway earlier than November 1st, giving his family added and unexpected value on the task.

The zigzag horizontal arrow represents the many linked Working Actions (WAs) being taken to move the Normal Work sit (the brick walkway) toward its objective. The dark vertical arrow represents the Improving Action (IA) being taken to increase the time on the task from 60 minutes per day to 90 minutes per day.

Also note that the sine wave of the work is now fluctuating at a higher level than before. This diagram is a picture of the leadership technique of *Standards-Betterment* and shows that Improving Actions are effective actions and are the *Preactive* type of leadership: *Leading in the absence of trouble.*

The Uptick in the Diagram

Looking more carefully now at Figure 3, notice the dramatic "uptick" (lifting or raising) of the *low standard* at the lower right side of the diagram. This uptick represents your decision to make Terry's old time standard better by working a new average of 90 minutes a day, instead of the old average of 60 minutes a day.

Remember, the Johnsons were happy with the old time standard. They hadn't complained or requested a change. You decided on your *own* to raise the old standard to a new level by means of an unexpected Improving Action.

We can safely assume that this free gift of an *earlier* completion date on the walkway will make the Johnson family happy and more loyal to you, and will make them more appreciative of your skills. That's the natural result of most Improving

Actions. But now let's shift gears and go negative for a moment. Now let's talk about three things that Improving Actions are *not*.

Improving Actions Are Not Correcting Actions

The first thing that Improving Actions are *not* is that they aren't Correcting Actions. Some leaders confuse the leadership technique of Standards-Betterment (the subject of this chapter) and the leadership technique of Cause-Removal (the subject of Chapter 9). Review Table 2, Row 2 on page 115 to see this. For example, let's pretend you own a company that makes gitwidgets, and you discover that your employees are shipping *defective* gitwidgets to your customers. You hurriedly find out what's *causing* these defects. You remove this cause, and soon your employees are shipping good gitwidgets again. You call a staff meeting, and proudly announce to your staff, "Folks, we 'improved' our gitwidgets today! We're making gitwidgets 'better' than ever, and our clients are happy again!"

But you *didn't* improve your gitwidgets.

What you did was find the True Cause of a Current Trouble in your gitwidgets and remove that True Cause with a Correcting Action. And that was a good thing. Nothing wrong with that. But it *wasn't* Standards-Betterment. It was Cause-Removal.

Here's another way to think about this. Clients don't expect (and usually don't ask for) Improving Actions. But clients *do* expect and usually *do* ask for Correcting Actions to remove defects in products and services. Organizations are obligated—usually by law—to remove defects from their products and services. That's why Correcting Actions are often legally binding in guarantees and contracts. There's a big difference between a *voluntary* Improving Action based on respect for a client, and an *involuntary* Correcting Action based on legal obligations to a client.

As we've said so often, *Preactive* leadership is founded on clear definitions. "Words *matter*," as we keep saying. A *Preactive* leader identifies his or her situations and actions and calls them by their proper names. Leaders must know which leadership technique they're using because the different leadership techniques have different *outcomes*. And the only way we can predict the outcome of our leadership is to know what situation we're acting on. Okay, the next thing that Work Improvement situations are *not* is that they're not always big.

Improving Actions Are Not Always Big

A second mistake some leaders make in the technique of Standards-Betterment is thinking that Improving Actions must be *big*. Think about that a moment. As we said earlier, many leaders tend to be impatient, to be impulsive, and to think that bigger is better. That's good to a point. Except that it makes us think improvements must be *big*, too. We think of "improvements" as building a new factory, developing a new product, or buying new machinery.

But that often backfires. Because we often don't have the time, energy, or budget for a new factory, a new product, or new machinery. So we give up and *don't do anything*. That's the trap in thinking big. It can keep us from taking any Improving Actions at all.

Instead, thinking *small* is often more effective. Thinking *small*, for example, is one of the principles in the continuous improvement movement. The books and seminars in this movement teach their followers to take continuous *small* Improving Actions all week long. That way, the loyalty and trust of recipients is earned slowly over time through dozens of small improvements.

Think for a moment about the two Improving Actions we talked about earlier on the Johnson's brick walkway. The first was upgrading Terry's bricks from MW Grade to SW Grade. The second was increasing your work schedule to finish the walkway early for the family.

Neither of these IAs was earthshaking. Neither was a giant leap forward. You didn't offer to finish Terry's walkway a month early, or to build a free walkway for him. Your improvements weren't "big," as we tend to think of big. But even though these improvements were *small*, they earned the family's appreciation and loyalty. That's the usual outcome of Improving Actions. Lastly, let's look at the third thing Work Improvement sits are *not*.

Customer Requests Are Not Improving Actions

A third mistake that some leaders make with Work Improvement sits is thinking that changes requested by the *recipients* of the leader's products and services are "Improving Actions." In other words, some leaders confuse improvements developed by the leaders themselves with changes requested by their customers, coworkers, or superiors. The key to identifying Work Improvement sits correctly is to realize that changes requested by *recipients* aren't voluntary actions by leaders.

For instance, in our story about the Johnson's walkway, if Terry had phoned *you*, and asked *you* to change from MW Grade bricks to SW Grade bricks (instead of you phoning *him* with the idea), the upgrading of the bricks would *not* have been an Improving Action. It would have been a change in a task standard requested by the client. The rule is that it's only when *we* voluntarily initiate upgrades in our old standards, without recipients requesting it or even knowing it, that we're taking genuine Improving Actions. Now, against this background and these examples, let's define an *Improving Action*.

The Definition
of an Improving Action

*Any **action** you choose and implement in a Work Improvement*
*situation to make a standard better, and to make it **exceed***
*a recipient's **expectations** in a surprising and pleasant*
new way with the least risk of Future Trouble.

This definition also let's us define the technique of *Standards-Betterment.*

The Definition of
Standards-Betterment

Choosing and implementing a best Improving Action to make
an existing standard in a Work Improvement situation better,
*and to make work **exceed** a recipient's **expectations** in a*
surprising way with the least risk of Future Trouble.

In one sentence, Standards-Betterment is making standards better so that work exceeds a recipient's expectations in a surprising new way. Now, with these definitions under our belts, let's shift gears again and talk about how to develop and implement Improving Actions.

How to Take
Improving Actions

The steps for taking Improving Actions are simple. We simply find an existing *standard* in one of our Normal Work sits—a standard that we're already meeting satisfactorily, and one that our recipient hasn't complained about—and we *raise*, *lower*, or *alter* that standard in a way that creates unexpected value for the recipient. (Remember, a recipient can be a friend, family member, civic club member, church member, coworker, corporate customer, or anyone else.)

Think back to our story about Sophia, the president's assistant at Apex Products. You'll recall that she started printing the president's monthly reports on pale yellow paper so he could find them easier on his desk. She identified a Work Improvement sit in one of her tasks. She recognized an old standard that she was already meeting (printing reports on white paper) and realized she could make that standard *better*. So she took an Improving Action. She upgraded the old standard

> **Improving Action**
> *Any **action** you choose and implement in a Work Improvement situation to make a standard better and to make it **exceed** a recipient's **expectations** in a surprising and pleasant new way with the least risk of Future Trouble.*

(white paper) to a new standard (yellow paper). Then she started printing the president's reports to meet this new standard. That made the president's job easier and earned more appreciation for Sophia.

The idea behind improvements is, therefore, simple: Find an old *standard* in a task that can be made *better* without the recipient asking for it—and then *make* it better. Raise the bar in a task, and start jumping that higher bar. There are at least eight ways to do that.

Eight Ways to Raise the Bar

In track and field events, the *bar* is a long rod suspended between two poles that the athletes try to jump. The judges slowly raise the bar higher and higher, until only the best athlete in the contest can jump it.

In this chapter, our "bar" is an existing *standard* in one of our tasks. We gradually make that bar better and better, until

---

Standards-Betterment

Choosing and implementing a best Improving Action to make an existing standard in a Work Improvement situation better and to make work **exceed** *a recipient's* **expectations** *in a surprising way with the least risk of Future Trouble.*

---

our work is the best in the "contest." Here are eight ways to raise the bar in our work.

1. We can clarify a smokescreen standard.
2. We can clarify the fuzzy words in a standard.
3. We can write a new standard where none exists.
4. We can increase, decrease, or alter an old standard to make it better.
5. We can eliminate a duplicated standard.
6. We can eliminate an inappropriate standard.
7. We can simplify a complicated standard.
8. We can define an undefined standard.

Note that the common denominator in all these approaches is that we're making an old standard more useful, suitable, and desirable, and we're adding value for recipients. We'll return to this subject in later pages and talk in greater detail about how you can implement Improving Actions on your own job. Right now, let's close with some thoughts about *continuous improvement*.

Continuous Improvement

The leadership technique we've been calling *Standards-Betterment* in this chapter can also be called continuous improvement, the continuous improvement process, continuous process improvement, and similar terms. The difference between these terms and our technique in this chapter is that we're showing you a *simplified* version of what is normally a highly technical (and often highly statistical) technique.

Many experts believe that Masaaki Imai of Japan founded the continuous improvement movement in 1986 when he wrote his best-selling book, *Kaizen: The Key to Japan's Competitive Success.* Imai's book is now published in 20 languages and is still a best-seller. The Japanese word *Kaizen* means "good change," and the lesson Imai teaches in his book is that improving the standards for our products and services should be a *daily* activity. Employees should make "good changes" in their task standards each and every day. That's why the movement uses the word "continuous" in its books and lectures.

Over the years, Imai's concepts have been folded into (totally or partially) many other "quality systems," and his teachings have been rehashed and renamed in dozens of books, articles, classes, and seminars. However, the truth is that continuous improvement has been around since the 1950s, and many of its principles have been taught for years by such statistical process control and total quality management writers as W. Edwards Deming, Walter A. Shewhart, Joseph M. Juran, and Philip B. Crosby, among others.

However, this chapter is about *leadership*. It's not about statistical process control or total quality management. So we'll leave the statistics and the high math to the engineers and statisticians. Instead, we'll limit *our* discussion of continuous improvement to the *situational* approach we're using in this book.

That settled, let's summarize Chapter 6 in one sentence: Every day in every way, look for an existing task standard in a product, service, or behavior that you can raise, lower, or change to make something *faster, quieter, cleaner, safer, longer-lasting, cheaper, easier, lighter, thinner, more simple, more colorful, more readable, more interesting, more modern, more convenient, more flexible, more complete, more accurate, more useful, more fun, or more profitable* for your recipient, at no cost or obligation to him or her.

Summary of Chapter 6

1. The Work Improvement situation (the WI sit) is the second Effective-Efficient situation we'll learn in this book.

2. The WI sit is one of the five situations that is *connected* to Normal Work sits and that is part of them.

3. Actions taken on WI sits are called Improving Actions (IAs), but they can also be called upgrading actions, raising the bar, continuous improvement, etc. The purpose of Work Improvement situations is to set *new normals* for products, services, and behavior. That's why we call this technique Standards-Betterment.

4. A Work Improvement sit is an existing standard in a Normal Work sit that's currently being met, but that can be raised, lowered, or changed in a way that exceeds the recipient's expectations in a surprising and pleasing new way, with the least risk of Future Trouble.

5. An Improving Action is any action you choose and implement in a Work Improvement situation to make a standard *better* and to make it *exceed* a recipient's *expectations* in a surprising and pleasant new way with the least risk of Future Trouble.

6. The technique of Standards-Betterment is choosing and implementing a best Improving Action to make an existing standard in a Work Improvement situation better and to make work *exceed* a recipient's *expectations* in a surprising way with the least risk of Future Trouble.

7. In one sentence, Standards-Betterment is making standards better so that work exceeds a recipient's expectations in a surprising new way.

8. The motive behind Standards-Betterment is respect and appreciation for the recipients of our work, and improvements must be made without any thought of reward. Improvements are *gifts* to recipients without cost or obligation to the recipient.

9. Common mistakes made in the technique of Standards-Betterment are confusing improvements with Correcting Actions, thinking that improvements must be big, or believing that changes requested by customers are improvements.

10. Simply put, Standards-Betterment is anything you do to clarify, define, simplify, explain, interpret, change, or modify an existing task standard to make that standard *better*.

11. Figure 3 shows symbolically a Work Improvement sit and an Improving Action.

12. Finally, the technique we call Standards-Betterment was made popular by the writers in the continuous improvement movement of the 1980s, spearheaded by the best-selling Japanese book, *Kaizen*.

Now, our next chapter is one of the most challenging in this book because it's about Trouble-Prevention—one of the most neglected and misunderstood techniques in leadership. In Chapter 7, we're going to talk about the mysterious *Likely Cause* situation and about the greatly misunderstood *Blocking Action*.

CHAPTER 7

LIKELY CAUSE
SITUATIONS

The Third
Effective-Efficient Situation
(See Table 1, Row 3, Page 114)

Description: A Weakness that will Probably Cause
a Performance to break a Task
Standard in an Unwanted Way

Existence in Time: The Present (*but will Cause Trouble
In the Future*)

Name of Action: Blocking Action

Leadership Technique: Trouble-Prevention

Leadership Type:	*Directing* Tasks with *Preactive* Strategies and Tactics
Action Statement Template:	*I want to choose the best (Blocking Action to prevent this Likely Cause from hatching in the work on this Normal Work situation).*

W e've now arrived at the second situation that's connected to Normal Work situations and is a part of them. This situation is also the *last* of the three generic Choice Situations we'll see that "masks" as an Effective-Efficient situation—this is the last situation that lets us *direct* work with an *offensive-minded* and *Preactive* type of leadership. This situation is described in Table 1, Row 3, page 114, and it plays a huge role in *Preactive* leadership—a fact that many books and classes give lip service to but don't fully understand.

This chapter is about the *Likely Cause* situation. Actions taken in this situation are called *Blocking Actions*. I use the abbreviations *LC* sits for Likely Causes, and *BAs* for the Blocking Actions taken in them. The purpose of actions taken in these situations is to *prevent* future defects, mistakes, oversights, and other troubles from developing in tasks.

Our action statement template for this situation is, "I want to choose the best (Blocking Action to prevent this Likely

Cause from hatching in the work on this Normal Work situation)." For instance, you might write, *I want to choose the best Blocking Action to prevent Laura Mitchell's lack of MX Machine experience from producing bad gitwidgets on her machine next week.*

Okay, let's open this chapter by discussing something that many books call "problem-prevention." I call the leadership technique in this chapter *Trouble-Prevention* because its purpose is to protect tasks from Future Trouble. Here's a closer look at the confusion some leaders have over *prevention.*

What is This Thing Called Prevention?

Many articles are written, speeches given, and seminars taught each year on "prevention." But many of them describe the wrong situation and teach the wrong action. True prevention has always been on the endangered species list and, over the years, surveys have shown that Blocking Actions are often the *least used* of the six leadership actions. For example, I heard of a survey some years ago that discovered that the average leader only spends *one percent* of his or her time taking Blocking Actions. Yet most leaders will agree that Blocking Actions are among a leader's most valuable actions and will say that they *take* many Blocking Actions during the workweek.

So why the disconnect?

Why do leaders claim to be taking BAs when surveys show that they *aren't*? Worse, why do they *think* they're taking prevention when they aren't? There are two reasons why leaders aren't more preventive. The first is that "problem-prevention" is a fuzzy phrase, and many speakers and writers haven't taken the time to clarify it. Of course, that means graduates of their seminars and readers of their books can work on the job thinking they're taking prevention—and really not be taking it. So a big purpose of this chapter is to clarify the fuzzy phrase "problem-prevention" for you.

The second reason leaders aren't as preventive as they should be is a more subtle. It's a psychological glitch that we recognize immediately when it's shown to us. This chapter shows you this glitch and explains it. Now, let's start unraveling the confusion over "prevention" with the definition of a *Likely Cause* situation.

The Definition of a Likely Cause Situation

*A Likely Cause situation is a **weakness** connected to the work in a Normal Work situation that's **not** causing trouble now but is threatening to cause trouble in the future and that can be prevented by a Blocking Action so the Future Trouble doesn't occur.*

Briefly, a Likely Cause is a *weakness* in the work on a task. It's a *weakness* in the skills, equipment, and experience surrounding a task that isn't triggering trouble now, but that could trigger it in the future. Let's also clarify the fuzzy word "weakness." The word weak refers to something that's likely to fail under pressure. So in this chapter a *weakness* is a person, thing, or system involved in our work on a task that's likely to fail if more pressure is applied to it (and of course, more pressure *will* eventually be applied to it).

Examples of weaknesses in our work would include places where a coworker is untrained (or poorly trained). Or where a coworker doesn't have enough experience (or has the wrong experience). Or where equipment is poorly maintained, old, or abused. Or where raw materials aren't the best ones for the application. Or where the design of a product or service is obsolete, and so on. You get the idea.

The point is, when more pressure is applied to such weaknesses, they usually "hatch" and create trouble. When more pressure is applied, that untrained coworker will make a mistake. That poorly maintained machine will break down. That raw material will fail. As the ancient Chinese Proverb says: "When the tide goes out, the rocks show."

So, Likely Cause sits are *weaknesses* in people, things, and systems in our work on tasks that may crack under additional pressure. But remember this principle: These people, things, and systems aren't causing trouble *now,* but they probably *will*

Likely Cause
Situation

*A Likely Cause situation is a **weakness** connected to the
work in a Normal Work situation that's **not** causing
trouble now but is threatening to cause trouble
in the future and that can be prevented by a
Blocking Action so the Future Trouble doesn't occur.*

---

when the heat's turned up. Worse, the trouble will usually strike
when we least expect it and when we're least prepared to cope
with them.

Okay, if LCs are weaknesses waiting to "hatch" in the work
on our tasks, what is a Blocking Action? And how does the technique of Trouble-Prevention come into play? Let's define these
terms next, starting with the definition of a *Blocking Action.*

The Definition
of a Blocking Action

*Any action you choose and implement to best **neutralize**
a Likely Cause situation connected to the work in a
Normal Work situation, **preventing** that weakness
from "hatching" and causing future costs,
losses, and trouble.*

The word *block* means to deliberately prevent something from moving forward in time and space. And that's exactly what we're doing with Blocking Actions. We're deliberately preventing Likely Causes from moving forward in our work on our tasks. That thought leads us to our next step, the definition of the leadership technique of *Trouble-Prevention*.

What is Trouble-Prevention?

Trouble-Prevention is a type of forecasting technique that identifies Likely Causes (weaknesses) in our work and then takes assertive advance action to keep them from "hatching." Said another way, Trouble-Prevention is a tool to fail-safe our work. It's a tool to guarantee the success of our work and to ensure that our tasks reach their goals. A participant in one of my seminars once said it this way, "The only trouble I ever really *solve* is the one I don't ever let start." That's the core of it. Next, putting all these thoughts together, here's our definition of *Trouble-Prevention*.

The Definition of Trouble-Prevention

*Choosing and implementing best Blocking Actions for Likely Cause situations connected to the work in Normal Work situations **before** those Likely Causes can "hatch," thus **preventing** future costs, losses, stress, and damage.*

Blocking Action

*Any action you choose and implement to best **neutralize** a Likely Cause situation connected to the work in a Normal Work situation, thus **preventing** that weakness from "hatching" and causing future costs, losses, and trouble.*

Simply stated, *Trouble-Prevention* is blocking Likely Causes before they can cause trouble. Note that Trouble-Prevention is always used *prior* to the start of failures, defects, and other troubles. Blocking Actions are always implemented *before* any trouble starts. The word *prevention* refers to something that comes *before* something else. Trouble-Prevention always comes before trouble starts and tries to keep that trouble from ever occurring.

To summarize, Trouble-Prevention is advance action that prevents Likely Causes from triggering Future Troubles. It intercepts LCs and neutralizes them before they can attack. That's why the military calls their Blocking Actions *preemptive strikes*.

Now, notice that we're emphasizing this "before" principle because this is exactly the place that so many books, speeches, seminars, and classes get it wrong. I've used this saying in seminars for years: True prevention is the *absence* of trouble—not the suppressing of trouble. The reverse is also true: False prevention is the *suppressing* of trouble—not the absence of trouble.

This means that if you have trouble in your work and you're taking action against that trouble, you're *not* working in prevention. You're working in suppression. You're taking Suppressing Action on a Current Trouble. (Or perhaps a Correcting Action on a True Cause. Review Table 2, Row 1 and Row 2 on page 115 to see this.)

The point is, if you had taken true prevention in your work, *the trouble you're acting on wouldn't be there.* The big mistake books and classes make is teaching that if you take heroic action on *trouble,* you're being preventive. They teach that because they believe that if you keep trouble from *spreading,* you're being preventive.

But that's a word-play. That misses the whole principle. Their mistake is that the trouble they're trying to keep from spreading *shouldn't have been there in the first place.* Said another way, the situation to which such leaders are responding is a Current Trouble—not a Likely Cause. (Compare Table 2, Row 1 to Table 1, Row 3 to see this.)

Trouble-Prevention

*Choosing and implementing best Blocking Actions for Likely Cause situations connected to the work in Normal Work situations **before** those Likely Causes can "hatch," thus **preventing** future costs, losses, stress, and damage.*

Let's take an example. Let's imagine a fire truck loaded with brave fire fighters and fire-fighting gear roaring to the scene of a burning home. Our question is this: What's the role of that truck, its fire fighters, and its fire-fighting gear at the house? Is their role to prevent a house fire? Or is their role to *suppress* a house fire? Isn't the answer easy? Isn't the main purpose of fire fighters is to suppress fires that are already burning? Isn't that's why fire-fighting equipment is often called "fire suppression" equipment?

The truth is, fire fighters are equipped and trained by local governments to be Suppressing Actions, not Blocking Actions. (To be specific, fire fighters are actually Preparing Actions that governments take as part of the Trouble-Readiness systems in communities. Then, when the fire fighters leap into action, they're acting out the roles of *Suppressing Actions*. See Table 2, Row 1 and Row 3 on page 115 to understand this.)

The key to this story is that if the homeowners had practiced true prevention by turning off the stove before they left town, there never would have been a house fire for the fire fighters to suppress.

Let's review. The main reason leaders don't take more Blocking Actions is that they don't understand the fuzzy word "prevention," and also they haven't identified the situation to which they're responding. The acid test is this. If even the smallest amount of trouble *physically exists*, you're already too late. You're already in suppression, correction, or a combination of both.

Here's another tip to help identify true prevention. I sometimes say that true prevention is "a bunch of *pre-* words." That refers to the prefix *pre-* on the front of many words—meaning *before*, as we said earlier. Thus, any time we see or hear a word with the prefix *pre-*, we're probably seeing or hearing about true prevention. Here's a list of typical *pre-* words you'll see and hear in business and family communications.

Pre- Words That Usually Indicate Prevention

Preview	Pretest
Preplan	Pretrain
Preschedule	Prearrange
Prepackage	Prepay
Preassign	Precode
Precondition	Preprocess
Precook	Preeducate
Preprogram	Preengineer
Presell	Presort
Prescreen	Preflight

As you read this list of *pre-* words, you might have been thinking, *Wait a minute. I never see any of these words in my life and job. Who would use such weird words, anyway?* If that thought passed through your mind, it may tell you something

202 | *Preactive* Leadership

about your actions, and about the actions of your friends, family, and coworkers. It may tell you that none of you is using as much prevention as you should. It may even tell that you and your coworkers are working in suppression and correction and calling it "prevention."

But it gets worse. There's yet another misunderstanding that occurs with true prevention. As we said earlier, some leaders confuse true prevention with *Trouble-Readiness*. They think that Preparing Actions are Blocking Actions. For instance, some leaders claim that installing fire extinguishers in buildings is "fire prevention." But it isn't. Fire extinguishers don't *prevent* fires. They *suppress* fires that have already started. Isn't that true? Ask yourself a simple question: When are fire extinguishers *physically used*? Before fires start or after fires start? If it's true that they're used after fires start, then fire extinguishers are designed to respond to Current Troubles—not Likely Causes. So fire extinguishers are another example of Preparing Actions and are a form of *Reactive* leadership.

In a side bar, let's repeat a lesson we've mentioned several times in this book. We're discovering once again how important it is for leaders to use the *proper names* for their situations and actions. Let's say it again: "Words *matter*." It's vital for leaders to correctly identify the situations they're facing, and to assign the correct names to the actions they're taking. That's the only way they can become *Preactive* leaders.

Okay, let's shift gears and talk about the second reason that many leaders don't take as much true prevention as they should. This is the *psychological* reason we mentioned earlier. It's time to deal with the mental glitch that many of us have.

The Fear of Being Negative

At the beginning of this chapter, we said that Trouble-Prevention requires us to think *negatively* about the people, things, and systems in our work and to identify the weaknesses in those people, things, and systems that might cause Future Trouble. That means prevention is a *negative* way of predicting how you, your friends, your family members, and your coworkers may not be experienced enough, mature enough, educated enough, disciplined enough, skilled enough, or motivated enough to do the assigned work. It's a way of thinking *negatively* about how people, things, and systems aren't fast enough, efficient enough, or effective enough for the work they're supposed to be doing.

In short, prevention is thinking negatively for a constructive purpose. However, most of us don't like *negative* thoughts, and we don't like *people* who think negatively. *That's* the mental glitch we're talking about in this chapter: The fear of being negative.

Yet negative thinking for a *constructive* purpose is the launching pad of prevention. If we're hesitant to identify the

Likely Causes of Future Troubles in our work and hesitant to take Blocking Actions against those Likely Causes, we can't be *Preactive* leaders. In truth, Trouble-Prevention is probably the most psychological of the six leadership techniques we're learning. It's probably rooted in a *mental attitude* more than any of the other techniques. Earlier, we mentioned a survey revealing that leaders were spending less than one percent of their time on Blocking Actions. Now we know why. They were afraid of being called "negative thinkers" by their friends and coworkers.

Many of us were told in childhood to *"Stop being negative. Look for the positive in life. Nobody likes a pessimist. Every cloud has a silver lining. Every problem is only an opportunity in disguise."* In other words, we were conditioned in childhood to delete negative thoughts from our mental hard drives. But that backfires as adults. That makes us hesitant to think negatively about the Likely Causes all around us. It makes us hesitant to identify—and act on—the weaknesses in the people, things, and systems around us.

Instead, we find ourselves hoping that, somehow, those weaknesses will evaporate. Somehow, things will work out. Somehow, if we just ignore the weaknesses we see, things will be okay. But the weaknesses won't evaporate, work out, or be okay. Instead, at a moment when we least expect it, and at a moment when we're least prepared to handle it, one of those weaknesses will lunge out of the darkness and grab us by the throat.

In summary, a professional negative attitude is the foundation of prevention. Prevention requires us to professionally think about the weaknesses around us—and then to professionally take Blocking Actions against them.

Of course, all of that runs counter to childhood conditioning. But the rewards are great. Blocking Actions usually have the biggest pay-offs of any actions we take. I heard about a study some years ago that showed Blocking Actions have a *one-thousand-fold payoff* in prevented costs and losses. That is, each dollar invested in Blocking Actions yielded one thousand dollars in prevented costs and losses.

Think about how much it could *save* in your own work if you could *prevent* ten percent of your Future Troubles. Or twenty percent. Or fifty percent. Or seventy percent.

Or look at that in reverse. Think about how much it will *cost* in your own work if you *don't* prevent ten percent of your Future Troubles. Or twenty percent. Or fifty percent. Or seventy percent.

At the beginning of this chapter, we had an action statement for Trouble-Prevention that read like this: *I want to choose the best Blocking Action to prevent Laura Mitchell's lack of MX Machine experience from producing bad gitwidgets on her machine next week.* Let's think more deeply about Trouble-Prevention by seeing the story behind that statement.

The Case of
Laura Mitchell's MX Machine

Once upon a time in a far-away city, a small manufacturing plant operated a line of MX machines that assembled gitwidgets for the company's customers. The MX machines were good machines, except they were purchased from a foreign country, and were difficult for operators to run. So it came to pass in those days that the operator of MX machine number 13 retired, and the company hired a new operator named Laura Mitchell to take over the machine. Laura had worked in factories before and was an experienced operator. But she had never operated an MX machine.

Laura's supervisor, Harry Dolt, told top management, "Laura has a good background. She catches on fast, so I'm letting let her teach herself. Her production is slow right now because she's practicing, but she'll learn the skills in a few days."

William James, the plant superintendent, is listening to this. He trusts Harry's judgment. But he knows something Harry doesn't know. A flood of new orders is due next week from a new customer, and all the MX machines in the plant will be running at full capacity on Monday morning. William starts to think about this negatively for a constructive purpose.

Laura Mitchell's lack of experience is an obvious weakness in the work Laura is being asked to do. Her lack of experience is a threat to both the quality and quantity of next week's production. Her lack of experience is a Likely Cause threatening the plant's production schedule for gitwidgets. Laura isn't making any bad gitwidgets now. But when her machine starts running at full capacity on Monday she probably will. So William begins to think, *What if Laura has bad runs next week? What if she ends up shipping bad gitwidgets to our new customer?*

William decides to be *Preactive* on the Likely Cause he's identified. He calls Laura's supervisor over for a discussion of the threat. "Harry," he says, "I'm not comfortable with letting Laura teach herself at this point. I'm expecting pressure from new orders on Monday, and I think we need to take the best Blocking Action possible to keep Laura's lack of MX experience from hurting us. We don't want her shipping bad gitwidgets to our new customer next week."

Harry nods. "I agree, chief. But what are ya' thinkin' about doing?"

"Well," William answers, "we want to be creative. We want to give Laura the best help we can, at the least cost to us, with the least interruption of production. We want to produce next week's orders on-time and on-quality, but we want to give Laura the best MX training we can. Is that a good summary of our needs?"

"Yes," answers Harry. "We need to run her machine in order to meet our production schedule. But we don't have the time to put her in a training program, and we can't let her continue to teach herself. We don't have a substitute operator available, and we don't have time to hire and train one. So I'm stumped. What *can* we do, chief?"

"Tell you what," laughs William. "Let's try something I saw several years ago in another plant. Laura is operating machine number 13. So let's have the operators on machines 12 and 14 on each side of Laura take turns teaching her for an hour each how to run her machine, while they continue to run their own machines at the same time.

"That way, nobody gets too tired, and Laura learns the ropes from two different expert MX operators. Of course, this will make all three machines run a few cycles slower than normal. But it won't make them so slow that we'll fall behind in production and, more importantly, it'll prevent Laura from producing bad gitwidgets."

"Whoa," exclaims Harry, "I never heard of that."

William grins and asks, "Do you see any Future Troubles in my tentative choice?"

Harry thinks a moment and answers, "Well, I never like to distract operators, and helping Laura might distract our other operators a little. But as I think about it, it shouldn't distract them enough to make them start producing bad gitwidgets themselves. No, I think we're okay."

"Then it's settled," says William. "Go tell the three operators what we're going to do, and let's implement our Blocking Action."

Okay, to see the principle here, let's look at this example sequentially:

1. William James, the superintendent, thought negatively for a constructive purpose. He recognized that Laura's lack of MX experience was a Likely Cause threatening his work to produce quality gitwidgets on time.

2. William knew even though Laura wasn't producing bad gitwidgets now, she probably would when her machine started running at full capacity next Monday.

3. So William took a bold Blocking Action against the Likely Cause (Laura's lack of experience). He thought up a creative Blocking Action: The operators on each side of Laura could alternate training her for an hour at a time, while continuing to run their own machines. None of the machines would run too slowly, and Laura could be trained without producing bad gitwidgets.

Also notice something else important. Even though the story was presented in a conversational format (in the *Mental-Verbal Format* we saw in Chapters 2 and 3), William and Harry obeyed all the required steps for accurate decision-making. They started with an action statement, discussed their needs, discussed alternatives, made a tentative choice, discussed hidden troubles in the tentative choice, and implemented a final decision. In short, they satisfied the needs of a Likely Cause sit by choosing a best Blocking Action.

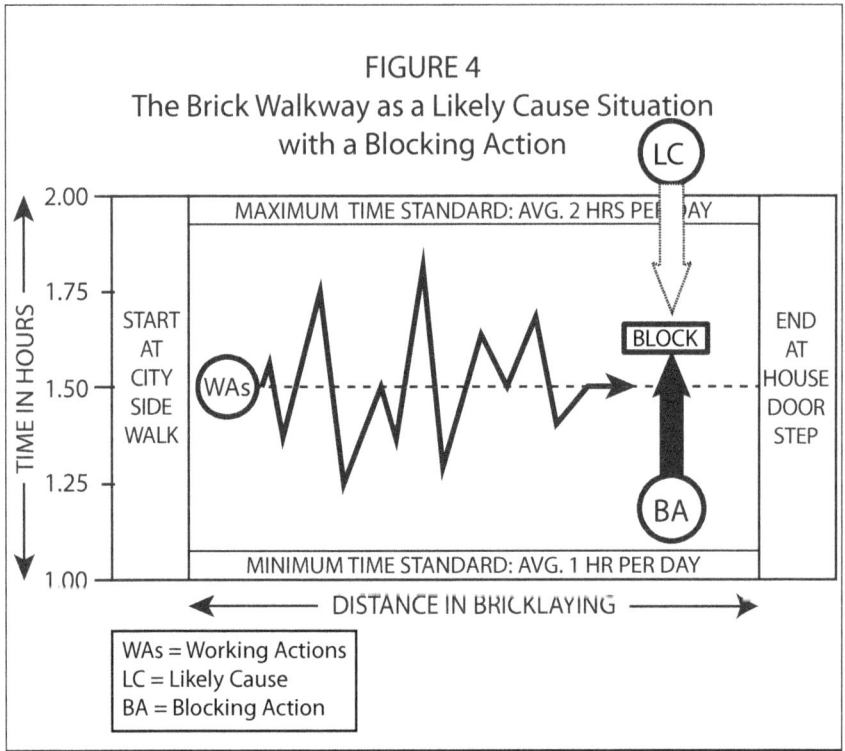

FIGURE 4
The Brick Walkway as a Likely Cause Situation
with a Blocking Action

WAs = Working Actions
LC = Likely Cause
BA = Blocking Action

Okay, now let's see what a Likely Cause sit and a Blocking Action look like in diagrammatic form. Let's return to the diagram we've been using in the previous chapters and let's update it for prevention.

Figure 4 is a continuation of the diagrams we've used in previous chapters illustrating the brick walkway you're building for Terry Johnson. This time a Likely Cause situation is added as well as a Blocking Action preventing that LC sit from "hatching."

The dotted arrow menacing the zigzag work arrow represents a *Likely Cause* situation (LC). LCs are weaknesses in the people, things, or systems connected to the work that are not causing trouble now but are threatening to cause it in the future. If they do, they will push the work arrow outside of the minimum time standard of one hour per day set for the work by the Johnson family creating a Current Trouble in the work— the work will be in non-conformance with the family's standards.

The black arrow represents a *Blocking Action* (BA) being taken in advance *before* the Likely Cause "hatches." BAs are preemptive strikes against LCs that are taken to prevent them from ever impacting the work. This diagram is a picture of the leadership technique of *Trouble-Prevention*. Note that BAs are effective and that they are *Preactive* leadership: *Leading in the absence of trouble.*

Examples of Common Everyday Blocking Actions

The purpose of Figure 4 is to illustrate how Working Actions proceed through time and space and what can threaten them as they move forward toward their goals. So now, let's think about how this principle might apply to your work on the brick walkway for the Johnsons.

Imagine that you've cut a section of grass out of the family's lawn, and you're filling the empty space with bricks, carefully obeying Terry's standards to have all the bricks lay flat on the ground with quarter-inch spaces between them. Then you glance at your watch and realize that it's time to stop work for the day. What are some of the common sense things you might do as you wrap up your afternoon's work?

Well, you might spread a piece of plastic over the newly laid bricks. You might gather up the tools and, using the key Terry loaned you, lock them in the Johnson's garage. You might twist the top of the bag of mortar tightly closed, and seal it with duct tape. You might rope off the newly laid area of bricks with yellow caution tape. You might ring the doorbell and tell the Johnson family you were stopping for the day, but that you'd be back at such-and-such a time the following afternoon.

Now, if you did these things, you would be taking common, everyday *Blocking Actions*. As an experienced bricklayer, you realize that there are some typical Likely Causes threatening your bricklaying for the Johnson family. For example, you know that it might rain during the night and dilute your new mortar. So you spread plastic over the new bricks.

You know that thieves might steal Terry's tools during the night, so you lock them in the garage. You know that the mortar bag might absorb moisture overnight and harden, so you seal the bag tightly with duct tape. You know that children might run across your new bricks while playing and unseat them, so you rope off the wet bricks with yellow caution tape. You know that the Johnson family might be planning a lawn party or other social event tomorrow afternoon that your work would interrupt, so you ring the doorbell and let them know your intended schedule.

What we're saying is that in many ways Trouble-Prevention is just common sense. But as someone once said, "It might be common sense, but sense ain't so common." A strange twist in prevention is that we often *do* take Blocking Actions at home and during hobbies and recreation, but we often *don't* take them on the job because we're too busy, tired, stressed, and distracted. Also, we don't want to be called "negative thinkers" by coworkers and superiors, as we said earlier.

So we're often not as aware of prevention on the job as we are when we're more relaxed. In the brick walkway story, you're working quietly and privately on your own. You have full authority over your work, and you're able to take prevention without asking anyone's permission.

But on the job, Likely Causes are often weaknesses in coworkers, superiors, and subordinates, or in other departments, equipment, vendors, clients, people, and things over which we have no authority. That complicates matters and makes it difficult to take Blocking Actions.

But perhaps it will give us more courage if we realize that the word "blocking" is a highly respected technical word that's used in chemistry, medicine, psychiatry, sports, electronics, and military applications—all with the same meaning: to professionally and intelligently *intercept* a threat to the work on a task to guarantee a positive outcome.

Thus, when you take a Blocking Action on the job, you're professionally intercepting trouble in your work to guarantee a positive outcome. So you shouldn't be timid about it. You aren't doing anything bad, you're doing something good. You're doing something that leaders *should* do. What's good enough for chemists, psychiatrists, sports figures, electronic engineers, and military commanders should be good enough for you.

Now—back to our discussion of Figure 4. Notice in the diagram that a Likely Cause is threatening your bricklaying at the upper right of the diagram (it's the arrow marked *LC*). Also notice you're taking a Blocking Action at the bottom right of the diagram to block this Likely Cause (it's the arrow marked *BA*). These arrows could represent any of the LCs and BAs we just listed above for Terry Johnson's walkway.

The Likely Cause arrow could represent the threat of rain during the night, or of tool thieves, or of the mortar hardening in the bag, or of children unseating the wet bricks, or of you interfering with a Johnson family social event.

Likewise, the BA arrow could represent the plastic cover over the wet bricks, or locking the tools in the garage, or sealing the mortar bag, or roping off the wet bricks, or ringing the doorbell to advise the family of your schedule.

Now, let's change the subject a moment and look at another side of Likely Causes. We've established that leaders are often hesitant to think *negatively*. So let's try to make Likely Causes less intimidating to ourselves and coworkers by treating them with humor. This humor will also explain why I often refer to Likely Causes as "hatching" in work.

Time Bombs
and Alligator Eggs

During my years of teaching *Preactive* leadership seminars internationally, I've used several mental images to help participants visualize Likely Cause situations in a humorous way. My two favorite images are *time bombs* and *alligator eggs*. The lesson in these amusing images is that Likely Causes *might* create trouble in work at some future time—but they haven't *yet*—and so maybe they can be blocked.

We've all seen Hollywood suspense films in which the villain plants a time bomb, and the brave hero or heroine must disarm it. Every few seconds, the camera zooms in on the bomb's clock mechanism. This usually consists of bright red numbers rapidly counting down, showing the audience that time is almost up. Meanwhile, the hero or heroine fumbles desperately with a pair of household wire cutters, trying to decide whether to cut the red, yellow, or black wire.

Okay, stop the clock (no pun intended). Why is a *time bomb* a good image of a Likely Cause? It's a good image because a time bomb can cause serious trouble if it's not disarmed in advance. The hero or heroine knows this, and he or she is trying to take a Blocking Action—with handy-dandy household wire cutters.

Such Hollywood plots are examples of true prevention. The time bomb represents a Likely Cause about to create a Future Trouble, and the hero or heroine is thinking negatively for a constructive purpose and taking advance action regardless of personal fear and danger.

Next, the second mental image I've used for Likely Causes is the image of an *alligator egg*. (That's why, throughout this book I talk about Likely Causes as "hatching.") As a native of Florida, I often tell stories about the alligator farms that once lined Florida highways to attract tourist dollars, and about how tourists fed the alligators bread from a bridge, and about how the children screamed when the alligators leaped out of the water to get the bread.

So, I often use the word *alligator* to represent a Current Trouble—as we'll see in the next chapter—and I often use the phrase *alligator egg* to represent a Likely Cause (after all, alligators come from alligator eggs). In a later chapter, we'll refer to our search for Likely Causes as "going on alligator egg hunts."

Special note: Alligators are large freshwater reptiles that grow up to 19 feet in length and that are native only to the U.S. and China. They breed in the spring, and during the summer the females build nests in the marsh vegetation holding as many as 50 eggs each. Strangely, ranchers and farmers actually do have alligator egg hunts to harvest the eggs; and strangely, there really are people who have the job title of Alligator Egg Hunter. So my humorous analogy isn't as far-fetched as it might seem.

To put these images together, let's imagine a science fiction film in which the hero is crawling through a desolate swamp, trying to find a large alligator egg in the muddy reeds. The egg has been treated with radioactivity by a mad scientist, and the hero knows that if it's allowed to hatch, a huge Godzilla-type alligator will emerge to create havoc among the residents of the local village. Worse, the nesting area is in reeds infested by deadly snakes and other dangerous creatures, so the hero may not survive the adventure. Still, he crawls onward through the mud, determined to save the village. Now, if such a corny film had ever been made, it would have been an example of true prevention. The radioactive egg would be a Likely Cause threatening Future Trouble for the village, and the hero would be trying to *preempt* the hatching of the egg by finding it and destroying it with a Blocking Action.

The lesson in the story is that finding Likely Causes in your work, and in the work of others, is a *good* thing—not a bad thing. Trouble-Prevention serves a *good* purpose. So you shouldn't be timid about using it, even if you need to keep it in perspective by calling your Likely Causes time bombs or alligator eggs.

I hope these amusing images make Likely Causes more approachable for you, and that they give you the boldness to *identify* the LCs in your work and to *take* Blocking Actions against them before they "hatch." That's the way to prevent trouble, damage, and failure in work, and earn financial and emotional rewards for doing so.

Summary of Chapter 7

1. Likely Cause situations (LC sits) are the third and last of the three Effective-Efficient situations we'll learn, and Blocking Actions are the third and last of the three actions we'll learn that we can use to *direct* work toward its goals with *Preactive* and *offensive-minded* strategies and tactics.

2. Blocking Actions (BAs) can also be called "preemptive strikes" and other such terms because they prevent attacks on products, services, and behavior, and because they intercept the costs, losses, and damage of Future Troubles.

3. Some books, classes, and seminars confuse the *Preactive* technique of Trouble-Prevention with the *Reactive* techniques of Trouble-Control, Cause-Removal, and Trouble-Readiness. (Review Table 2, page 115.)

4. Surveys show that some leaders don't take as many Blocking Actions as they should because they're afraid of being called "negative thinkers" by friends and coworkers.

5. A Likely Cause situation is a *weakness* connected to the work in a Normal Work situation that's not causing trouble now but is threatening to cause trouble in the future and that can be prevented by a Blocking Action so the Future Trouble doesn't occur.

6. A Blocking Action is any action you choose and implement to best *neutralize* a Likely Cause situation, thus *preventing* that weakness from "hatching" and causing future costs, losses, and trouble.

7. The leadership technique of Trouble-Prevention is choosing and implementing the best *Blocking Actions* for the Likely Causes threatening the work in Normal Work sits before the LCs can "hatch."

8. The word *weak* refers to something that's likely to fail under pressure. So a Likely Cause is a person, thing, or system connected to the work on a task that's likely to fail if additional pressure is applied to it.

9. The motto of true prevention is: "The *absence* of trouble—not the *suppressing* of trouble." (Likewise, false prevention is the *suppressing* of trouble—not the *absence* of trouble.)

10. In one sentence: Trouble-Prevention is blocking Likely Causes before they can "hatch" and create Future Trouble.

11. Prevention is rooted in a mental attitude more than any of the other six techniques because of our natural fear of being called *negative* thinkers by family, friends, and coworkers.

12. Figure 4 illustrates a Likely Cause situation with a Blocking Action intercepting it.

13. The word "blocking" is a respected professional word used in chemistry, sports, the military, and many technical fields. It means to *intercept* something to achieve a positive re-

sult. Thus, we shouldn't be shy about using the term in our own lives and careers.

14. Two humorous images for Likely Causes are *time bombs* and *alligator eggs*. These phrases can make discussions of Likely Causes less intimidating to our coworkers and us.

One final thought for this chapter is this. Blocking Actions are the *only* trouble-blockers in the field of leadership. If you're not taking Blocking Actions in your work, it's only a matter of time before you'll experience trouble. We'll return to the subject of Trouble-Prevention later and be more specific about how to be preventive in your own life and career.

But next, in Chapter 8, we cross the great divide in leadership. We cross the Grand Canyon that separates the three Effective-Efficient situations from the three Ineffective-Inefficient situations. In Chapter 8, we begin to see the vast difference between *Preactive* leadership and *Reactive* leadership.

PART III

THE THREE
INEFFECTIVE-INEFFICIENT
SITUATIONS

CHAPTER 8

CURRENT TROUBLE SITUATIONS

The First
Ineffective-Inefficient Situation
(See Table 2, Row 1, Page 115)

Description: A Performance that is Breaking a Task Standard in an Unwanted Way

Existence in Time: The Present (*But Originated In the Past*)

Name of Action: Suppressing Action

Leadership Technique: Trouble-Control

Leadership Type: *Correcting* Tasks with
                               Reactive Strategies and Tactics

Action Statement
Template: *I want to choose the best (Suppressing Action to suppress this Current Trouble in the work on this Normal Work situation).*

Starting with this chapter, we're now on the far side of the great divide, the deep chasm that divides leadership into two opposing types. This chapter is about the third situation that's connected to Normal Work situations and that's a part of them. But this chapter is about the *first* of the generic Choice Situations that "mask" as Ineffective-Inefficient situations. This chapter is our first look at a situation in which we're *correcting* work with a *defensive-minded* and *Reactive* type of leadership.

This situation is described in Table 2, Row 1, page 115 and, sadly, it's one of the most frequently seen situations in our lives and on our jobs. The *Reactive* situations are the opposites of the *Preactive* situations that we've been discussing, and I often say that leaders who're responding to these *Reactive* situations are "leading in the presence of trouble."

This chapter is about the *Current Trouble* situation. Actions taken in this situation are called *Suppressing Actions*. I use the abbreviations *CT* sits for Current Troubles and *SAs* for Suppressing Actions. This is the situation people are joking about when they say, "I'm up to my ears in alligators today!" The purpose of actions taken in this situation is to *control* mistakes, accidents, and failures that have popped up in work. We call the leadership technique in this chapter *Trouble-Control*, and we saw an example of it in the previous chapter with our story about the fire truck racing to the scene of the house fire to suppress the flames with fire suppression equipment.

The action statement template for this situation is, "I want to choose the best (Suppressing Action to suppress this Current Trouble in the work on this Normal Work situation)." For instance, you might write, *I want to choose the best Suppressing Action to suppress the 30% of our gitwidgets that have been defective on assembly line three since the start of second shift last Monday.* Now, let's open this chapter by thinking about what *trouble* is.

What is "Trouble"?

The root of the word *trouble* means to be confused or to inflict pain and discomfort on someone. That gives you a good sense for what trouble does. But we need a more practical definition that we can apply to everyday tasks. So here's a more specific definition of a *Current Trouble*.

The Definition of a Current Trouble Situation

*Any **performance** of any person, thing, or system that was previously satisfying a set, clear, and agreed on standard in a Normal Work situation but is now **breaking** that standard in an **unwanted** way.*

A Current Trouble is something that has gone *wrong* in work. It's work that's *breaking* a standard it was supposed to satisfy. It's behavior that was once acceptable, but is now *unacceptable*. It's something *bad* that wasn't happening before but is happening now—and we don't like it. Here are some examples.

1. An employee who was once punctual is now late each morning.
2. A molding machine that was once on schedule is now too slow.
3. A printer that once printed smooth sheets is now printing wrinkled sheets.
4. The grass in a lawn that was once green is now turning brown in patches.
5. A dog that was once warm and lovable is now biting the children.

But there's something else involved in the word "trouble" that makes it hard to define: It has too many *synonyms*. We've mentioned synonyms several times in previous chapters, but now let's really crank down on them.

The Treachery of Synonyms

Synonyms are words and phrases that are interchangeable in casual writing and speaking. They're words and phrases that mean approximately the same thing, and so people switch them around in written and verbal communications. For instance, a person might say, "My boss made a (*decision, choice, judgment*) about the new stock option plan." Any of the three italicized words shown in the parentheses would work in the sentence because they're synonyms.

The term *synonym* came from a Greek root that meant the *same name*. And the words decision, choice, and judgment are close enough in meaning to serve as the same name in the sen-

---

Current Trouble Situation

*Any **performance** of any person, thing, or system that was previously satisfying a set, clear, and agreed on standard in a Normal Work situation but is now **breaking** that standard in an **unwanted** way.*

tence. But synonyms are treacherous because they can confuse coworkers. We already know that there are six different situations in leadership, and we've been learning how to talk and write about them. That's hard enough. But it becomes much harder when we discover that each of the six situations has *dozens* of different synonyms, and when we realize that if we carelessly use these synonyms, our coworkers will get lost in the verbiage.

Said another way: Unless our coworkers have the ability to quickly "decode" synonyms in their heads (and many *don't*), they'll soon lose track of which situation a leader is describing. Here's an illustration. Let's imagine a leader calls a Monday morning staff meeting and presents the following situation statement to gathered coworkers.

"I called this meeting to be more selective about the variations in the paint our vendors have been delivering to the paint department for the past two weeks. From the symptoms I've seen, the vendors on our short-list have a range of anomaly too wide for us to handle, and we need to do something about it immediately."

Yes, unfortunately, some leaders really *do* talk this way. But what's worse is that the employees listening to this rambling statement would quickly be confused about the true identity of the situation the leader is trying to describe. Here's why. This leader used three different *synonyms* in the same situation statement to describe the same Current Trouble. But how many of the coworkers gathered for the meeting can mentally interpret synonyms fast enough to stay focused on the real situation the leader is describing? Probably not many.

To see this fallacy even more clearly, here's a sampler of common synonyms for the word "trouble." You'll see and hear these synonyms anywhere people are working on tasks. Note that the three different synonyms that the leader used in our paint department example are *italicized* in the list.

Common Synonyms for the Word Trouble

Problem	Undesirable
Deviation	Breakdown
Variation	Unacceptable
Stress	Difficulty
Complaint	*Symptom*
Anomaly	Confusion
Damage	Nonconformance
Malfunction	Rejects
Substandard	Failure
Alligator	Things-Gone-Wrong

By the way, the last two synonyms in the columns are especially interesting. *Alligator* is a humorous synonym for trouble that's used mostly in the U.S., and *Things-Gone-Wrong* is an unusual synonym for trouble that's used mostly in England.

But back to our illustration. Why was it necessary for the leader in our paint department example to use *three* different synonyms to describe *one* Current Trouble? Wasn't that repetitive? Didn't that just triple the chances for employees to get confused? I think so. And that's why our Identification Tables on pages 114-115 are so important. These tables give standardized names for the six leadership situations and actions and, if leaders use *only* the names on pages 114-115 when discussing situations and actions, they exponentially increase their chances of success.

For example, what if the leader in our paint department example had avoided using synonyms? If he or she had done so, the situation statement in our paint department example might have sounded something like this, "We need to choose the best way to immediately suppress the variations in the brand of unleaded paint our vendors have been delivering to our paint department for the past two weeks."

With that, let's stop and ask the same question we've already asked several times in other chapters of the book: Which of the two situation statements we've seen in our paint department example would give the employees of that department the best chance for efficient action—the leader's original version with the synonyms in it or this latest clarified version we just read? Isn't the answer obvious? The lesson is this: We learned in earlier chapters not to use fuzzy words and smokescreen statements to describe situations and actions. But now we've added a third rule. We can't use *synonyms* to describe situations and actions, either.

We've said it before: "Words *matter*." It's extremely important for leaders to use clear and specific words when speaking and writing about situations and actions. Next, let's continue with this principle of clear definitions with the definition of a *Suppressing Action*.

The Definition of Suppressing Action

*Any action you choose and implement to best **control, limit, fix,** or **minimize** the costs, losses, stresses, and damages of a Current Trouble in the work on a task and to keep those costs, losses, stresses, and damages from spreading.*

To understand Suppressing Action better, let's also see some of the *synonyms* for it that we'll see and hear at home and in the workplace.

Common Synonyms for
Suppressive Action

Minimizing action	Limiting action
Coping action	Contingency action
Restraining action	Emergency action
Evading action	Stonewalling action
Controlling action	Temporary action
Fixing action	Stalling action
Disciplinary action	Stopgap action
Holding action	Adapting action

Any time you see or hear any of these terms at home or on the job, you're probably reading or hearing about someone who's taking *suppression*. That's not a good thing because, as we're about to see, Suppressing Actions are extremely inefficient. Worse, they have many unintended negative consequences. But before we get to those principles, let's first define

---

Supressing Action

*Any action you choose and implement to best **control**, **limit, fix,** or **minimize** the costs, losses, stresses, and damages of a Current Trouble in the work on a task and to keep those costs, losses, stresses, and damages from spreading.*

the technique *Trouble-Control* since it's based on Suppressing Actions.

The Definition of Trouble-Control

*Choosing and implementing the best Suppressing Actions to **control, limit,** or **minimize** the costs, losses, stresses, and damages of Current Troubles in the work on a task and to keep those costs, losses, stresses, and damage from **spreading**.*

In one sentence, Trouble-Control is controlling existing trouble in an effort to fix it and keep it from spreading. Now, while we're on the subject of using the proper names for our situations and actions, let's also springboard off these last two definitions to eliminate a very confusing phrase in leadership. In fact, it's one of the most confusing phrases in the whole vocabulary of leadership. It's the fuzzy phrase *problem solving*.

The Phrase "Problem Solving" Should Never Be Used

Have you noticed that we haven't used the phrase *problem solving* yet in this book? Does that surprise you in a book about leadership? The truth is, I never use that phrase in seminars or when consulting with clients. Why not? I don't because it's too fuzzy and has too many synonyms. Using it only confuses seminar participants and consulting clients. Let me explain.

In daily conversation, the term "problem solving" can represent *any* of the seven—or *all* seven of the seven—leadership techniques we're learning in this book. Let's see how that can happen. Each of the following examples takes one of the seven techniques we're learning in this book and describes it by using the fuzzy phrase "problem solving."

1. Work-Accuracy: Let's do some *problem solving* and produce this within standards.

2. Standards-Betterment: Some *problem solving* will help improve this standard.

3. Trouble-Prevention: If we do some *problem solving*, this machine will be safer.

4. Trouble-Control: Let's do some *problem solving*, and repair these defective parts.

5. Cause-Removal: With creative *problem solving*, we can make this trouble go away.

6. Trouble-Readiness: Given our extensive *problem solving*, we're ready for this trouble.

7. Decision-Making: Let's do some *problem solving* and make a good decision on this.

This list shows that the fuzzy phrase "problem solving" is one of the most dangerous terms in leadership. It's so fuzzy that it's meaningless as a leadership term. It can be used to falsely

---

Trouble-Control

Choosing and implementing the best
*Suppressing Actions to **control, limit,** or*
minimize *the costs, losses, stresses, and damages*
of Current Troubles in the work on a task and to keep
*those costs, losses, stresses, and damage from **spreading**.*

---

describe any of the seven leadership techniques in this book. But item number 7 on the list is the most confusing of all because in it we're using the fuzzy phrase "problem solving" to describe the foundational technique of leadership—the platform on which the other six techniques are built—the technique of *decision-making*.

Many leadership textbooks, seminars, DVDs, and classes make a serious mistake by teaching a mixture of the leadership techniques and then calling their *mixture* either "problem solving" or "decision-making," depending on which lesson they're trying to teach. This is a mistake because, as we saw in Chapters 2 and 3, decision-making is a separate technique all to itself. It is the tool that guides all our actions and has nothing to do with "problem solving." Thus, it's vital to keep decision-making intact in our minds as an independent technique and to never call *decision-making* "problem solving."

But let's go deeper. Even if we tried to limit the use of the fuzzy phrase "problem solving" to Current Trouble situations as we're learning them in this chapter—it *still* won't work. The reason is because the word "solving" in the phrase is also too fuzzy to use. The word *solving* means finding the solution to something. And that's good. Except that we can take any one of *four* different actions to "solve" a Current Trouble.

1. We could *suppress* its damage—which is what we're learning in this chapter.
2. We could *remove* its cause—which is what we'll learn in the next chapter.
3. We could do *both* in a sequence—suppress the damage, then remove the cause.
4. We could do *both* in the opposite sequence—remove the cause, then suppress the damage.

To summarize, the fuzzy phrase "problem solving" is like a chameleon. It can change itself into so many colors that, as we said earlier, it's *meaningless* as a leadership phrase. That's why we don't use it. To drive this nail home, let's see one final illustration. Imagine you give a subordinate this situation statement, "George, I want you to do as much *problem solving* as possible today on the defective gitwidgets that Laura Mitchell is producing on MX machine 13."

Now, what are you asking George to do?

Are you asking him to *suppress* the defective gitwidgets being produced on machine 13—such as replacing them, repairing them, or remaking them? Or, are you asking him to remove the *cause* of the defective gitwidgets on machine 13?

Or, are you asking him to do *both* in some sequence: either suppress the defective gitwidgets first, and remove the cause second? Or, maybe remove the cause first and suppress the defective gitwidgets second?

Who knows? Maybe even *you* don't. That's why the fuzzy phrase "problem solving" and the single word "solving" are so confusing. And that's why our Identification Tables on pages 114 and 115 are important. As we said earlier, *Preactive* leaders *only* use the names in the tables to discuss situations and actions and, by doing so, they increase their chances of success exponentially. Okay, next let's continue our discussion of Suppressing Actions and talk about how *inefficient* they are.

Why Suppressing Actions are Inefficient

At the beginning of this chapter, we gave a sample action statement that went like this, *I want to choose the best Suppressing Action to suppress the 30% of our gitwidgets that have been defective on assembly line three since the start of second shift last Monday.*

Now, imagine that this is *your* assignment. What Suppressing Action will you take on the defective gitwidgets? You probably can't answer that question since the alternatives are literally endless. For starters, here are *nine* different Suppressing Actions you could take to limit the costs and losses of the defective gitwidgets on assembly line three.

1. You could shut down line three to stop the defective gitwidget production.
2. You could increase production on another line to replace the defective gitwidgets.
3. You could add a new night shift to replace the defective gitwidgets.
4. You could buy good gitwidgets from a competitor to replace the defective gitwidgets.
5. You could recall any defective gitwidgets you've already shipped to customers.
6. You could apologize to customers who've already received defective gitwidgets.
7. You could work the day shift overtime to replace the defective gitwidgets.
8. You could send the defective gitwidgets to the Rework Department to be reworked.
9. You could do combinations of any or all of these in various sequences.

There are many more actions we could add, but we won't use the space here. The point we're trying to make is that there's something interesting about all these actions. All of them are *ineffective* and *inefficient*. If this were a real situation in a real factory, you probably wouldn't want to take any of these actions because all of them are costly, embarrassing, and disruptive in the plant. That's a big clue to the nature of Suppressing Actions: They're always costly, embarrassing, and disruptive.

Said another way, Suppressing Actions always have *negative* side effects. They often create more trouble than we had before we took them. They usually create more badness than the goodness they do. Think back to the fire truck story we told in the previous chapter. Did you know that the *water* fire fighters use on flames often does more damage than the flames themselves? Water damage is a *negative* side effect of fire suppression. Other negative side effects of fire suppression might include high-speed accidents in fire trucks, fire fighters injured on the job, hoses and other fire suppression equipment damaged at the scene, and so forth.

The leadership principle we're learning is that Suppressing Actions often *magnify* the trouble they're supposed to be limiting. That's why convicts often leave prison more criminalized than before they entered. That's why children are often more rebellious after punishment than before. That's why riots often intensify when the riot police arrive.

This tendency to magnify the trouble is one reason the technique of Trouble-Control is listed as one of the Ineffective-Inefficient techniques in Table 2 on page 115. But to brighten an otherwise gloomy subject, let's mock the *negative* side effects of Suppressing Actions by calling them "Alligator Training" and "Booby Traps."

Suppression is Like Alligator Training

I sometimes say taking a Suppressing Actions is like trying to *train an alligator*. With Suppressing Actions, we're trying to make a Current Trouble (the "alligator") obey us. We're trying to control damage by acting forcefully against it. Indeed, the word *suppress* comes from a root that means to hold down by force. So when we take suppression, we're trying to hold an alligator (a trouble) down by force. That's what fire fighters are doing when they hose water on fires. That's what police officers are doing when they handcuff bank robbers. That's what soldiers are doing when they open fire on the enemy. Fire fighters, police officers, and soldiers are trying to *hold down trouble by force*.

But notice an important principle. When we use suppression, we're *not* preventing trouble and we're *not* removing a cause of trouble. We're only fighting the *trouble* itself. That makes a big difference in efficiency. To put it another way, training alligators isn't very efficient.

If that's not bad enough, it gets worse. Not only are Suppressing Actions inefficient, they also tend to backfire. The second *negative* side effect of Suppressing Actions is that they have hidden *booby traps.*

Suppression Has Booby Traps

The second negative side effect of Suppressing Actions is that they usually have hidden *booby traps.* Every time we use suppression, unexpected negative consequences pop out and explode in our faces. For example, let's suppose an employee is injured on the job. Acting as a Suppressing Action, coworkers pick up the injured employee and try to place him or her on a stretcher. But in their excitement, the coworkers handle the victim incorrectly and make the injury *worse*—an unintended booby trap in their suppression.

Imagine a small fire breaks out in a corner of a warehouse. Acting in the role of a Suppressing Action, the overhead sprinkler system is activated. The fire is extinguished, but the water *ruins* the warehouse's inventory of paper products—an unintended booby trap of the suppression.

Or, let's suppose some miners are trapped in a coal mine. In the role of a Suppressing Action, rescuers arrive and attempt to reach the trapped miners. But the drilling equipment used by the rescuers causes another cave-in, and some of the trapped miners are *killed*—an unintended booby trap of the suppression.

These examples tell us that a second *negative* side effect of Suppressing Actions is that they often contain unintended consequences that suddenly explode. That's another reason leaders should avoid suppression as much as possible. Suppression should always be used as a last resort only—after everything else has failed. With that in mind, let's see a diagram of a Current Trouble and a Suppressing Action.

In Chapter 2, we introduced a diagram illustrating in symbolic format the brick walkway you're laying for the Terry Johnson family. The diagram's purpose is to display how a Normal Work situation is assigned and executed and what can happen to it as it moves forward in time and space. In this chapter, Figure 5 on page 243 shows a Current Trouble attacking your bricklaying task and illustrates a Suppressing Action trying to limit the damage.

The Attack of the Alligator

As we said earlier, one of the humorous synonyms people use for Current Troubles is to call them *alligators*. So in Figure 5, we see an alligator attacking your bricklaying work for the Johnsons. The sine wave of your bricklaying proceeded normally from left to right within its low and high standards, until it reached a point toward the right of the diagram. Then, the sine wave suddenly nose-dived and broke the bottom *when* (time) standard that you and Terry negotiated requiring you to

FIGURE 5
The Brick Walkway as a Current Trouble Situation with a Suppressing Action

MAXIMUM TIME STANDARD: AVG. 2 HRS PER DAY

TIME IN HOURS

2.00
1.75
1.50
1.25
1.00

START AT CITY SIDE WALK

WAs

END AT HOUSE DOOR STEP

CT

MINIMUM TIME STANDARD: AVG. 1 HR PER DAY

DISTANCE IN BRICKLAYING

WAs = Working Actions
CT = Current Trouble
SA = Supressing Action

SUPPRESS

SA

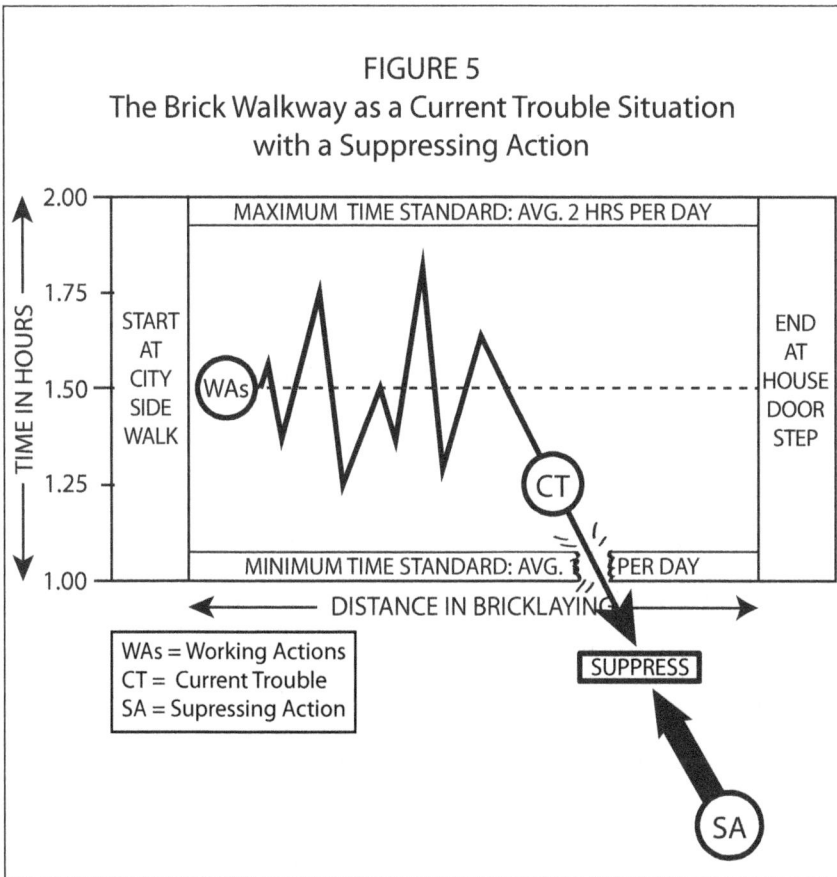

work a minimum average of one hour per day. Your bricklaying is now a Current Trouble situation (see arrow marked *CT*).

Symbolically, this nose-dive shows that your bricklaying has come to a screeching halt. No bricks are being laid. You're breaking your promise to the Johnsons to work a minimum average of two hours per day. You're in nonconformance. You're no longer doing quality work. An "alligator" exists in your work.

Also notice that you're taking a Suppressing Action at the bottom right of the diagram trying to limit the damage (see arrow marked **SA**). We'll talk about what that action is in a moment. But first note that SAs are ineffective, and that they're *Reactive* leadership: *Leading in the presence of trouble.*

Now, let's understand Figure 5 more clearly by explaining your bricklaying for the Johnson family. As you recall, a local building supply store is delivering pallets of Severe Weather Grade bricks to your job site on the family's lawn. The building supply store's truck delivers these pallets during the morning hours while you're on your day job, and leaves them on the grass. You arrive for your bricklaying that afternoon, cut the straps and shrink-wrap off the pallets.

But this afternoon there's trouble. As you cut open the brick pallet you find that the bricks are the *wrong color.* They're completely different from the bricks you've been laying. You can't use them. All you can do now is take *Suppressing Action* on the trouble.

Greatly irritated, you drop your tools, jerk out your cell phone and dial the supply store. After punching through several long menus with growing anger, you finally reach the brick department. You ask for the manager. He's out. You ask for the assistant manager. She's out, too. You ask for *anyone.* A young trainee comes on the line, and you soon find the cause of your trouble: The trainee misread your work order and loaded the wrong color of bricks on the delivery truck.

The trainee apologizes, and promises to *replace* the bricks as soon as he can. When will that be? He doesn't know. He doesn't have the authority to replace bricks without permission, and both the manager and the assistant manager are out of town attending an efficiency seminar.

This story illustrates once again that suppression is *ineffective* and *inefficient*, and that it often causes more trouble than we had in the first place. In a perfect world, we wouldn't need suppression. We'd take Blocking Actions against all the Likely Causes that threaten our tasks, and there wouldn't be any trouble to suppress. But we don't live in a perfect world. Worse, there are some Likely Cause situations that we, as private citizens, can't prevent. Things like tornados, floods, wars, and recessions can't be prevented by us as individuals. All we can do is to take Preparing Actions such as buying flood and storm insurance, storing emergency food, keeping emergency cash in a safe deposit box, and so forth.

But let's return to our bricklaying story. You have bricks on your jobsite that are the wrong color, and there's nothing you can do about it but have them *replaced*. And using the word "replaced" here opens the door to our next principle. I often say that Suppressing Actions are a bunch of "re-" words. Whenever you see or hear a word with the prefix *re-*, you're usually reading or hearing about someone who's using suppression.

The prefix *re-* means to do again or to do over. And that's often what we're doing when we take suppression. We're reordering, replacing, and reworking things. We're doing things for the second time—trying to get them right after failing in our first attempt. In the case of Terry's walkway, you're being forced to have a load of bricks *reordered*, *redelivered*, and *replaced*. The identifying tip here is that each of these words is a *re-* word, so you know you're dealing in suppression. There are many *re-* words abroad in the land, but here are a few that you'll see and hear at home and on the job.

"Re-" Words That Usually Indicate Suppression

Redo	Rework
Rewrite	Revise
Refine	Rethink
Retrain	Restore
Recall	Repair
Reassign	Redeliver
Retest	Reschedule
Repack	Reorder
Recount	Reappoint
Redefine	Regroup

Do you ever see or hear any of these *re-* words in your life and career? Think about it. Many companies have a *rework* department to *repair* their defective products. Many cars are *recalled* to *repair* factory defects. Many inventories have to be *recounted* because someone made a mistake. Many products and services need to be *redesigned* because they didn't work the first time. You get the idea. All these *re-* words are synonyms for Suppressing Actions.

In later pages, we'll talk more about how to identify Suppressing Actions and how to use suppression less in your own life and job. But right now, let's return to Figure 5 for a final lesson on how *sine waves* operate in the work on a task.

Sometimes It's Good to Break a Standard

In this chapter, we're defining a Current Trouble as work that's *breaking* a standard it was once meeting. That's normally a *bad* thing. But it's also interesting to know that all work that breaks all standards isn't bad. Sometimes extreme peaks and valleys in the sine waves on tasks are desirable and even planned.

Said another way, not all sine waves that break standards are unwanted. Sometimes leaders try to *make* them happen. Here's why. Any work that breaks any standard is *technically* a Current Trouble by our definition. But there are special situations, such as when a new type of airplane is trying to break a speed record, or a new type of car is trying to break a mileage record, or a new type of product is trying to break a sales re-cord, when it's *desirable* for work to break an old standard.

Figure 5 is displaying a typical, classic, textbook type of Current Trouble situation—one that's bad. What we don't show in Figure 5 is that the sine wave of your work on the walkway *could* have zoomed upward and *could* have broken the high standard set for your work. It could have zoomed up and bro-ken your ceiling standard. This would show symbolically that you were working *longer* than two hours a day on the job—and the Johnsons didn't want you to do that. So that would have been *bad* because it was *unwanted* and the Johnsons would have asked you to suppress it.

However, as we said, sometimes leaders use research and development to try to *create* sine waves that break low or high standards for a *good* purpose. They try to *force* the work on a project to exceed previously set standards. For instance, a qual-ity control technician may want to reduce the number of defec-tive parts *below* previous levels. Or, a maintenance expert may want to reduce the number of machine breakdowns *below* pre-vious levels. Or, as we just said, engineers may want to *exceed* previous levels of speed, mileage, or sales.

That's why we define Current Trouble in this chapter as work that's breaking standards in an *unwanted* way. If stand-ards are being broken in a desirable and intended way, the lead-ers involved don't consider the situation a form of trouble. So what do we call it when low or high standards are purposefully broken or old standards are purposefully raised to new levels? We call it Standards-Betterment (see Table 1, Row 2 on page 114). We learned all about raising the bar to new levels with Improving Actions back in Chapter 6.

To summarize these sine wave principles, if work breaks a standard in an *unwanted* way, it's a Current Trouble and we express it in *negative* terms—we say it's creating losses, costs, stresses, and damages. However, if work breaks a standard in a *desired* way, it's a Work Improvement, and we express it in *positive* terms—we say it's creating benefits, better customer relations, higher quality, and more sales.

Now, as we come to the end of Chapter 8, our study of Current Troubles sometimes leave us with some big questions on the job. What caused a Current Trouble? What attacked our work in such an unwanted, negative way? To paraphrase the old-time murder mysteries, "Who or what dun' it?" These questions are answered in our next chapter.

Summary of Chapter 8

1. This chapter puts us across the great divide between *Preactive* leadership and *Reactive* leadership, and the two are very different because *Preactive* leadership is always used *before* trouble starts, and *Reactive* leadership is always used *after* trouble starts.

2. The Current Trouble situation (the CT sit) is the first *Ineffective-Inefficient* situation we've seen, and the Suppressing Actions (SAs) taken in it are the first actions we've seen that try to *correct* troubles with a *Reactive* and *defensive-minded* type of leadership.

3. A Current Trouble situation is any performance of any person, thing, or system that was previously *satisfying* a set, clear, and agreed on standard in a Normal Work situation but is now *breaking* that standard in an *unwanted* way. Most simply put, "trouble" is anything that's breaking a clear standard in an undesirable way.

4. Some of the synonyms for a Current Trouble include: problem, deviation, defect, alligator, complaint, reject, failure, symptom, nonconformance, disobedience, damage, and things-gone-wrong.

5. A Suppressing Action is any action you choose and implement to *best* control, limit, fix, or minimize the costs, losses, stresses, and damages of a Current Trouble in the work on a task, and to keep those costs, losses, stresses, and damages from spreading.

6. Some common synonyms for Suppressing Actions include: coping, restraining, stalling, fixing, repairing, regulating, emergency, and disciplining actions.

7. The technique of Trouble-Control is choosing and implementing the *best* Suppressing Actions to *control*, *limit*, or *minimize* the costs, losses, stresses, and damages of Current

Troubles in the work on a task and to keep those costs, losses, stresses, and damages from *spreading*.

8. The popular terms "solving" and "problem solving" are too fuzzy and have too many synonyms to be used in *Preactive* leadership because they confuse coworkers.

9. Suppressing Actions often have unexpected *negative* side effects, and often make matters worse than they were before the action was taken. Leaders should avoid SAs as much as possible, and the best way to do that is to focus on the three Effective-Efficient situations in the workplace. This tends to diminish the number of SAs that need to be taken.

10. Figure 5 in this chapter illustrates symbolically a Current Trouble situation and a Suppressing Action being taken to limit the damage.

11. If work breaks a standard in an *unwanted* way, it's a Current Trouble. But if work breaks a standard in a *wanted* way, it's a Work Improvement.

12. In one sentence, Trouble-Control is suppressing existing trouble in an effort to fix it and keep it from spreading.

In closing, there's another side of Current Trouble situations that we hinted at a moment ago but haven't covered in this chapter. When we're faced with a Current Trouble, one of the first thoughts that often pops into our heads is: *Why? Why did this trouble happen? What caused it?* To show this more clearly, let's return to the five examples of Current Troubles we listed at the beginning of the chapter and this time let's put the word "why" before each question.

1. *Why* is an employee who was once punctual now late each morning?
2. *Why* is a molding machine that was once on schedule now too slow?
3. *Why* is a printer that once printed smooth sheets now printing wrinkled sheets?
4. *Why* is the grass in a lawn that was once green now turning brown in patches?
5. *Why* is a dog that was once warm and lovable now biting the children?

In other words, many times in life and on the job we want to know the *True Cause* of a trouble so we can remove the cause and make the trouble go away. That's our subject in Chapter 9. We're going to learn how to find and remove True Causes.

CHAPTER 9

TRUE CAUSE
SITUATIONS

The Second
Ineffective-Inefficient Situation
(See Table 2, Row 2, Page 115)

Description:	The Reason that a Performance is Breaking a Task Standard in an Unwanted Way
Existence in Time:	The Present (*But Originated In the Past*)
Name of Action:	Correcting Action
Leadership Technique:	Cause-Removal

Leadership Type: *Correcting* Tasks with
Reactive Strategies and Tactics

Action Statement
Template: *I want to choose the best (Correcting Action to remove this True Cause from the work on this Normal Work situation).*

This chapter is about the next of the three generic Choice Situations that "mask" as Ineffective-Inefficient situations in our lives and work. In these pages, we continue our discussion of situations in which we're *correcting* work with a *defensive-minded* and *Reactive* type of leadership. This chapter is about the True Cause situation and the actions taken in it that we call Correcting Actions. I use the abbreviations *TC* for a True Cause and *CA* for a Correcting Action.

This situation is described in Table 2, Row 2 on page 115 and the purpose of the actions taken in this situation is to remove an existing *cause* of trouble in work. In other words, this chapter is about how to find, verify, and remove True Causes of Current Troubles so that those troubles wither on the vine and disappear.

Our action statement template for this situation is, *I want to choose the best (Correcting Action to remove this True Cause from the work on this Normal Work situation).* For example, you might write, *I want to choose the best Correcting Action to remove the improper power settings on machine nine so it'll stop producing 10% of the defective gitwidgets on first shift.*

Now, let's open this chapter by talking about an unpleasant fact—a fact that some leaders haven't thought about. The sad truth is that many of the troubles we encounter in our lives and on our jobs are caused by *repeating* causes.

Our Persecution by Repeaters

We already know that removing True Causes is *Reactive* leadership, and that its costly and stressful. But even though that's true, the technique of Cause-Removal can still be useful at times because of this unhappy fact: Research shows that as much as *80 percent* of our troubles is created by causes that are called *repeaters.* Said another way, people tend to endure the *same* troubles over and over, year after year because they haven't taken the time (or haven't had the skills) to remove the *repeating* causes of those troubles.

Ask yourself a question: What percentage of your *own* troubles is caused by repeaters? In other words, are the troubles you experience at home and on the job always something *new and different* that you've never seen before? Or, do your troubles tend to be the *same* old troubles that you always experience? If you're like many people, the latter answer is closer to the truth.

Think back to the Introduction of this book, to the story of the young assistant supervisor who earned a promotion in 15 minutes. After you're read this chapter, you'll understand that what he did was find, verify, and remove a *repeating* cause that had haunted his assembly line for four years. His repeater had caused costs, losses, stresses, and damages month after month, year after year. But nobody on the staff had taken the time (or had the skills) to remove it. They simply suppressed the trouble and swallowed the costs. Then the young assistant supervisor came along and, using skills he'd just learned in the seminar, applied the technique of Cause-Removal and eliminated the repeater.

What the young man's story tells us is that, even though Cause-Removal is a *Reactive* technique, and even though it takes knowledge and practice to use it, sometimes it *must* be used when people have forgotten to take prevention. Now, let's continue our discussion with the definition of a *True Cause.*

What is a True Cause?

Back in Chapter 7, we said that Likely Cause situations could be called *alligator eggs* and *time bombs*. We talked about the importance of taking Blocking Actions to keep such eggs and bombs from "hatching" or "exploding" in our tasks—and we agreed that Blocking Actions are some of the most effective actions leaders can take.

But in this chapter there are no more amusing images. In this chapter the eggs have already *hatched*. The bombs have already *exploded*. It's too late for prevention. So for an overview of our subject, let's say that a True Cause is a Likely Cause that nobody prevented and that somebody allowed to *hatch* in a task or project.

Notice there's a lesson hidden in this last sentence. Reading between the lines, you can see that we're comparing *Preactive* leadership to *Reactive* leadership, and that we're underscoring once again how inefficient *Reactive* leadership is. Acting after trouble has started is always inefficient. As a participant in my seminar once said, "You can't un-break an egg or un-ring a bell." He meant that once a Likely Cause has *hatched* and become a True Cause, we can't do anything but fight it and lick our wounds.

To summarize, a True Cause is a Likely Cause that nobody prevented and that was allowed to "hatch" in work creating stresses, costs, and damages. Having digested this principle, let's see the full definition of a *True Cause*.

The Definition
of a True Cause

*Any **verified** mental, physical, or technical **trigger event**
that forced the performance of a person, thing, or
system to break a previously set, clear, and
agreed on task standard in an unwanted way.*

To understand True Causes more clearly, here are some everyday phrases we'll hear at home and on the job that usually refer to the True Cause of an existing trouble.

Common Synonyms
for True Causes

The taproot	The underlying event
The reason	The motive
The source	The influence
The spark	The trigger
The flashpoint	The guilty party
The origin	The cue ball
The why	The stimulus

So a TC is the *verified* event that created a trouble, and that forced work to break a standard we didn't want it to break. But note carefully that True Causes must be verified. The word *verified* means to prove the truth by investigation and evidence. Thus, an investigative process must be implemented to find out what *really* caused a trouble and then, after we know for sure what really caused it, we take Corrective Action to remove that True Cause.

You can sense from this that a mistake some leaders make is *guessing* what's causing a trouble and then taking action on that *guess*. Said another way, some leaders take action on the *possible* causes of troubles—instead of the True Causes of troubles. Think about how ineffective and inefficient that is.

For example, suppose a subordinate comes up to you and says, "I think Roger is the troublemaker in our department, and I want him out of here!"

So you have the human resources department issue Roger a pink slip, and he leaves the organization. But all the time the actual troublemaker in the department was Jake. Yes, Roger and all the other employees in the department

> **True Cause**
>
> Any **verified** mental, physical, or technical **trigger event** that forced the performance of a person, thing, or system to break a previously set, clear, and agreed on task standard in an unwanted way.

were *possible* causes of the trouble. But Jake was the True Cause of it. So you fired a possible cause, and the True Cause stayed on at full salary and benefits to cause more trouble.

This shows why acting on possible causes is inefficient, but it happens every day in organizations of every kind and size. *Preactive* leaders avoid this like the bubonic plague, and we'll talk more about jumping to causes and false correcting actions in a moment. But first, let's look at another interesting fact about True Causes. There are five different kinds, and all them can be repeaters.

The Five Types of True Causes

Type 1: *Known* True Causes that don't need to be investigated and that *can* be removed with Correcting Actions. (If necessary, the troubles can be temporarily controlled with Suppressing Actions until a CA can be taken.)

Type 2: *Known* True Causes that don't need to be investigated but *can't* be removed with Correcting Actions, so the troubles can *only* be controlled with Suppressing Actions.

Type 3: *Unknown* True Causes that *can* be found through investigation and that *can* be removed with Correcting Actions. (If necessary, the troubles can be temporarily controlled with Suppressing Actions while the TC is found.) *This is probably the most common type of cause we face in life and on the job and this is the type we'll emphasize in this chapter. It was a Type 3 that the young assistant supervisor found and removed in the Introduction of this book.*

Type 4: *Unknown* True Causes that *can* be found through investigation but that *can't* be removed with Correcting Actions, so that the troubles can only be controlled with Suppressing Actions.

Type 5: *Unknown* True Causes that *can't* be found through investigation and thus *can't* be removed with Correcting Actions, so the trouble can only be controlled with Suppressing Actions.

Now, don't panic. You don't need to memorize these five types of True Causes, or even remember all of them. Instead, you can use this list for on-the-job reference. The point we're making is that, regardless of their type, True Causes are vicious, mean, and unnecessary. They create stress, fear, anger, and trouble—and worse of all, it's inefficient to be forced to spend the time, money, and energy to find and remove them.

To make these types more understandable, let's see an example of each one. To do that, let's return to the list of troubles we had at the end of the previous chapter. That was the list that included the late employee, the slow molding machine, the wrinkled printer paper, the lawn with the brown spots, and the dog that was biting the children. Let's assign one of the five types of True Causes to each of the troubles now to illustrate how the types fit.

1. *Why* is an employee who was once punctual now late each morning? Let's assign a *Type 1* True Cause to this trouble. Let's assume that we know the employee's car is in the shop and that he or she is bumming rides to work. No investigation is needed and, as a Correcting Action, we ask the driver of the company car to pick the employee up each morning until the employee's car is repaired.

2. *Why* is a molding machine that was once on schedule now too slow? Let's assign a *Type 2* True Cause to this trouble. Let's assume we know that the machine is old and can't run any faster. No investigation is needed and we can take any number of Suppressing Actions—such as running the machine overtime, supplementing its low production by buying moldings from an outside vendor, or by buying a new molding machine.

3. *Why* is a printer that once printed smooth sheets now printing wrinkled sheets? Let's assign a *Type 3* True Cause to

this trouble. Let's assume that we *don't know* why the sheets are wrinkling. So for *investigation,* we open the printer's access doors and discover that one of its rollers is worn out. As a Correcting Action, we arrange for a service rep to deliver and install a new roller.

4. *Why* is the grass in a lawn that was once green now turning brown in patches? Let's assign a *Type 4* True Cause to this trouble. Let's assume that we *don't know* why the grass is turning brown. So for *investigation,* we arrange a visit by an expert from the local garden shop. He tells us that the lawn is infested with root-eating nematodes, and that nothing can be done to remove them. The best suppressive alternatives are digging up the lawn, burning the grass, and re-sodding the lawn. So as Suppressing Actions, we dig up the lawn and re-sod it.

5. *Why* is a dog that was once warm and lovable now biting the children? Let's assign a *Type 5* True Cause to this trouble. Let's assume that we *don't know* why the dog is biting the children. The children deny any wrongdoing, and we *can't* investigate because dogs can't talk. We could guess at some *possible causes* such as accusing the children of secretly pulling the dog's tail, but we know guessing is inefficient. Thus, the True Cause in this case is unknown and can't be verified. All we can do is take Suppressing Actions in the situation, such as putting the dog in a pen, attempting behavior modification with doggie treats, sending the dog to obedience school, and so on. However, we'll never know why the dog is biting the children

and, worse, he may not *stop*, thus requiring an ultimate form of suppression.

Notice that these five True Causes are listed in order of their difficulty. *Type 1* is the easiest to remove, and *Type 5* can't be removed. In fact, only two of them can be removed at all (*Types 1* and *3*). We can't do anything about the other three except control the trouble with Suppressing Actions. This proves once again how inefficient it is for us to allow Likely Causes to "hatch" into True Causes. Once a TC has "hatched" and created its trouble, our chances for being *Preactive* leaders have already flown the coop.

Summary: The best of all worlds is to have *no* True Causes, and the best way to do that is to take plenty of Blocking Actions as we learned in Chapter 7. In later pages, we'll return to this thought and talk more about how to avoid a lifestyle of suppression. But to be practical for the rest of this chapter, we're *only* going to discuss *Type 3* causes from this point forward. They're the most common causes we encounter and, as we said, they're a hidden kind that can be found and removed. Let's start by looking at a *profile* of a *Type 3* cause, and as we show its parts, let's illustrate each part with the young assistant supervisor's story from the Introduction.

A Profile of a
Type 3 True Cause

1. *Type 3* True Causes are *hidden* at first. (In the young assistant supervisor's story of the assembly line, no one knew what was causing the trouble.)

2. With *Type 3* True Causes, we only see the *trouble* at first. (Everyone in the plant could see the trouble on the young man's assembly line.)

3. *Type 3* True Causes are often *repeaters*, creating the same trouble over and over. (The same trouble had haunted the young assistant supervisor's assembly line for four years.)

4. *Type 3* True Causes *can* be found through investigation. (The young assistant supervisor used the investigative skills he learned in the seminar to find the cause of the trouble on his assembly line.)

5. *Type 3* True Causes *can* be verified by a test. (The young assistant supervisor verified the True Cause on his assembly line and demonstrated the verification to his superior.)

6. *Type 3* True Causes *can* be removed by a Correcting Action. (The young assistant supervisor removed the cause on his assembly line and demonstrated his Correcting Action to his superior.)

7. *Type 3* True Causes *can* be treated in the same inefficient way that we can treat all causes: We can *control* the damage they're creating with Suppressing Actions until someone takes

the time, or has the skills, to find and remove the cause. (Sadly, this is what the staff in the assembly line story had chosen to do. They had chosen to suppress the trouble permanently without ever finding and removing its cause.)

As you can see, the young assistant supervisor's story from our Introduction fits this profile of a *Type 3* cause perfectly. The lesson is—as we said in earlier pages—if the young assistant supervisor could do what he did then, you can do what he did now. To prepare you for that level of cause-finding skill, let's now dial in on *Type 3* causes and learn how to find, verify, and remove them. Remember as we continue now that we're only talking about *Type 3* causes from this point forward.

How to Find, Verify, and Remove True Causes

When trouble strikes, we usually don't see the cause of it at first; we only see the *trouble*. That leaves us three obvious alternatives.

1. We can *ignore* the trouble and hope it'll go away.
2. We can *control* the trouble with suppression and endure the stress and cost.
3. We can *investigate* the trouble to find, verify, and remove its True Cause.

Obviously, alternative three is the best choice, and it's the one assertive leaders pick (even though they know it's a *Reac-*

tive type of leadership). Assuming that all of us are assertive leaders, alternative three is our choice, and we're going to learn how to investigate causes with the technique of *cause-finding*. This is the same technique used by scientists, police detectives, private investigators, crash investigators, and research analysts the world over.

The logical principle we're obeying is this: *Before a True Cause can be removed, it must first be found and verified.* That's the theme of this chapter. But how do we do that? Let's begin by looking at cause-finding backwards. Let's see what *not* to do in an investigation.

The Case of the Tardy Subordinate (What Not to Do in Cause-Finding)

All troubles have many possible causes. But they only have one True Cause. For example, let's assume you have a male subordinate who arrives two hours late for work one bright and sunny Wednesday morning. That's a Current Trouble. The subordinate has violated a previously set, clear, and agreed on standard in the *when* (time) category, and he's never done it before.

So the question becomes: *Why* is the subordinate late? (What's the True Cause of his lateness?) Of course, you could just ask him why he's late. But to keep our story rolling, let's not do that (anyway, he might not tell the truth).

Continuing, there are dozens of *possible* causes for your subordinate's tardiness. Maybe he overslept. Or got lost taking a short cut. Or had a snack attack and stopped for breakfast. Or was pulled over for speeding. Or parked along the road to view the beautiful sunrise. The possible causes are endless, but the two key questions are:

1. Which of the dozens of *possible* causes is the one *True* Cause?

2. How can we *prove* that the cause we tentatively identify is really the True Cause?

Of course, we could always take the easy way out and *suppress* the subordinate's tardiness, perhaps by giving him a written reprimand. But that wouldn't remove the cause of his lateness. Worse, his tardiness might then become a repeater out of spite. Or, we could take the second easiest way out and *jump to causes* with *false correcting actions*. Ah, that'd be fun, wouldn't it? Let's do that.

Let's assume you decide that the best way to keep your subordinate from ever being tardy again is to take action on the five possible causes of tardiness that you've thought up. So you take the following five steps.

1. You buy a new alarm clock for his bedroom.

2. You install a new GPS system in his car.

3. You provide him with a free baggie breakfast each morning.

4. You install a new cruise control in his car.

5. You buy a picture album full of beautiful sunrise photographs for him to study.

Then you smile serenely, confident that your subordinate will never be tardy again. But he probably will. In fact, you've probably wasted your time and money by taking your five false correcting actions because the *True* Cause may be something you haven't even considered yet. Chances are, you've thrown your time and money down a rat hole with these false actions. What we're trying to show in this silly story is just how inefficient it is to *jump to causes* and take *false correcting actions*. "Jumping" is nothing but guessing. And "false" actions are nothing but actions taken on guesses. So here's the first big principle in cause-finding.

Act Only on Verified True Causes

*Take Corrective Actions **only** on verified True Causes—never act on one of the many **possible** causes of a Current Trouble.*

The scientific term for what we call a "possible cause" is a *hypothesis*. This word comes from a Greek root meaning to suppose or to guess. So we never act on a hypothesis. We never take action on guesses.

Except that in real life we often *do*. Guessing is human nature, and the cause-finding technique we're learning in this chapter must control that natural urge. Think back to our earlier example of the dog biting the children. Let's imagine for a moment that the parents who own this dog are sitting at their kitchen table trying to figure out *why* the dog is biting their children. What investigative method will they probably use? Their technique will probably sound something like this.

Father: "I think Rover's just mean."

Mother: "No, he's not mean. It's just that his breed bites a lot."

Father: "Well, I bet the children are pulling his tail."

Mother: "They said they weren't. I think we're feeding him too many table scraps."

Father: "Maybe, but he's not fat. I just think he needs more exercise."

And so it goes. Do you see what's happening? The parents are simply *guessing*. They're throwing out hypotheses (possible causes) to discuss and debate. But where's their logical investigative technique?

That's often what happens when an individual or a group is confronted with a Current

> ### Acting on Verified True Causes
> *Take Corrective Actions **only** on verified True Causes—never act on one of the many **possible** causes of a Current Trouble.*

Trouble. They start guessing at causes. Worse, they often end up taking an action on one of their guesses. So how do we cope with this natural urge? How do we find, verify, and remove a True Cause *without guessing*? We do what scientists and detectives do: We search for them using a process of elimination.

The Process of Elimination

Logical investigation, whether performed by detectives, scientists, or assertive leaders, must eliminate the *possible* causes of troubles and reveal the one *True Cause* of those troubles. If we visualize a household funnel, such as we might use to pour oil into an engine or cider into a bottle, we have the picture. Logical investigation is a "funnel technique" that weeds out possible causes. It tosses out everything that *could* have caused a trouble and leaves the one thing that *did* cause the trouble.

How does the process of elimination work? It's based on a technique you've already learned. It starts with the five *what-who-when-where-amount* factual categories we used in previous chapters. The idea is simple. If a possible cause doesn't fit the *five factual categories* of the trouble you're investigating, then it can't be the True Cause, and it's dropped from consideration.

A good way to see this is to watch the technique used by the fictional heroes in a typical murder mystery. We've all seen the plot in dozens of TV episodes and movies. As the heroic detective arrives on the scene of the murder, there are always several colorful suspects. The detective's job is to eliminate all the innocent suspects (all the possible causes) and to reveal the true murderer (the True Cause). In fact, what makes these mysteries entertaining is watching the detective's process of elimination as he or she identifies the villain. Consider a typical case.

Murder on the Siberian Express

Similar to an Agatha Christie murder mystery, our story unfolds on a dark and stormy night. It happens on a luxury train speeding across the Siberian wasteland. In the dining car, a frightened group of people is seated on maroon velvet seats. Standing sternly before them is the famous detective, inspector Steelbrain of Scotland Lard. Steelbrain is glaring at each colorful character in the group. One is a retired British army officer wearing a monocle and carrying a swagger stick. Another is a dark-haired oriental woman in a bright red dress, holding a strange porcelain doll on her lap. Another is an elderly single school teacher wearing a plaid shawl and carrying a knitting basket. And so on around the circle.

Inspector Steelbrain locks the doors at each end of the dining car and announces loudly, "I have determined that the killer is in this car! One of you is the guilty party! One of you stabbed poor professor Labrat thirty-four times with a dagger as he was eating dinner in this very car, and you stole his brief-case full of priceless NASA secrets!"

The group gasps and stares fearfully at one another. In-spector Steelbrain begins with the first person in the group and points to each person in turn.

"It couldn't have been you, Miss Ironpants," he says to the elderly school teacher, "because your arms are paralyzed, and this heinous crime was committed with a heavy, left-handed dagger. Besides, you left the dining car immediately after din-ner and never came back.

"And it couldn't have been you, Colonel Ramrod," he says to the retired army officer, "because you were in a coma at 11:10 pm when the murder was committed, and you didn't wake up until after the evil deed was done.

"And it couldn't have been you, Madam Kong," he says to the oriental woman holding the doll, "because you had din-ner in your compartment, and you never entered the dining car where the murder was committed."

In like manner, inspector Steelbrain eliminates the sus-pects one by one, testing them against the *what-who-when-where-amount* factual categories of the situation. Finally, the detective turns to face the last person in the circle—a muscular man wearing a fedora and trench coat, his face hidden behind dark glasses.

"Therefore," Steelbrain shouts triumphantly, "the killer must be *you*, Señor Deviate! You're the only person here who's left-handed. You're the only person here who flagged down the train from camelback using a red lantern and boarded at 11:00 pm. You're the only person here who was seen entering the dining car at 11:10 pm. And you're the only person here with bulges under a trench coat that must be the dagger and the missing briefcase!"

Señor Deviate leaps to his feet with an oath, switches off the lights, and tries to fight his way out of the darkened car. But he's quickly wrestled to the floor and handcuffed by inspector Steelbrain and his team of burly assistant officers.

Okay. What just happened in our typical murder mystery?

Did you notice the process of elimination that inspector Steelbrain used to isolate the killer? Steelbrain used the five *what-who-when-where-amount* factual categories of the situation as a funnel technique to eliminate all of the suspects but one: Señor Deviate. Let's look more carefully at inspector Steelbrain's *investigative funnel*.

The Eight Levels in the Funnel

To see how Steelbrain's funnel operated, let's look at the structure of the process of elimination he used. The structure has eight sequential levels of elimination, and you already know the first five levels from earlier chapters. Here are the eight levels.

1. What
2. Who
3. When
4. Where
5. Amount
6. Critical Change
7. Probable Cause
8. Verification

To gather the necessary facts for the levels, here are the eight questions we mentally ask ourselves:

1. What: *What clear and agreed on standard was broken?*
2. Who: *Who was present during the breaking of the standard?*
3. When: *When was the standard broken? Did the breaking of the standard have a fluctuating pattern in time?*
4. Where: *Where was the standard broken? Did the breaking of the standard have a fluctuating pattern in location?*
5. Amount: *How Much or How Many people, things, or systems broke the standard?*
6. Critical Change: *What was the critical change in, about, or around the five factual categories of the situation?*
7. Probable Cause: *What was there about this critical change that could have caused the trouble?*
8. Verification: *What test, experiment, or research can be performed to prove that this probable cause is actually the True Cause?*

Let's now see what facts inspector Steelbrain gathered as he mentally asked himself these eight questions in the dining car of the train. But let's break the eight questions into three parts, and learn one part at a time. The first part is composed of the five factual categories you learned in earlier chapters:

1. What: *Poor professor Labrat was murdered with a heavy, left-handed dagger.*

2. Who: *Miss Ironpants, Colonel Ramrod, Madam Kong, Señor Deviate, and the other passengers were present in, about, and around the murder scene.*

3. When: *The murder was committed on this day and this date at 11:10 pm.*

4. Where: *The murder was committed at the professor's table in the dining car of the express train as it was speeding across the Siberian wasteland.*

5. Amount: *There was one victim; he was stabbed thirty-four times; one briefcase full of NASA secrets was stolen.*

Now as we said, you already know these first five steps of the investigative funnel because you learned them in Chapters 2 and 3 for accurate decision-making, and then you saw them again in Chapter 4 for clarifying smokescreen statements. Here in Chapter 9 we're using the same five categories as an elimination funnel for the possible causes of a Current Trouble.

Next, let's add a *new* principle to the process of elimination. You haven't seen this one before. This new principle has special cause-finding powers because it adds a powerful level of elimination to the funnel. It's called the principle of *the critical change.*

The Principle of the Critical Change

The word *change* comes from a root meaning to be different or to make something different. In our elimination funnel, we're using the phrase to refer to something that has been modified or altered in the situation, or something that is new, unusual, or unique in the situation.

Of course, every situation has dozens of changes happening in, about, and around it each day. But Current Trouble situations always have one *critical change* in, about, or around them through which the True Cause struck. Let's state the principle clearly.

Trouble is Always Preceded by a Critical Change

*The start of a Current Trouble is always **preceded** by a **critical change** in one of the factual categories of the situation that allowed the True Cause to strike.*

We can also read this principle backwards. A True Cause *can't* strike unless a critical change occurs in one of the situation's categories through which it can attack. Special note: Often a critical change is visible in more than one of a situation's factual categories. But, it's *always* visible in at least *one* of them. For example, in our murder mystery, Señor Deviate was visible in three of the situation's categories. He was visible in the *who*, *when*, and *where* categories, making him the obvious suspect for inspector Steelbrain.

> # Trouble is Always Preceded by a Critical Change
> *The start of a Current Trouble is always **preceded** by a **critical change** in one of the factual categories of the situation that allowed the True Cause to strike.*

The good news about critical changes is that they're always tangible and physical. They always obey the laws of chemistry and physics. That makes them easy to identify. We can sense them with our five senses. Critical changes in situations can be observed, studied, analyzed and then used to "point" to the True Cause. Of course, *all* the changes in, about, or around situations aren't connected to the True Cause and don't point to it. But *one* of them does, and that's the one we're trying to identify.

Okay, time out. What *is* a critical change? How do we recognize one? We've already said critical changes are physical and tangible, and that we can detect them with our five senses. But here's a more exact definition.

The Definition of a Critical Change

*A critical change is anything **new, moving, different, unique,** or **unusual** in one of the factual categories of a Current Trouble situation. It's **connected** to the True Cause of the trouble and was the channel that the True Cause used to create the trouble.*

Note that the critical change in a situation is *not* the True Cause itself. But it's always connected to the True Cause, it's always the channel that the True Cause used to create the trouble, and it always "points" to the True Cause. For example, in our murder mystery, the True Cause of the murder of poor professor Labrat—if we want to be specific—was a *left-handed dagger.*

But that dagger entered the dining car and was able to stab professor Labrat, by using the channel of a critical change. That critical change was Señor Deviate. He boarded the train with the dagger hidden under his trench coat and later used it on the poor professor. Thus, Señor Deviate was the *channel* through which the dagger was able to enter the dining car and do its dirty work.

A critical change can be a new employee, a moving part in a machine, a different system being implemented, a unique process being activated, an unusual chemical being added to a mixture, and so on—whether or not these things are *authorized*, *routine*, or *expected* by the staff.

That last sentence needs some explaining. There's an odd twist in the way people think that causes some leaders to be *blind* to critical changes. Some leaders will ignore critical changes by explaining them away, saying the changes are "routine," "authorized," or "expected," and therefore unimportant.

As an example, let's imagine that a temporary employee arrives for work in a certain department on a certain morning, and immediately afterwards trouble breaks out in the department. Some leaders would be *blind* to this temp as a *critical change* because they'd say, "Oh, but we always use that same temp agency, and she's been a temp with us many times before, so she's not a change."

But she *is a change.*

Think about it. We said changes are physical and tangible, and that we can detect them with our five senses. Thus, this female temp physically walked into the department, tangibly sat

---

Critical Change

*A critical change is anything **new, moving, different, unique,** or **unusual** in one of the factual categories of a Current Trouble situation. It's **connected** to the True Cause of the trouble, and was the channel that the True Cause used to create the trouble.*

down at a desk and began work in a way we can detect with our five senses. She was something new, moving, different, unique, and unusual in the department that morning. In fact, like Señor Deviate in our murder mystery, she was a change in three of the five factual categories in the department: She was a change in the *who*, *when*, and *where* categories and it wasn't relevant that she was authorized, routine, and expected by the staff.

In our murder mystery, what if we had discovered that Señor Deviate rode the same express train every week, that the conductor knew him and liked him, and that he possessed a railroad pass that allowed him to flag down the train at any time, board it, and partake of a free meal in the dining car? *None* of that would have mattered. The point was not that Señor Deviate was routine and authorized. The point was that he was something physically moving in the *who*, *when*, and *where* categories of the murder situation.

One last example. Let's assume some large tractor parts are going down an assembly line and soon trouble breaks out on the line. While looking for a critical change, some leaders would say, "Oh, those tractor parts always move down the assembly line that way. They're supposed to do that. That's been our procedure for many years. Those parts aren't a change, and they can't be connected to the cause of our trouble."

But the tractor parts *are a change*.

Think about it again. They're physically *moving* in time and space as they flow down the assembly line. If you put a chalk mark on the edge of the assembly line and watched the mark, you'd see the tractor parts passing the chalk mark at a rate of several per minute. In other words, you'd see tractor parts changing in the *when* and the *where* categories of the situation at a rate of several per minute. It wouldn't matter that the parts "always" moved down the line that way, or that they were "supposed" to do so. The only relevant fact would be that they *were* moving down the line. That makes them a physical change to be analyzed in the case.

As we said, the critical change in a situation *won't* be the True Cause itself. But it'll always be *connected* to the TC and will be the *channel* the TC used to strike. To apply this principle, all we do is analyze each of the five *what-who-when-where-amount* categories in our situation, looking for something new, unusual, or moving in one (or more) of the categories that the TC could have used as a channel for its attack.

Let's apply the principle of critical change now by returning to the process of elimination in our murder mystery, and by adding a level for the critical change to the previous five levels of our funnel:

6. Critical Change: *Señor Deviate boarded the train as a new passenger and was a change in the passengers (the* who *category). He stopped the train and boarded it in the middle of the night at 11:00 pm and was a change in the time schedule (the* when *category). He walked to the dining car and entered it and was a change in the dining car (the* where *category). As a result,*

Señor Deviate was a change in three of the five factual categories of the situation. This told inspector Steelbrain that Señor Deviate was probably the critical change that the left-handed dagger (the TC) had used as a channel to board the train and commit the murder.

The next step in our process of elimination is to develop a *probable cause* from our discovery of the critical change.

The Probable Cause

Once inspector Steelbrain realized that Señor Deviate was a critical change in three of the five factual categories of the murder situation, he sensed that Señor Deviate was the *probable cause* of the murder (the prime suspect for the murder).

Probable causes are developed by speculating about *how* the critical change we've discovered could have been the channel for the True Cause to attack. So let's return to the inspector Steelbrain mystery now and add a seventh level to our funnel to develop the probable cause:

7. Probable Cause: *As a critical change in three categories of the situation, Señor Deviate is also left-handed (he could use a left-handed dagger), and in addition, he has bulges under his trench coat that could be the dagger and the stolen briefcase. Thus, we can surmise that Señor Deviate is the probable cause— he is probably the "channel" through which the True Cause of the murder (the left-handed dagger) was able to board the train, en-*

ter the dining car, and stab the professor. That is, Señor Deviate is the probable murderer.

So far, so good. But we're not done yet. A probable cause is still only a highly suspicious possible cause until it's verified. So now we must do a *verification test*.

The Verification Test

At the eighth and final level of inspector Steelbrain's process of elimination funnel, he must perform a verification test of some kind to prove that what he *thinks* is true really *is* true. That is, he must prove that the probable cause of the murder (*Señor* Deviate) is actually the true person who killed poor professor Labrat.

This final step is overlooked in some leadership books, seminars, and classes—but until the probable cause is factually proven to be the True Cause, it's still only a probable cause and can't be acted on. Said another way, a probable cause is only a highly likely *possible cause* until it's verified, and we know we can't act on possible causes.

There are many kinds of tests, interviews, research, and experiments that can be used to verify probable causes. We can use laboratory experiments, medical and chemical analyses, surveys, interrogations, audio tapes, films and surveillance footage, computer data bases, eye witness accounts, photographs, and many other types of files, papers, legal documents, and evidence. In practical field tests, we can switch equipment on and off to see if the trouble stops and starts. We can alternate raw materials on assembly lines to see if the trouble comes and goes. We can move an employee in and out of departments to see if the trouble follows the pattern of his or her movements, and so on.

By doing these things, we're trying to prove by a physical test that the probable cause we've identified is in fact the True Cause of the trouble. Said another way, if we can artificially *manipulate* our probable cause and the trouble stops and starts on *command*, then we know we have our finger on the True Cause. As a simple example of this technique, if we've identified chemical X as the probable cause of a trouble in a certain mixture of chemicals, and if we add chemical X to the mixture and remove chemical X from the mixture several times in a row—and the trouble starts each time we add chemical X and stops each time we remove chemical X, then we've verified that chemical X is the True Cause of our trouble in the mixture.

In our inspector Steelbrain murder mystery, as a verification test inspector Steelbrain could have arrested *Señor* Deviate and searched him for the dagger and briefcase. Or he could have fingerprinted Señor Deviate and run his fingerprints through Interpol to see if Deviate was a known assassin. Or he could have used sleep deprivation during Deviate's interrogation to make him confess and so forth. But in our story, Señor Deviate verified *himself* by starting a fight and trying to escape.

Let's now add this last level to inspector Steelbrain's process of elimination. Let's add a verification test level to the funnel:

8. Verification: *Since Senor Deviate switched off the lights in the dining car and tried to escape, he verified himself as the murderer of poor professor Labrat. However, as additional verification tests (perhaps for use in court), inspector Steelbrain can use DNA tests, fingerprint tests, interrogation techniques, Interpol searches, and other such tests and legal evidence to prove that Senor Deviate is the true murderer.*

And thus, our exciting story of inspector Steelbrain and his cause-finding funnel technique comes to a close. Nothing's left for us to do now but talk about the easiest part of the chapter—removing causes with Correcting Actions after we've verified them. Let's start with a definition of a *Correcting Action.*

The Definition of a Correcting Action

*Any **action** you choose and implement to best remove, cancel, or neutralize the **True Cause** of a Current Trouble in a Normal Work situation, after that cause has been **verified** as the True Cause of the trouble.*

Next, let's see a full definition of the technique of *Cause-Removal.*

The Definition of Cause-Removal

*Choosing and implementing the best Correcting Actions to remove, cancel, or neutralize the **verified True Causes** of Current Troubles in Normal Work situations.*

Briefly put, the leadership technique of Cause-Removal is finding, verifying, and removing the True Causes of Current Troubles in work. And now, for more practice in Cause-Removal, let's return to your bricklaying adventures with the Terry Johnson family.

In Figure 6 on page 288, we return to our diagram of your bricklaying project for the Terry Johnson family. This time, our diagram shows your work on the walkway with a new True Cause attacking it—and a new Correcting Action you're taking to remove that True Cause. For more experience in cause-finding, let's consider this new case next.

Correcting Action

*Any **action** you choose and implement to best remove, cancel, or neutralize the **True Cause** of a Current Trouble in a Normal Work situation, after that cause has been **verified** as the True Cause of the trouble.*

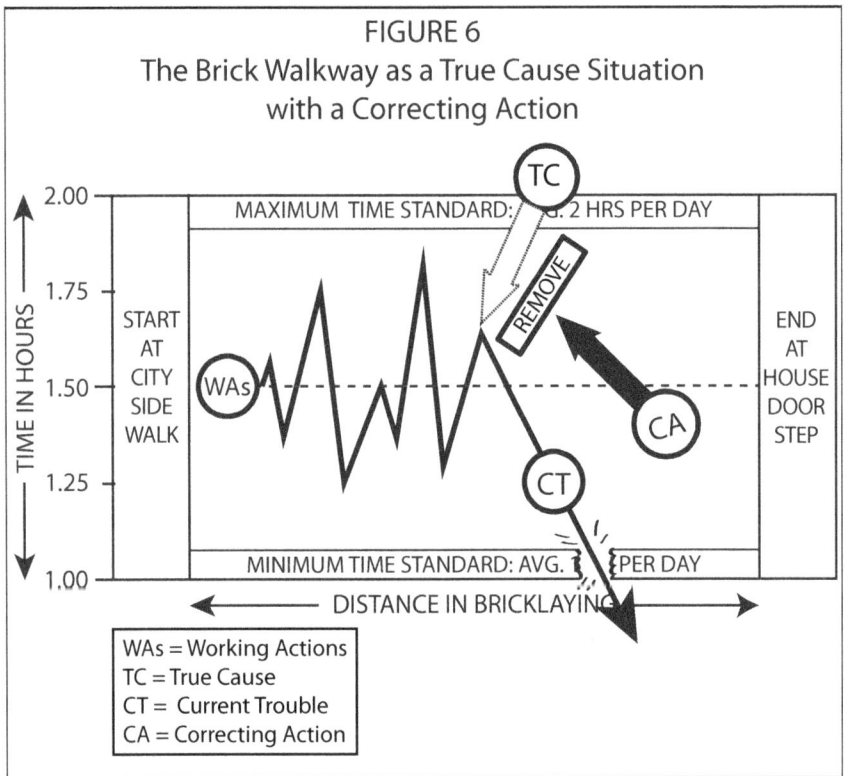

FIGURE 6
The Brick Walkway as a True Cause Situation
with a Correcting Action

WAs = Working Actions
TC = True Cause
CT = Current Trouble
CA = Correcting Action

The downward turn in the zigzag arrow of linked Working Actions (WAs) represents a Current Trouble situation (CT) that has occurred in the bricklaying. Work has stopped, breaking the minimum time standard of one hour per day set by the Johnson family.

The dotted, white arrow represents the *True Cause* situation (TC) that created the trouble. The TC will usually continue to create the trouble until it is identified and removed.

The black arrow represents a *Correcting Action* (CA) being taken to remove the True Cause and return the work to its normal sine wave within standards. This diagram is a picture of the leadership technique of *Cause-Removal.* Note that CAs are ineffective and that they are *Reactive* leadership: *Leading in the presence of trouble.*

The Attack of a Second True Cause

In Figure 6, we see a second True Cause occurring in your bricklaying for the Terry Johnson family. You'll recall from the previous chapter that your work has already been stopped once because a trainee at the building supply store delivered you a pallet of off-color bricks. You took Suppressing Action on that trouble because you had no control over the trainee or his duties, and you had to re-order the right bricks and have them re-delivered to you.

But here in this chapter, let's imagine that a second True Cause attacks your bricklaying. In Figure 6 your work has again been stopped and you have another Current Trouble attacking your work (the arrow marked "CT"). Also, you're taking a new Correcting Action to remove this second cause (the arrow marked "CA").

Cause-Removal

*Choosing and implementing the best Correcting Actions to remove, cancel, or neutralize the **verified True Causes** of Current Troubles in Normal Work situations.*

In addition, following the theme of this chapter, let's assume this second cause is a *Type 3*, so you'll be able to find, verify, and remove it. Here's the story behind the second attack shown in Figure 6.

The Disappearing Tools Caper

Let's imagine that one balmy Monday afternoon, you arrive for work at the Terry Johnson home to lay more bricks in the walkway. But when you unlock the garage with your loaner key, you're surprised to see that all the tools the family has been letting you use are missing from their customary garage shelf. You're looking at a *Current Trouble* because for weeks you've been using the family's hammer, bag of nails, tape rule, saw, and lumber to build wooden frames around your bricks. Today all the tools are missing, along with the roll of duct tape you've been using to seal your mortar bag each night.

Your agreement with the Johnson family includes the use of these tools and materials for your work, so you ring the doorbell and ask Mrs. Johnson what happened to the tools. She's home alone, the children are outdoors playing somewhere, and Terry is at work. She hasn't seen the tools and knows nothing about them. So the *True Cause* of your new trouble is unknown. You decide to ignore the cause temporarily to complete your day's work. So you take a Suppressing Action: You walk home to get your personal tools for the job.

However, the next afternoon when you arrive at the Johnsons carrying your bag of personal tools and unlock the garage, to your surprise the Johnson's tools are back on the garage shelf as usual. So you put your own tool bag down and use the Johnson's tools for work.

But the following afternoon you're angered to find the Johnson's tools missing again, and you must walk home to get your personal tools. The day after that, the Johnson's tools are back on the shelf again and the following day, they're gone again.

Thoroughly frustrated, you realize that you're facing a *repeating* True Cause that's attacking your bricklaying—and that it has a fluctuating pattern in time. You know from experience that when a TC fluctuates in time, location, or both, it's easier to find and verify than other types of causes. So you decide to start an immediate cause-finding investigation. You ring the doorbell and talk to Mrs. Johnson again. She says she asked Terry and the children about the tools (the Johnson's have two young girls named Abby and Gracie and a little boy called Little Pete), but Terry and the children all said they had no idea what was happening to the tools.

Terry told her that he was puzzled too because when he walks through the garage each morning about 8:00 am to leave for work, the tools are always on the shelf. When he comes home for a late lunch each day about 1:00 pm, the tools are still there, and the tools are there about 7:00 pm each evening when he comes home for the night. Thus, the tools seem to be disappearing and reappearing between 1:00 pm and 7:00 pm in the evenings. Even more puzzling, the Johnson's garage is always locked and only family members have access to a key.

So the plot is thickening. Why are the tools disappearing and reappearing with such a precise time pattern, and why don't the family members know why? So you continue with your investigative funnel. You always keep a small calendar, notebook, and pen in the pocket of your work shirt, so you take them out, study the calendar a moment, and start to write down the eight levels of your process of elimination funnel like this:

1. What: *The Johnson's tools that I use in bricklaying are disappearing and reappearing.*

2. Who: *Terry, Mrs. Johnson, the three children, and I all have access to the tools and have been in, about, and around the tools and the family garage.*

3. When: *The tools disappeared on Monday, Wednesday, and Friday, and reappeared on Tuesday, Thursday, and Saturday with a fluctuating pattern; they disappear after 1:00 pm and reappear by 7:00 pm.*

4. Where: *The tools disappear and reappear from same shelf in the same locked garage.*

5. Amount: *One hammer, one bag of nails, one tape rule, one saw, and one roll of duct tape are disappearing; they have disappeared three times this week.*

You're now ready to find a critical change. You ring the doorbell and ask Mrs. Johnson if she can think of anything new, different, or unusual that happens in, about, or around her family between 1:00 pm and 7:00 pm on Mondays, Wednesdays, and Fridays.

She looks puzzled and shakes her head in the negative. So you ask her if she can think of anything that's *different* about the family's habits or schedules on Mondays, Wednesdays, and Fridays compared to the other afternoons of the week.

She reflects a moment. Then she answers, yes, those are the three afternoons each week that Little Pete plays outdoors with the other neighborhood boys. He gets off the school bus about 2:30 pm, and plays until she calls him in for dinner about 6:30 pm. She explains that the boys can't play outdoors on Tuesdays, Thursdays, and Saturdays because Little Pete and the other boys are on a soccer team that practices on those afternoons. You thank Mrs. Johnson and return to your notebook. You've identified the critical change in the situation. You add it to your notes:

6. Critical Change: *Little Pete plays outdoors with the other boys on Mondays, Wednesdays, and Fridays from about 2:30 pm to about 6:30 pm. So his outdoor play on these three days is a fluctuating change in the when (time) category of the disappearing tools situation, and must be the critical change.*

Now you're ready to develop the probable cause. You think for a moment and write the following in your notebook:

7. Probable Cause: *Little Pete must be doing something with the tools during his play afternoons on Mondays, Wednesdays,*

and Fridays. He must take the tools after he gets off the school bus about 2:30 pm, and he must return them when Mrs. Johnson calls him in for dinner at about 6:30 pm. But he won't confess this for some reason.

You ring the Johnson's doorbell again and explain to Mrs. Johnson what you believe is the probable cause of the disappearing tools. You ask her whether she and Terry would be willing to talk to Little Pete about the tools that evening, and to find out whether he used them for some reason on Monday, Wednesday, and Friday of this week between 2:30 pm and 6:30 pm. Mrs. Johnson agrees to ask Little Pete, but says she can't imagine why he wouldn't have admitted it if he was using the tools.

Later that evening, your phone rings. It's Terry. He says Little Pete has admitted to using the tools. He and the other boys on the neighborhood soccer team have formed a secret club, and they're building a tree house in some nearby woods to use as a club house. Little Pete wouldn't admit taking the tools because the boys took a vow of secrecy when the club was formed. So the probable cause is verified. Little Pete is the True Cause of the disappearing tools.

At this point, a best Correcting Action must be taken to remove the True Cause of the trouble. In other words, an action must be taken to stop Little Pete from using the tools. You explain this to Terry and point out that, as agreed with the family, you need the tools yourself to finish the brick walkway.

Terry agrees and says he'll call you back in an hour or so with a decision.

Later that evening your phone rings. It's Terry. He says that as a Correcting Action he phoned the other soccer parents on the boy's team. He explained the tool situation, and asked them if they'd be willing to donate some of their own tools to the tree house project. Several of the soccer parents became interested and agreed to provide the boys with tools, nails, wood, tarpaper, tape, and anything else they need to finish the tree house.

Thus, the mystery of the Disappearing Tools Caper is closed, and our study of the technique of Cause-Removal comes to an end. You now possess the same eight-level, cause-finding funnel as inspector Steelbrain in our murder mystery and as the young assistant supervisor in our Introduction. With experience and practice, you can now find, verify, and remove True Causes with the same skill that they had.

Summary of Chapter 9

1. The True Cause situation (the TC sit) is the second Ineffective-Inefficient situation we've learned, and its Correcting Actions (CAs) are the second action we've learned that is a *corrective*, *defensive-minded*, and *Reactive* type of leadership.

2. A True Cause situation is any *verified* mental, physical, or technical *trigger event* that forced the performance of a per-

son, thing, or system to break a previously set, clear, and agreed on task standard in an unwanted way.

3. Some common synonyms for True Cause sits are: the taproot, the reason, the cue ball, the spark, and the source.

4. A Correcting Action is any *action* you choose and implement to best remove, cancel, or neutralize the *True Cause* of a Current Trouble in a Normal Work situation, after that cause has been *verified* as the True Cause of the trouble.

5. There are five types of True Causes: In *Type 1*, you know the cause of the trouble and can remove it. In *Type 2*, you know the cause of the trouble but can't remove it. In *Type 3*, you don't know the cause of the trouble but can find it and remove it. (This is the most common type and the type we've emphasized in this chapter.) In *Type 4*, you don't know the cause of the trouble but can find it, then can't remove it. In *Type 5*, you don't know the cause, can't find it, and can't remove it.

6. The technique of Cause-Removal is choosing and implementing the best Correcting Actions to remove, cancel, or neutralize the *verified True Causes* of Current Troubles in Normal Work situations.

7. We always take Corrective Action on a *verified* True Cause only, never on one of the many *possible* causes of a trouble. Guessing at TCs is called *jumping to cause*. Acting on such a guess is called a *false correcting action*. Both are inefficient forms of leadership.

8. A critical change is anything *new, moving, different, unique,* or *unusual* in one of the factual categories of Current Trouble situation. It's connected to the True Cause of the trouble and was the channel the True Cause used to create the trouble. Thus, identifying the critical change in a situation always "points" to the True Cause and adds a valuable level to the process of elimination funnel.

9. The best way to find and verify an unknown True Cause is to write out the eight-level process of elimination. The eight levels in the investigative funnel are:

1. What	5. Amount
2. Who	6. Critical Change
3. When	7. Probable Cause
4. Where	8. Verification

10. Research shows that as much as 80 percent of the troubles in people's lives and jobs are caused by True Causes that are *repeaters.* That is, the same causes are triggering the same troubles over and over again. This happens because people don't take the time—or don't have the skills—to find, verify, and remove the repeating True Causes of their troubles.

11. The big lesson in this chapter is that True Causes are costly, and that finding, verifying, and removing them is stressful and time-consuming. The best of all worlds is not to *have* any True Causes, and the best way to do that is to take plenty of Blocking Actions on the Likely Causes in our work.

12. Figure 6 illustrates a situation with a Correcting Action being taken to remove it.

13. In one sentence, Cause-Removal is finding, verifying, and removing the True Causes of Current Troubles in tasks.

To close this chapter, let's admit that in a strange way cause-finding can be exciting and fun. Everybody loves a good mystery, and people who find and remove True Causes in their organizations are usually recognized and rewarded for it (as the young assistant supervisor was in our Introduction).

But in a perfect organization, there wouldn't *be* any cause-finding because there wouldn't *be* any True Causes. All the Likely Causes of all the troubles in all the work of the organization would be preempted by Blocking Actions. But we don't live in a perfect world. So the Cause-Removal technique is necessary at times.

And now there's only one situation left to discuss. In Chapter 10 we'll finish our discussions of the six situations in leadership by looking at one last situation—the Future Trouble situation.

CHAPTER 10

FUTURE TROUBLE SITUATIONS

The Third
Ineffective-Inefficient Situation
(See Table 2, Row 3, Page 115)

Description: A Performance That Could Break
a Task Standard in an Unwanted Way
at a Future Time

Existence in Time: Will Originate and Exist in the Future

Name of Action: Preparing Action

Leadership Technique: Trouble-Readiness

Leadership Type: *Correcting* Tasks with
                         Reactive Strategies and Tactics

Action Statement
Template: *I want to choose the best (Preparing*
                         Action to wait to suppress this Future
                         Trouble if it happens in this Normal
                         Work situation).

T his chapter is about the last of the three generic Choice Situations that "mask" as Ineffective-Inefficient situations. This is the last situation in which we *correct* work with a *defensive-minded* and *Reactive* type of leadership. The *Future Trouble* situation is our subject in this chapter, together with the *Preparing Actions* that we take in them. This situation and action are described in Table 2, Row 3 on page 115, and I use the abbreviations *FT* for a Future Trouble and *PA* for a Preparing Action.

The purpose of the Preparing Actions in this chapter is to arrange people, policies, and paraphernalia to *wait* for the chance to *suppress* a Future Trouble if one occurs. Examples of Preparing Actions are installing fire extinguishers, buying insurance, making backup files, wearing seat belts, and establishing police and fire departments.

In everyday slang, Future Troubles can be called future damage, potential problems, future losses, unexpected breakdowns, and similar terms. The point is, we live in an imperfect world where bad things happen—no matter how careful we are. And often, all we can do about those bad things is suppress them. Said another way, there are hundreds (maybe thousands) of *Likely Causes* in our lives and careers, and no matter how many Blocking Actions we take, we're bound to miss a few. The worst news of all is that some Likely Causes are *unpreventable*, as we'll discuss in detail in a moment.

Because of these future threats that we all face, this chapter is about the preparations all of us make from cradle to grave to handle them. Even though we realize such preparations are *Reactive* and, therefore, inefficient and expensive, we continue to make them out of habit, tradition, childhood training, and various local, state, and federal laws.

Our action statement template for this situation is, *I want to choose the best (Preparing Action to wait to suppress this Future Trouble if it happens in this Normal Work situation).* For example, you might write, *I want to choose the best Preparing Action to wait to suppress the damage of a fire in our paint booth if one happens while painting our tractor parts.*

Now, let's go negative a moment and begin this chapter with some thoughts about *Future Troubles* in our lives, jobs, and careers.

Things That Go Bump in the Night

As long as there have been people, there have been things that go bump in the night. People have always been afraid of the dark, the unknown, the unseen, and the unknowable. In short, people have an instinctive dread of Future Trouble, and it's right for them to do so.

For example, in Chapter 8, we admitted there are some Likely Causes of Future Trouble that *can't* be prevented by us as individuals and citizens. These include things like inflation, recession, lightening, tornados, floods, wars, gas line explosions, city-wide fires or riots, water shortages, famines, terrorism, plane crashes and, of course, death and taxes.

Think about it. What can we, as individuals, do to prevent such things? The answer is *nothing*. All we can do is take Preparing Actions that wait to *suppress* the damage if the dreaded event occurs. That is, we make preparations that wait (sometimes for years) for the chance to control the future damages we fear.

How do we do that? We do it in many ways. We purchase insurance policies, stockpile gold, build tornado shelters, store emergency food and water, wear life preservers when we're in small boats, buy cars with air bags, and evacuate inland as hurricanes approach.

In the briefest terms, all we can do about cataclysmic future disasters is prepare to limit, minimize, and control their costs, losses, and damages. In fact, when you think about it, a great deal of our personal money, organizational money, and societal money is spent on Preparing Actions that wait to suppress Future Troubles. As a quick example, let's talk about a little thing called an *annual physical.*

Why Do People Have Annual Physicals?

Many organizations require their employees to have annual physicals, and the organizations spend a lot of time and money on these programs. The paperwork for such physicals often refers to them by terms such as preventive medicine, preventive health care, preventive services, and so on. Except that annual physicals aren't preventive.

Ask yourself a question. What's the purpose of an annual physical? Why does the doctor perform the blood tests, X-rays, EKGs, and other examinations during the checkup? Does the doctor perform them to *prevent* trouble in the patient's body? Or does the doctor perform them to *detect* trouble in the patient's body?

As we'll see in a moment, such doctor's tests are examples of trigger reports. Their purpose is to detect *trouble* and then to trigger Suppressing Actions to try to control that trouble—in this case, medicine, radiation, operations, therapy, and so forth. Think about it. When annual checkups are completed each year, doctors usually say one of two things. They either say, "You're as healthy as a race horse. See you next year!" Or they say, "Hmmm. We've got some work to do, don't we? Your weight's up, your cholesterol's high, and your sugar's above normal. We've got to put you on a special diet and exercise program that will…."

See the point? Annual physicals don't *prevent* illness. They *detect* it. Then after the detection, doctors prescribe medical Suppressive Actions to combat the illness. The fact is, doctors and their knowledge, medicine, and equipment are primarily Preparing Actions that society has established to detect and suppress illnesses that walk in the door.

Let's repeat that for clarity. A doctor's knowledge, medicine, and equipment don't prevent illness; they detect and suppress it. This means doctors are a Trouble-Readiness technique that society has installed. That being true, why do we call annual physicals *preventive* medicine? Logically, shouldn't we call them *suppressive* medicine? Indeed, isn't that why many of the drugs that doctors prescribe are called *suppressants*?

We'll talk more about *suppressive-bias* in a moment. But the lesson here is that much of society's time, money, thought, and energy are spent preparing systems to detect Future Trouble so it can be suppressed after detection. Sadly, a much smaller percentage of society's time, talent, and treasure are spent trying to *block* the Likely Causes of Future Trouble so it never occurs in the first place.

Let's pause here to think about a related principle. We've been talking about how to prepare for trouble, how to detect trouble, and the difference between preventing and suppressing trouble. So let's talk a moment about the *two types of reports* that leaders use.

The Two Types of Leadership Reports

Leaders use two basic kinds of reporting systems. The first is the trigger system, and the second is the milestone system. Since we've been talking about the medical tests in doctor's offices, let's start by talking *trigger reports.*

Trigger Reports

Think about the number of fire alarms and burglar alarms you've seen in recent few days. Probably dozens. You may even have one (or both) in your home. Most of the shops and stores you entered during the past week certainly had them.

The word *alarm* comes from a Latin root meaning "to arms!" in the sense of being called out to arm yourself against an attack. Because of this root, an alarm is a signal that calls people out to fight a trouble that's occurring. Said another way, an alarm is a signal that notifies people to implement a Suppressing Action. Thus, doctor's tests, together with burglar and fire alarms, are examples of *trigger reports*. They detect trouble and then activate people, policies, and paraphernalia that have been arranged to fight that trouble.

Other trigger reports include things like tornado sirens, air raid sirens, the severe weather alerts that crawl across our TV screens during our favorite programs, car horns, flashing lights on ambulances, ringing bells at railroad crossings, and so forth. In industrial terminology, trigger reports are sometimes called trigger points, order points, and similar terms. Other types of organizations call them warning signals, distress signals, red alerts, and so forth. Here's our full definition of a *trigger report*.

The Definition of a Trigger Report

*Any audible and/or visual signal that **waits** to be triggered by a **Current Trouble** situation, and that activates a Suppressing Action to limit the damage of that trouble.*

Note that trigger reports only activate *after* trouble has been detected or at least after the first traces or trend of it has been detected. That makes them *Reactive* in nature. The good news is that when trigger reports *do* detect trouble, they report it immediately. There's no delay in the notification. Also note that the only purpose a trigger report serves is to call in a Suppressing Action to fight the trouble that has been detected. In short, what trigger reports are designed to "trigger" is a Suppressing Action. That's why trigger reports are always connected to Suppressing Actions. Fire alarms are connected to fire stations, burglar alarms are connected to police stations, air raid alarms are connected to Air Force bases, and so on. Next, let's define our second leadership report, the *milestone report.*

Milestone Reports

The word *milestone* comes from the ancient Roman habit of installing numbered stones at each mile on their paved roads. These numbered stones showed travelers how far they were from the city of Rome. (Such markers are also called mileposts and mile-markers.) Because of this history, milestone reports are sequential, periodic reports that show the degree to which work is within standards as it moves toward goals. Said another way, milestone reports measure the sine waves of the work being done in a task.

Setting up milestone reports is part of the planning process for a task, and they typically report progress at periodic points in *time*—hourly, daily, weekly, monthly, quarterly, semi-annually, or annually. But they can also report progress in the

---

Trigger Report

*Any audible and/or visual signal that **waits** to be triggered by a **Current Trouble** situation and that activates a Suppressing Action to limit the damage of that trouble.*

---

what, amount, or any of the other factual categories, such as reporting it by volume, pressure, height, weight, depth, distance, or speed, etc. Here's our full definition.

The Definition of a Milestone Report

Any audible and/or visual signal that measures—either continuously or at intervals—the work on a Normal Work situation and reports the degree to which that work is meeting standards.

Of course, milestone reports can also report *trouble* if it occurs. But they can *only* report it at their prearranged report points. For instance, if a milestone report makes its report on Fridays, it can only report trouble on Fridays, even though the trouble might have begun the previous Wednesday. This type of delay is called *lag time,* and it's a weakness in milestone reports—trouble goes *unreported* until the next report point.

That also means the damage goes *unsuppressed* until the next report point and piles up until someone sees the milestone report and acts on it.

Thus, both types of reports—trigger reports and milestone reports—have weaknesses. Trigger systems are weak because they can report trouble, but can't report progress. Milestone systems are weak because they can report progress, but can't report trouble (except at their next report point).

As examples, the annual physicals in doctor's offices that we were discussing earlier are examples of *milestone* reports. They measure the progress of an employee's health over time, with report points scheduled for once a year. Of course, that means that if a serious illness develops in the employee's body during the lag time between checkups, it goes undetected until the patient arrives at the doctor's office several months later. Then the *trigger* reports that the doctor has installed in the office (the X-Rays, EKGs, MRIs, and other equipment) sound the alarm. But sometimes that's too late.

The dangers of the lag time in milestone reports are even more obvious if we think about

> **Milestone Report**
>
> *Any audible and/or visual signal that measures—either continuously or at intervals—the work on a Normal Work situation, and reports the degree to which that work is meeting standards.*

the surveillance cameras in quick shops. They're a special kind of milestone system that has no set report point. They simply film the shop constantly, and the clerks occasionally change the tapes. Worse, there's no trigger report in the camera. So, even if the cameras film a robbery, they have no way to call the police. All the police can do is view the films later, looking for clues to the identity of the robbers.

Because of this lag time, quick shops often install a secret button under the counter to serve as a trigger system. Thus, quick shops often have two reporting systems: a milestone camera to film criminals, and a trigger button to call police. But that's still inefficient, since the clerk may not be able to reach the secret button during a confrontation with a robber.

Thus, due to these obvious weaknesses in each of the two systems, leaders sometimes develop a combination alternative, and fold the two types of reports into one. That overcomes both weaknesses: The work is constantly monitored and trouble is instantly reported. An example of such a combined report is a common automobile speedometer, which usually has a red line on the dial. The speedometer is a milestone system constantly measuring the speed of the car until the needle reaches the red line. At that point the speedometer becomes a trigger report calling for suppression—the driver needs to slow down or risk damage to the engine.

Let's recap. Milestone reports are connected to the work on tasks, and their purpose is to actively measure and periodically report on the progress of that work toward its goals and objectives. Trigger reports are also connected to the work on tasks, but their purpose is to passively wait until trouble is detected in the work and then to call in suppression. Combined reporting systems do both of these things at once.

This means that milestone reports are *Preactive* because they involve advance planning, setting clear standards, and actively measuring the sine waves of work. Trigger reports are *Reactive* because they passively wait for trouble and are connected to suppressive response systems.

Now, building on this deeper understanding of report systems, detection, and suppressive responses, we're ready to think about some insights into human societies.

Society's Suppressive-Bias

The theme of this book is that—in order to be a *Preactive* leader—we must correctly identify the situations we're facing each week, and then focus *Preactively* on the Effective-Efficient situations in our environment. At the same time, we must try to avoid being forced to *React* to any of the Ineffective-Inefficient situations in our environment.

With these leadership principles in mind, it's disturbing to realize that many human societies tend to do this exactly backwards. Societies tend to do the exact opposite of what we're saying here. They tend to focus *Reactively* on the Ineffective-Inefficient situations in their environment. They tend to be *corrective* and *defensive-minded*, and to use *Reactive* strategies and tactics.

We'll talk in more detail about this inefficient focus in later pages. Right now, let's crank down on some examples of the *Reactive* attitude that prevails in many societies. Think about the following list of major social systems that we all take for granted every day.

1. Police departments
2. Fire departments
3. Army, Navy, Air Force, and Marine military units
4. Hospitals, emergency rooms, and clinics
5. Drug stores and pharmaceutical companies
6. Doctors, nurses, and medical workers
7. Life, home, auto, fire, and theft insurance
8. Emergency medical services (EMS units)
9. Courts, jails, lawyers, judges, and prisons
10. Psychologists, psychiatrists, mental health facilities
11. Maintenance departments and repair shops
12. Welfare and social support programs

Okay, you get the point, don't you? Many of society's largest and most expensive systems are designed, organized, and funded primarily as *Reactive* systems—systems that respond to trouble and try to suppress it, instead of trying to predict it and prevent it. We could ask this same question in reverse. Can you think of a major social system that *isn't* designed primarily to *React* to trouble?

Naturally, we know that some of society's systems do play a dual purpose: They're *Preactive* to some degree and *Reactive* to some degree, all in one system. So, to identify whether a system is primarily *Preactive* or *Reactive*, we apply what's called the *51% Rule*. We'll discuss this rule in more detail in a later chapter. Right now, let's see a picture of it. Let's envision a uniformed bank guard standing in the lobby of a bank. If a gang of robbers was casing the bank, he would be playing a *Preactive* and preventive role to some degree since they might be deterred by his presence.

But later, when the robbers return to rob the bank, the guard plays a *Reactive* and suppressive role to a degree as he fires his pistol at the robbers, sets off the alarm, calls for help on his walkie-talkie, and tries to memorize the faces of the robbers and the license plate number of their getaway car.

So, which one *is* the guard: Is he primarily a *Preactive* system? Or is he primarily a *Reactive* system? Let's use the *51% Rule* to find out.

Which role is the guard playing *51% or more* at the bank? Is his majority role to scare robbers away, so that no robberies occur? Or is his majority role to cope with robbers who're attacking the bank? Said another way, was the bank guard trained, armed, and paid by a bank primarily to scare robbers away? Or was he trained, armed, and paid by the bank primarily to resist robbers who're attacking?

After thinking about it, many people would agree that even if the bank guard's job was as high as 49% for the purpose of scaring robbers away—at least *51%* of his job would be for the purpose of resisting robberies that were in progress. Thus, we identify the bank guard as primarily a *Reactive* and suppressive system. In fact, we can identify him as primarily a trigger report system connected to the police station.

We can ask this same *51% Rule* question about many of the great social systems on our list several paragraphs back. For instance, what's the primary role of a police department? Is it to *Preactively* block the Likely Causes of crime in a city so that none exists? Or is it to *Reactively* suppress crimes that have already occurred or are in the process of occurring?

What about a fire department? Is its primary purpose to *Preactively* block the Likely Causes of fires in a city so that none exists? Or is its primary role to *Reactively* suppress fires that have already started? What about the maintenance department in a factory? Is its main role to block the Likely Causes of wear in a factory's machinery so that none exists? Or is its main role to minimize, control, and repair wear that's already occurring in the factory's machinery?

To summarize, while many of our great social systems do play *Preactive* roles to a lesser extent, most of them have a primary role that's *Reactive*. Our conclusion? Society relies heavily on *Reactive* strategies and tactics, and thus has a *suppressive-bias*. That's probably why the first rescue workers to arrive at the scenes of car wrecks and house fires are proudly called "first responders," and are honored by society for playing that role. That's probably why police dispatchers tell panicking callers, "Sorry, ma'am, but we can't come out there until he actually does something to you. The law doesn't allow us to arrest people until *after* they've committed a crime."

Why Do Societies Have a Suppressive-Bias?

If all this is true (and it probably is), *why* do societies have a *suppressive-bias*? What's the True Cause? Some of the possible causes include a lack of knowledge, skill, training, and ability by our social leaders. It's simply easier for leaders to *wait* for trouble to happen and then *respond* to it, than it is for them to invest the necessary time, talent, and treasure to identify the Likely Causes of Future Trouble and then to design social systems to block those LCs.

Worse, as we said earlier, some Likely Causes are unpreventable—things such as tornados, hurricanes, and recessions. So it may be that the highly visible damage of these very dramatic troubles keeps social leaders focused on *responding* to overwhelming damage.

No matter what it was centuries ago that created today's societal *suppressive-bias*, many people *are* suppressively biased and, worse, that costs society billions of dollars a year. Even worse than that, those billions are a frozen asset. It's money invested in Preparing Actions that sits idle most of the time, waiting for trouble to appear.

The point of all this is that, to be a *Preactive* leader, *you* must not allow yourself to be trapped in *suppressive-bias. You* must not allow yourself to have the habit of waiting for trouble to occur before you act. We'll return to this principle in coming chapters and discuss how you can keep yourself from being a suppressive leader. But right now, let's continue our discussion of Future Trouble situations and Preparing Actions with the definition of a *Future Trouble* situation.

The Definition of a
Future Trouble Situation

*A Future Trouble situation is any performance of a person, thing, or system that **isn't** breaking a clear and agreed on task standard now but that **could** break one in an unwanted way in the future.*

While we're defining things, let's also define a *Preparing Action.*

The Definition of a Preparing Action

*Any action you choose and arrange that **waits** to control the cost, loss, stress, and damage of a Future Trouble situation in work and that **waits** to keep the damage from spreading if the trouble does happen.*

You might notice that this last definition is similar to the definition for a Suppressing Action that we had in Chapter 8. That's because Preparing Actions *are* Suppressing Actions—they're just *delayed* Suppressing Actions. They're prepared and installed for implementation later. Let's see a real-life example of how inefficient that can be.

The Case of the Flammable Paint Spray

At the beginning of the chapter, we gave this example of a action statement for a Future Trouble situation, *I want to choose the best Preparing Action to wait to suppress the damage of a fire in our paint booth if one happens while painting our tractor parts.*

Now let's do some role-playing. Let's imagine that you're the superintendent of an assembly plant for the famous Kat-

> ## Future Trouble
> ## Situation
>
> *A Future Trouble situation is any performance of a*
> *person, thing, or system that **isn't** breaking a clear*
> *and agreed on task standard now but that **could***
> *break one in an unwanted way in the future.*

erpuller tractor company that manufactures farm tractors. For many years, your paint department employees have hand-painted the metal parts of your tractors by wearing facemasks and using hand-held spray guns.

However, in a recent efficiency move, you built an enclosed, automated paint booth for the plant. Now the tractor parts hang on padded hooks and move through the new paint booth on an overhead chain. As the parts move through the booth, revolving nozzles spray all sides of them, and they exit the far end of the booth gleaming with your company's traditional bright pink color. This is much more efficient than the old system, and you're pleased with it.

Except for one thing.

The vendor who sold you the booth said that, under certain air temperatures and humidity levels, the paint spray in the booth becomes flammable and can ignite in a flash fire. The vendor said that this explosive condition can't be prevented

---

Preparing Action

*Any action you choose and arrange that **waits** to*
control the cost, loss, stress, and damage of a
*Future Trouble situation in work and that **waits***
to keep the damage from spreading
if the trouble does happen.

---

but, since such flash fires aren't very frequent, you needn't worry about them.

You ignore this advice and think about the situation. You can't control the temperature and humidity in the new paint booth because your large factory doors open and close to the outside weather all during the day, and nearby hot machines stop and start continuously, adding to the changes in the internal air. You realize that you have a classic Future Trouble situation facing you—unwanted flash fires could ignite at any moment, and apparently, they can't be prevented.

So what *can* you do? You decide to implement a package of Preparing Actions to suppress future flash fires if they occur. So you take the following steps.

1. You hang heavy-duty fire extinguishers around the paint booth.

2. You install extra overhead fire sprinklers over the booth.

3. You hold fire drills for the booth operators.

4. You print a manual telling the operators how to escape during a fire.

5. You install a red phone at the booth that's connected to the fire department.

6. You buy fire retardant work clothes for the booth operators to wear.

Then you sit back with great satisfaction, feeling deeply gratified that you've taken every Preparing Action that a reasonable leader could reasonably take in such a situation. And maybe you have. But none of these Preparing Actions will *prevent* a flash fire in the paint booth. All of them are designed to *wait* to suppress the damage and injuries of flash fires after they ignite.

So think about this. There's a sense in which all of this expense—the extinguishers, sprinklers, drills, manual, red phone, and fire retardant clothes—are *wasted*. They're dead weight on your company's budget unless and until a flash fire actually ignites. And that could be years from now, if ever.

Worse, if we multiply this paint booth story by thousands of similar situations in hundreds of similar organizations nationwide, we start to get a sense of the billions of dollars that business, industry, and society are *wasting* by the habit of *suppressive-bias*. *That's* why Preparing Actions are classified as ineffective and inefficient actions in Table 2, Row 3 on page 115.

So here's a question to ponder. We admitted earlier that some Future Troubles are unpreventable, and that nothing can be done about them except to install Preparing Actions to fight them later. So that means we're all doomed to lives of *Reactive* living and *suppressive-bias,* right? No, that's not right. Instead of waving a white flag in the face of the enemy, let's play the *What If* game at the Katerpuller factory.

The What If Game

Many leaders roll over and play dead in the face of Future Trouble. As we said, societies have a strong *suppressive-bias.* They accept *Reactivity* as a mandate of their environment, instead of being creative and looking for new ways to be preventive. In short, they don't play the *What If* game. Let's play it now.

Let's practice the *What If* game by returning to our Katerpuller assembly plant and, instead of accepting the vendor's statement that flash fires can't be prevented, let's play the *What If* game in our paint booth.

Let's imagine that as the plant superintendent, instead of implementing the Preparing Actions that we listed earlier, you stop and ask yourself, "But *what if* the Likely Causes of flash fires in our paint booth *could* be prevented? *What if* the paint booth vendor was giving me incorrect advice?"

So you crank up your courage and assertiveness, and phone a local industrial paint expert. Craig, the paint expert, comes on the line, and you explain your Future Trouble situation to him and how the vendor said flash fires were unpreventable.

Craig replies, "What do you mean, flash fires are *unpreventable*?"

"Well," you answer, "the vendor said it's impossible to control the inside temperature and humidity of our booth, so we can't prevent the air from reaching flash point."

Craig chuckles and says, "But you don't *need* to prevent the air from reaching flash point."

"What are you talking about?" you respond with irritation.

"Look, you don't need to worry about the *air* at all," Craig answers, "because I can give you a brand of paint that's non-flammable. And if you don't want to change paint brands right now, I can give you a chemical additive for your current paint that'll make it non-flammable, too."

"Wow," you reply, "tell me more!"

And—presto—you just saved your company thousands of dollars by *not* listening to the vendor, and by *not* falling into the *suppressive-bias* trap of implementing the Preparing Actions you were planning. Instead, you were creative and assertive enough to play the *What If* game. You focused on *Preac-*

tive leadership instead of *Reactive* leadership. You blocked the Likely Cause of future flash fires in your paint booth in a bold new way.

Here's the lesson. Too often, we take the easy way out and accept *Reactive* thinking from friends, relatives, coworkers, customers, and vendors without question. However, if we played the *What If* game, we could be more *Preactive* in more situations. So here's our lesson: Take the time to be *Preactive*. Use *Preactive* techniques before trying anything else. Cave in to *Reactive* strategy and tactics *only* as a last resort. Our guideline is: *Use Preparing Actions only if Blocking Actions are physically impossible.*

When we think about the dozens of everyday Preparing Actions that we all take for granted in our lives (things like fire extinguishers, seat belts, first aid kits, spare tires, insurance policies, police cars, fire trucks, jails, courts, prisons, most of the medicines in our medicine cabinets, etc.), we should probably stop and ask ourselves, "Wait a minute, isn't it at least possible that some of the Likely Causes of the Future Troubles I'm afraid of could be blocked by creative Preventing Actions?" Then we could start to play the *What If* game. "*What if* it *was* possible to...."

Let's now shift gears and define the leadership technique of *Trouble-Readiness*.

The Definition of Trouble-Readiness

*Choosing and implementing the best Preparing Actions to **wait** to **control** the costs, losses, stresses, and damages of Future Troubles in Normal Work situations if they happen and to keep those damages from growing worse and spreading if they do occur.*

Thus, the technique of Trouble-Readiness is the act of getting ready to control Future Trouble and then waiting to fight the damage of that trouble if it happens. As a picture of the technique of Trouble-Readiness, let's return to our diagram of the brick walkway that you've been building for the Terry Johnson family.

Figure 7 on page 325 shows that your work is proceeding normally—with *dotted lines* showing your work proceeding into the *future*. The dotted downturn in the zigzag arrow of linked Working Actions (WAs) represents a *Future Trouble* situation (FT) that *may* occur in the bricklaying at some *future* time. If it does, it will push the work arrow outside the minimum time standard of one hour per day set by the Johnson family, thus becoming a Current Trouble situation at that time and falling into non-conformance with the family's standards.

FIGURE 7
The Brick Walkway as a Future Trouble Situation
with a Preparing Action

MAXIMUM TIME STANDARD: AVG. 2 HRS PER DAY

TIME IN HOURS

2.00
1.75
1.50
1.25
1.00

START
AT
CITY
SIDE
WALK

WAs

END
AT
HOUSE
DOOR
STEP

FT

MINIMUM TIME STANDARD: AVG. ... PER DAY

DISTANCE IN BRICKLAYING

WAs = Working Actions
FT = Future Trouble
PA = Preparing Action

SUPPRESS

PA

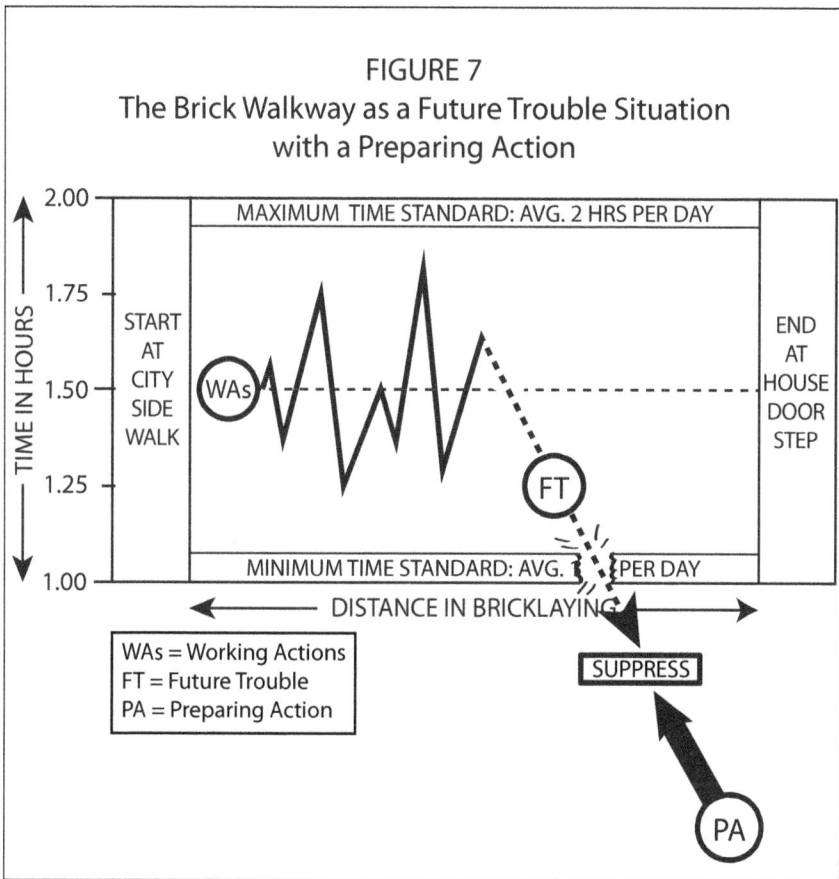

The black arrow represents a *Preparing Action* (PA) you have arranged to suppress this Future Trouble if it actually ever becomes a Current Trouble. Notice that PAs are delayed Suppressing Actions. This diagram is a picture of the leadership technique of *Trouble-Readiness.* Note that PAs are ineffective and that they are *Reactive* leadership: *Leading in the presence of trouble.*

The Threat of the Unseasonable Snowstorm

Here's the story behind Figure 7. You started work on the brick walkway for the Johnson family in the month of September. Your agreement with them was that you'd finish the walkway by November 1st. But let's imagine that your area of the country is known for freak snowstorms that hit early in the fall—often as early as October. These freak storms melt quickly and things soon return to normal, but they can accumulate several inches of damp snow at the time and that snow can linger for several days. As you think about your commitment to build a high-quality walkway for the Johnsons, you realize that if one of these unseasonable snowstorms strikes, it could ruin a lot of your work.

As an experienced bricklayer, you know that the mortar between your bricks must cure for a minimum of two weeks, or it won't harden sufficiently to produce a long-life walkway. In other words, the cold pressure of a damp pre-

---

Trouble-Readiness

*Choosing and implementing the best Preparing Actions to **wait** to **control** the costs, losses, stresses, and damages of Future Troubles in Normal Work situations if they happen and to keep those damages from growing worse and spreading if they do occur.*

mature snow could dilute your mortar, and the finished walkway would lack the quality the Johnsons are expecting from you. Indeed, if your mortar doesn't cure for at least two weeks, the bricks in the walkway could start to unseat in just a few months.

Obviously, you can't block freak snowstorms. It's physically impossible for you to block this Likely Cause of mortar dilution in the walkway. There's no way to be *Preactive* in this situation. So you'll have to punt and be *Reactive.* Here's your action statement, *I want to choose the best Preparing Action to wait to suppress the dilution of the mortar in the Johnson's walkway if a freak snowstorm hits it before November 1st.*

After thinking about this action statement and making a decision by the *Mental-Verbal Format* that we learned in Chapter 2, you make the following preparations.

1. You buy a tarp wide enough to cover the width and length of the brick walkway.

2. You roll up this tarp, tie it securely, attach a tag to it explaining its purpose, and put it on the tool shelf in the Johnson's garage.

3. You ring the Johnson's doorbell, tell them about the tarp, and explain that it's important for them to phone you if they hear a freak snowstorm is approaching. If they can't reach you for any reason, they're to unroll the tarp themselves, spread it over the entire walkway, and anchor it with scrap lumber and extra bricks.

4. You explain that this is a Preparing Action you're taking to be ready to suppress the dilution of the mortar in the walkway by a freak snowstorm, and that you hope the tarp will never be used. You thank the family for their role in helping you arrange the Preparing Action, and you walk home for dinner.

However, notice that you're probably wasting your money on the tarp and that you're probably wasting your time teaching the family how to use it. We've agreed that Preparing Actions are often wasted money and time. But we've also agreed that Preparing Actions can be helpful if Blocking Actions are impossible in a situation and if the pending future damage would be severe.

Okay, what we've said in this chapter is that none of us appreciates the pain, expense, and stress that Future Troubles can create in our lives. But sometimes the Likely Causes of those Future Troubles are unpreventable. So all we can do is arrange to suppress them if they happen. That's good, right, and proper.

Except that Preparing Actions can become a bad habit, and we can forget that Blocking Actions are some of the most effective and efficient actions any leader can take. That's why the goal of this book is to teach you to be a fair and balanced leader. That is, to teach you to use Blocking Actions whenever possible and to only use Preparing Actions when Blocking Actions *aren't* possible.

Summary of Chapter 10

1. The Future Trouble situation (the FT sit) is the *last* of the Ineffective-Inefficient situations we'll learn, and Preparing Actions (PAs) are the *last* of the actions we'll learn that *correct* trouble with *defensive-minded* and *Reactive* strategies and tactics.

2. A Future Trouble situation is any performance of a person, thing, or system that *isn't* breaking a clear and agreed on task standard now, but that *could* break one in an unwanted way in the future. FT sits can also be called potential problems, future damage, possible losses, and future breakdowns, among other things.

3. A Preparing Action is any action you choose and arrange that *waits* to control the cost, loss, stress, and damage of a Future Trouble situation in work and that *waits* to keep the damage from spreading if the trouble does happen.

4. A Trigger Report is any audible and/or visual signal that *waits* to be triggered by a Current Trouble situation and that activates a Suppressing Action to limit the damage of that trouble.

5. A Milestone Report is any audible and/or visual signal that measures—either continuously or at intervals—the work on a Normal Work situation and reports the degree to which that work is meeting standards.

6. The technique of Trouble-Readiness is choosing and implementing the best Preparing Actions to *wait* to *control* the cost, loss, stress, and damage of Future Troubles in Normal Work situations if they happen and to keep those damages from growing worse and spreading if they do occur.

7. Society has a strong *suppressive-bias* and tends to focus on *corrective*, *defensive-minded*, and *Reactive* strategies and tactics. One reason for this may be the highly visible damage of disasters such as earthquakes and floods that keeps social planners focused on preparing for overwhelming damage. Another reason may be that social planners don't have the knowledge, skill, training, or ability to be more preventive. However, the lesson is that with proper leadership, any organization or social system can be *more Preactive* than normal.

8. Preparing Actions are good and necessary when the Likely Causes of future damage are *unpreventable*—such as with tornados, hurricanes, forest fires caused by lightning, and so on. However, many more Likely Causes could be blocked at home and on the job if we focused less on *suppressive-bias*, and played the *What If* game more often to think up bold and creative new Blocking Actions.

9. Figure 7 illustrates a Future Trouble situation with a Preparing Action arranged to wait to control its damage if it occurs.

10. The technique of Trouble-Readiness is the act of preparing to control Future Trouble and then waiting to fight the damage of that trouble if it happens.

And that concludes our discussion of the six "masks" that generic Choice Situations can wear in our homes and in the workplace. It's time now to put all the pieces from all the previous chapters together and see what picture they create. Now let's talk about the overall strategy of *Preactive* leadership and to talk about how that *strategy* applies in our lives and on the job. In Chapter 11, we start to sense the leadership *strategy* that the first ten chapters of this book have so carefully built.

P A R T IV

LEADERSHIP STRATEGY AND TACTICS

CHAPTER 11

STRATEGIC *PREACTIVE* LEADERSHIP

At last the puzzle is complete. At last we can see the whole picture of *Preactive* leadership. Now let's look closely at that picture and see how logical and practical *Preactive* leadership really is and how it gives us hope for better lives and jobs.

Chapter 11 is important because in the previous chapters we were standing quite close to each of the six leadership situations and, as sometimes happens in an art gallery, if we stand too close to a painting, we can see its parts, but we can't grasp its whole. But, if we step back a few feet, we can see the full impact of the painting. That's what we're doing in this chapter. We're stepping back a few feet to see the full impact of *Preactive* leadership as a personal and group strategy.

One thing we're going to discover is that leadership strategies apply the *same* way whether we're leading a corporation, civic club, church, government agency, family, or ourselves. We're also going to discover that there are two *types* of leadership strategies, that each of them has two *parts*, and that each of them has two *applications*. While we're discovering these things, we're going to answer six questions about leadership:

1. What are leadership strategies?
2. What leadership strategies are best?
3. What are leadership styles?
4. What leadership styles are best?
5. What are leadership cultures?
6. What leadership cultures are best?

However, before we begin to answer these questions, let's back up and get a running start by reviewing the definitions we learned in Chapters 1 and 2. Let's recall what leadership is and then let's tie that definition to the concept of *strategy*.

A Review of Leadership

In Chapter 1, we said that a leader is an action-taker. We said that leadership is action-taking in the presence of others that influences them enough to create a positive change in their behavior. In Chapter 2, we gave this full definition of leadership.

Taking the best Decision Actions in Choice Situations
to positively influence the behavior of others in
directing *and* **correcting** *activities.*

In Chapter 2, we didn't emphasize the two italicized words at the end of this definition, but notice them now. Think about how *directing* tasks and *correcting* tasks are two different things. Those words were an early clue back in Chapter 2 that there are two basic *types* of strategies and that they serve two very different purposes.

As we're going to see, the purpose of the first type of strategy is to *direct* the work on tasks toward goals in a creative, preventive way. The purpose of the second type is to *correct* trouble in the work on tasks in a rectifying, suppressive way. Those are totally different purposes when you stop to think about them.

So *Preactive* leadership is another name for leadership strategies that *direct* work in an *offensive-minded* way. *Reactive*

> **Leadership**
> *Taking the best*
> *Decision Actions in*
> *Choice Situations to*
> *positively influence the*
> *behavior of others in*
> **directing** *and*
> **correcting** *activities.*

leadership is another name for leadership strategies that *correct* work in a *defensive-minded* way. With that, let's now begin answering our six questions, starting with the definition of the word strategies.

What are Strategies?

The word *strategy* was originally a military word. It comes from a Greek root that referred to the general of an army. Because of that military root, today the word refers to the general (overall) *values* and *actions* a person is using in leadership. It doesn't matter whether the leader's goal is to win a war, write a book, increase a market share, invent a product, or occupy the White House. The principle is still the same. A leader's "strategy" is the overall *values* and *actions* he or she is using. With that bit of history, here's our full definition of *leadership strategy*.

The Definition
of Leadership Strategy

*The general, overall set of **values** and **actions** a*
*leader uses to **direct** and **correct** personal*
or group work toward a goal in the most
effective and efficient way.

This definition means that both types of strategies (*Preactive-directing* and *Reactive-correcting*) divide into two parts.

1. *A set of values.* These are the personal *style* or *ethics* that guide a leader in his or her leadership decision-making.

2. *A set of actions.* These are the *tactics* or *behaviors* a leader uses to move his or her work forward toward its goals.

This definition also means that all leadership strategies do one of two things: They either *direct* work using a set of values and actions, or they *correct* work using a set of values and actions. To see examples of these two types of strategies implemented with their sets of values and actions, let's pause to read the tales of two physicians.

The Doctor's Memoirs

Our first physician, Dr. Patterson, is elderly and wealthy and has a personal goal of writing his memoirs. His desire is to share with the medical world the discoveries he made during his career. He establishes a writing schedule for evenings and weekends, buys a new computer, makes notes about his plot and the content of his chapters, and starts to write. Here's how we'd break down Dr. Patterson's leadership strategy.

> **Leadership Strategy**
>
> *The general, overall set of **values** and **actions** a leader uses to **direct** and **correct** personal or group work toward a goal in the most effective and efficient way.*

1. His goal: To write a book.

2. His situation: A Normal Work situation.

3. His values: To help other people, teach his discoveries, be open and honest with readers, communicate clearly, and improve medical practices and public health.

4. His actions: To set clear standards and to choose the best Working Actions to write his book and move it toward his goal of publication.

5. His strategy: The key point in this story is that Dr. Patterson's strategy is *not* a response to trouble. (He's taking action *before* any trouble has been reported to him.) Specifically, he's responding to a Normal Work situation—one of the Effective-Efficient situations in Table 1 on page 114. For these reasons, Dr. Patterson's strategy is a *directing* and *Preactive* strategy. Next, let's read the tale of our second physician.

The Doctor's Thefts

Our second physician, Dr. Watson, is also elderly and wealthy, but he has a different purpose. He's the senior partner in a medical clinic, and he and his partners have the group objective of stopping drug thefts in their clinic. Several thousand dollars of addictive drugs have gone missing in recent months, and the partners suspect an "inside job" by a new employee who joined the clinic at about the time the drugs began disappearing. Their desire is to verify this probable suspect and arrest the true thief. After several meetings, the partners hire a private detective to pose as a male nurse in the clinic, and they install surveillance cameras inside their drug cabinets to film evidence. Dr. Watson and his partners now wait for verification of the thief. Here's how we'd break down our second physician's strategy.

1. His objective: To catch a thief.

2. His situation: A True Cause situation.

3. His values: To stop drug thefts, remove a thief, and punish a crime.

4. His actions: To use cause-finding skills and a best Correcting Action.

5. His strategy: The pivotal point in this story is that Dr. Watson's strategy is a response to trouble. (He's taking action *after* trouble has been reported to him.) In fact, the intent of his strategy is to find and remove the source of a trouble that has been reported to him. Specifically, he's responding to a True Cause situation—one of the Ineffective-Inefficient situations in Table 2 on page 115. For these reasons, we identify Dr. Watson's strategy as a *correcting* and *Reactive* strategy. Let's continue now and see some even deeper lessons hidden in these tales.

The Two Types of Leadership Strategies

As the tales of two physicians show, there are two basic *types* of leadership strategies that are rooted in the two basic *types* of leadership and, as we've seen, they can be identified using the Identification Tables on pages 114-115. Let's review how that's done. If a leader's actions are in response to one of the three Effective-Efficient situations in Table 1, that leader's strategy is *Preactive, directive,* and *offensive-minded.* This was the case with Dr. Patterson in our first tale.

On the other hand, if a leader's actions are in response to one of the three Ineffective-Inefficient situations in Table 2, that leader's strategy is *Reactive, corrective,* and *defensive-minded.* That was the case with Dr. Watson in our second tale.

Note carefully that the key to identifying a strategy is whether or not trouble has *already started* in the situation that the strategy is intended to resolve. If a leader is responding to a goal and not to trouble, his or her strategy is *offensive* in nature. But if a leader is responding to trouble (or planning to respond to it), his or her strategy is *defensive* in nature.

Another lesson we saw in the doctor's tales is that there are two *applications* for strategies: They can be used by an individual leading him or herself in a private task—as we saw in Dr. Patterson's tale. Or they can be used as a group leader in a group task—as we saw in Dr. Watson's tale.

To summarize, we've learned that there are two types of leadership strategies:

1. *Preactive, directive, offensive-minded* strategies (see Table 1, page 114).

2. *Reactive, corrective, defensive-minded* strategies (see Table 2, page 115).

Each of these strategies then subdivides into two parts:

1. A set of guiding *values* or *ethics*.

2. A set of tactical *actions* or *behaviors*.

Each strategy also has two applications:

1. As an *individual* leading him or herself.

2. As a person leading a group.

Finally, we saw that we can easily identify strategies by measuring them against the two Identification Tables.

Okay, now let's answer the next question on our list at the beginning of the chapter. It's this. Is either of these strategies better than the other? Is either more desirable? Let's find out.

Which Strategy is Best?

Our subject gets interesting at this point because *both* of these leadership strategies serve a good purpose when they're *needed*. For example, in our second tale about Dr. Watson, the group of doctors in the medical clinic *needed* to find, verify, and remove the thief. Thus, their *Reactive, corrective, defensive-minded* strategy was the best strategy at the time, even though it was a rectifying and suppressive type of leadership. (Let's not forget that if Dr. Watson and his partners had used more prevention in the clinic, there wouldn't have been any drug thefts to worry about.)

But let's press the issue. *All* things considered—is either of these two strategies preferable? Yes, one of them is preferable. The *Preactive* strategies are the best all-around strategies in every walk of life, and that's why this book was written. The reason for this is that if leaders emphasize *Preactive* strategies in their lives and on their jobs, they won't need *Reactive* strategies (or at least they won't need them as often). To see that more clearly, let's paraphrase some of the principles we learned in Chapter 7.

1. Since *Preactive* strategies are *offensive-minded* and are taken *before* trouble strikes, they're our most effective strategies and, since their purpose is to prevent trouble, they're also our most efficient strategies.

2. Since *Reactive* strategies are *defensive-minded* and are taken *after* trouble strikes, they're our most ineffective strategies and, since their purpose is to rectify trouble, they're our most inefficient strategies.

The result of these principles is that if leaders focus on *Preactive* strategies in their lives and jobs, they'll be more effective, efficient, and preventive in everything they do—and that glaring fact makes *Preactive* strategies the best ones overall. We'll say it many times in many ways: *Preactive strategies are the best strategies because they're the most effective, efficient way to reach goals and because they prevent trouble while doing it.*

In later pages, we'll talk in greater detail about how you can make your own leadership strategies predominately *Preactive*. But before we do that, let's change the subject a moment. As we saw in our tales of two physicians, both of the leadership strategies have a set of *values* or *ethics* guiding them. These values are vitally important. In fact, leadership strategies can't be understood without knowing how these values operate. So let's pause for a look at *values* in leadership, what some writers call "styles" of leadership.

Strategies and Values

In Chapter 5, we learned that "standards" are terms that describe what situations need and that tell us the degree to which our actions are satisfying those needs. We said there are over 200 synonyms for the word *standards* and that among them are such terms as "values," "styles," and "ethics." Thus, when we talk about the *values* that are guiding a leader's strategy, we're talking about the *style* he or she is using, or the *ethical* basis for what he or she is doing, or the *standards* he or she is obeying. Said yet another way, the words values, styles, ethics, and standards are all synonyms. They all mean the same thing in this context.

For example, when authors publish books on "leadership styles," they're using a synonym that refers to the values, ethics, or standards a leader is using. And since we want to stay in touch with what other authors are saying about leadership, we'll going to use the word "styles" in many of our sentences as a synonym for the *values* that are guiding a leader.

And so, speaking of what other authors have said about leadership, let's now look at what some of them have written about leadership *styles* (values) over the past 60 years.

What are Leadership Styles?

As we've said, the word "styles" is one of more than 200 synonyms for the terms values, ethics, and standards. Thus, anywhere you see the word "styles" in this chapter, it's referring to the values, ethics, and standards guiding a leader's decision-making. Against that backdrop, let's define a leadership *style*.

The Definition of a Leadership Style

*The set of **values** (ethics, standards) that*
are guiding a leader's decision-making
in a strategy.

Of course, entire textbooks, seminars, training DVDs, and college classes have been devoted to the subject of leadership "styles," and we can't cover all of those ideas here. Our aim is to always keep this book simple and practical. That's why I've purposely avoided including the usual footnotes, references, photographs and bios of famous leaders, multi-colored pie charts, and all the other paraphernalia that you'd expect in a book on leadership. Another reason I haven't included such materials is that—except for where I specifically mention a classic researcher's name—I developed the principles in these chapters myself during my years as an organizational consultant and seminar leader.

> **Leadership Style**
> *The set of **values**
> (ethics, standards) that
> are guiding a leader's
> decision-making
> in a strategy.*

But suffice it to say that all the discoveries by all the classic researchers since serious leadership research began in the 1940s agree with the techniques in these chapters. In alphabetical order, those classic researchers include such luminaries as: Clayton Alderfer of Yale; Chris Argyris of Yale; Ken Blanchard of Cornell; Fred Fiedler of the University of Washington; Paul Hersey of Northern Illinois University; Frederick Herzberg of Case Western Reserve; George Homans of Harvard; Edward Lawler of University of Southern California; Abraham Maslow of Brandeis; Doug McGregor of Massachusetts Institute of Technology; Lyman Porter of University of California Irvine; Ralph Stogdill of Ohio State University, and Victor Vroom of Yale.

However, to keep our discussion of leadership styles simple, in this chapter we're only going to talk about one discovery by one researcher. It's an easy one to remember. It's called *Theory X and Theory Y*. We're going to use it as our tool for interpreting the values, styles, ethics, and standards that leaders are using in their decision-making.

Theory X and Theory Y

Theory X and Theory Y leadership *styles* (values, ethics, standards) were discovered by Dr. Douglas M. McGregor at the Massachusetts Institute of Technology over 50 years ago, and were first described in his 1960 classic book, *The Human Side of Enterprise.* McGregor's research showed that, to one degree or another, all leaders tend to use one of two opposing sets of values in their leadership strategies. He called the first set of values *Theory X.* It's a set of values that are autocratic, control-oriented, numbers-oriented, production-oriented, and results-oriented. Theory X is a set of micromanaging values that's based largely on the threat of punishment, on the use of rigid supervision and, to a large extent, on instilling fear in followers.

McGregor found that leaders who use Theory X values are basing their leadership style on the assumption that people are lazy and incompetent and must be forced to work by strict discipline, strict recordkeeping, and strict micromanagement. Theory X values remind us of what Niccolo Machiavelli wrote about leadership in his book *The Prince* in the 1500s, when he said, "It is better to be feared than loved, if you cannot be both."

McGregor's second set of values is the exact opposite of the first. He called it *Theory Y.* Theory Y is best described as a set of values that are team oriented, relationship oriented, people centered, creative, and empowering. Theory Y is a set of team-working values that's based largely on open communications, listening to what followers have to say, group decision-making, and instilling confidence in subordinates.

McGregor found that leaders who use Theory Y values are basing their leadership style on the assumption that people want to work, enjoy work, and *will work* if they're treated with respect, and are motivated by trust, open communications, and clear standards. Theory Y values remind us something Ronald Reagan, the 40th American president, wrote about leadership in the 1980s when he said, "Surround yourself with the best people you can find, delegate authority, and don't interfere as long as the policy you've decided upon is being carried out."

But here's a related thought.

Let's ask ourselves the same question about these two leadership styles that we asked earlier about *Preactive* and *Reactive* strategies. Is either of these sets of values better than the other? Is either more desirable? Let's find out.

Which is Best:
Theory X or Theory Y?

Which one of McGregor's sets of leadership values is the best? We can answer that question the same way we answered it earlier for *Preactive* and *Reactive* strategies. Both Theory X and Theory Y values serve a good purpose when they're *needed*. Either one is best if the situation is "asking" for that set of values.

Dr. Fred E. Fiedler of the University of Washington proved this when he discovered what he called contingency leadership. He described it in his 1967 classic book, *A Theory of Leadership Effectiveness*. Later, in the decades following Fiedler's book, research on contingency leadership continued, and during the 1990s its best-known researchers were Paul H. Hersey of Northern Illinois University and Kenneth H. Blanchard of Cornell. Using Hersey's and Blanchard's words, most textbooks today call Fiedler's discovery situational leadership.

But what Fred Fiedler discovered in 1967 is that no *one* set of leadership values can be best in all situations. Some situations require Theory X autocratic values. Other situations require Theory Y teamworking values. The trick is for leaders to know the difference between the two, and to avoid using the *same* style in every situation since that would mean they were using the wrong style in some of their situations. Unhappily, that's exactly what many leaders do.

Research shows that Theory X (autocratic) values are the most frequently used values by leaders in every walk of life—regardless of what their situations need. In other words, many leaders use a rigid, non-negotiable, dictatorial, authoritarian set of values in *every* situation they face, whether or not the task is "asking" for that kind of style. Worse, they teach their subordinates to do the same thing, even though all textbook say this is a no-no. With that in mind, let's do some identification drills, and see *examples* of the kinds of situations that need these two different styles of action-taking.

The Kinds of Values that Situations Need

Let's start by repeating a principle we learned in our first chapter. Effective leaders always diagnose a situation's *needs* before taking any action. After they understand what a situation needs, they implement the style of action-taking that best satisfies those needs. Said another way, effective leaders identify the values a situation is "asking" for, and then they use that set of values in the situation. Here are some broad guidelines for deciding which set of values a situation needs.

1. *Situations that Need Theory X Values.* Situations that need an autocratic leadership style include all types of emergency situations—such as military situations, fire and police situations, crime situations, and medical crises. (Think of doctors shouting orders in the emergency room, army officers shouting orders on the battlefield, and fire commanders shouting orders at the scene of a blaze.)

Situations that need Theory X values include all types of urgent, new, and unknown situations where employees are in danger, confused, frightened, or don't know what to do. In a corporate setting, this might include such situations as introducing a new product, building a new factory, opening a new department, filling a rush order, and other such situations where the employees aren't sure what to do next. Such challenging and demanding situations require leaders to use a "firm hand" and to show and tell the employees what to do. As an example, in our earlier tales of two physicians, Dr. Watson was using a firm and assertive hand in the medical clinic to lead his partners in tracking down and capturing the drug thief. That makes him an example of Theory X style leadership being appropriately used.

2. *Situations that Need Theory Y Values.* Situations that need a teamworking leadership style include all types of creative and human relations situations—such as sales, advertising,

teaching, training, and writing tasks, as well as delicate technical tasks such as research, development, and experimental projects. They include all types of routine, normal situations where employees are calm, competent, experienced, and know their jobs. (Think of scientists wearing white coats in clean rooms, technicians hooking hoses to NASA astronauts, and skilled machine operators producing high-quality parts in spotless factories.)

Situations that need Theory Y values include all kinds of mature, stable, and safe activities, products, tasks, departments, assembly lines, and projects where employees are well trained, well matched, and well motivated, and where their work is on-budget, on-quality, and on-schedule. Such peaceful and routine situations are asking for leaders who can wear "kid gloves" and relate to employees with frequent group meetings to discuss plans and give employees the freedom to speak out, be creative, and make their own decisions. For example, in our earlier tales of two physicians, Dr. Patterson was using kid gloves on himself to plan and write a creative book for the benefit of humankind, and his sacrificial and thoughtful focus makes him an example of Theory Y style leadership being appropriately used.

Okay, now that we understand our two leadership styles, we've arrived at a big mistake some leaders make. We mentioned it earlier. It's a mistake that the classic leadership researchers have discussed for many years. It's the error of using the *wrong* values in situations.

Using the Wrong Values

Let's stop here and ask a question that the classic research-ers have probed for six decades: What happens if a leader uses the *wrong* values (the wrong style) in a situation? Said another way, what happens if the values a leader is using in a situation *aren't* the ones the situation is "asking" for?

Obviously, when that happens there are *negative* con-sequences: The leader's strategy is less effective and efficient. Progress toward goals and objectives is slower. Costs, losses, stresses, disappointments, and damages are higher. Profits are lower. Employee morale is lower.

The truth is, it makes no sense at all for leaders to use the wrong values in situations. But research shows that's exactly what many of them *do*. Let's talk bluntly for a moment about how leadership values are misapplied.

To repeat what we said earlier, research shows that Theory X values are the most frequently used values and many leaders use them in *every* situation they face regardless of whether or not the situation *needs* those values. This means many leaders are militant, rigid, autocratic, numbers-driven, results-driven, and time-driven even when the situation doesn't warrant that style of leadership. As a friend of mine used to say, such leaders are "treating everything like an emergency even when it ain't."

For years, I've called this error in values a *distorted sense of urgency*. This unrealistic feeling of urgency is wrong unless you're a soldier in combat, a police officer chasing a robber, a doctor in the operating room, or some similar Theory X situation. Frankly, there just aren't that many Theory X situations in today's normal workplace. In today's workplace, there tends to be an emphasis on team building, human relations, team communications, and employee motivation. In other words, there's an emphasis on *Theory Y* values. Thus, leaders who use Theory X values in all their situations are out of step with today's trends.

So let's talk True Cause a moment.

Why do so many leaders use X values? The answer is complex yet simple. Theory X values are easier, faster, and more self-empowering *on the front end* of tasks. To be blunt, it takes less effort, time, and humility to be an X leader. It's quicker and easier to just snap at employees, "I'm too busy to argue with you right now! Just do as I said!"

On the flip side, it takes more time, patience, respect, and inner strength to explain to employees *why* something needs to be done and to answer their questions about it. In Chapter 5, we learned the motto *Be Slow Right Instead of Fast Wrong.* We said that if leaders invest more time analyzing needs on the front end of tasks, they'll spend less time reworking defects, repairing damage, fighting law suits, and soothing hurt feelings on the back end of tasks.

So let's face it. Which set of values is *really* more time-consuming: being faster on the front end with Theory X values and slower on the back end with trouble and waste? Or being slower on the front end with Theory Y values and faster on the back end with quality and efficiency? The answer seems obvious.

The point is that if leaders *invest* the time in Theory Y values on the front end of their tasks (assuming those are the values the task needs), the increased employee motivation and communication produces higher quality and faster work on the back end. To be sure, tasks may be a few days slower getting started. But they'll finish easier, faster, more profitable, and more empowering for both the leader and the employees.

This principle is the first *Preactive* Conclusion to strengthen your personal leadership.

First Conclusion to Strengthen Your Leadership

Use Theory Y Values

Recognize which values your situations need and apply the correct X or Y styles, emphasizing Y values and using X values only when absolutely necessary.

But on top of everything else, there's even a bigger reason for avoiding Theory X values on the front-end of tasks wherever possible. I call it the error of riding *the down escalator*.

The Down Escalator

Let's ask a bold question. As long as the job gets done, does it really *matter* what values a leader uses? Yes, it really matters. In fact, that question makes no sense because the job usually *isn't* getting done when someone asks it. To see why that's true, let's discuss the different attitudes that *Theory X* and *Theory Y* values create in employees.

The word *attitude* comes from a root that means a state of mind. While some leaders don't realize it, the values they use in their leadership have an effect on the mental attitudes of their followers. Said another way, the leadership style a leader uses has an emotional effect on his or her subordinates—and that can be good or bad depending on *what* emotion the leader is creating in subordinates and on how *long* the leader creates it in them.

Dr. Christopher ("Chris") Argyris of Yale wrote on the dangers of wrong emotions in followers when he discovered immaturity-maturity cycles. He first described them in his 1957 classic book, *Personality and Organization.* The cycles Argyris wrote about are disturbing. In the simplest terms, he found that the longer employees are led with *Theory X* values, the more *immature* they become. It's as if they're on a downward spiral into immaturity. I call that "the down escalator." Theory X leadership takes employees aboard a moving staircase downward into career stagnation.

> ### First Conclusion to
> ### Strengthen Your Leadership
> *Use Theory Y Values*
> *Recognize which values your situations need and apply*
> *the correct X or Y styles, emphasizing Y values*
> *and using X values only when absolutely necessary.*

Happily, Argyris found the reverse to also be true. He found that the longer employees are led with *Theory Y* values, the more *mature* they become. It's as if they're on an upward spiral into maturity. I call that "the up escalator." Theory Y leadership takes employees aboard a moving staircase upward into career growth and excitement.

To understand these two escalators, we need to stop and clarify the fuzzy words *maturity* and *immaturity*. By "immature" employees, we mean employees who lack confidence, who aren't assertive, who're close-minded, unhappy, and creatively unfulfilled. They have weak decision-making skills and are overly dependent on the leader in the bad sense that they rely too heavily on the leader's opinions during decision-making.

By "mature" employees, we mean employees who're confident, assertive, open-minded, happy, and creatively fulfilled. Such employees have strong decision-making skills, and are independent of the leader in the good sense that they *don't* rely too heavily on the leader's opinions during decision-making.

To repeat, Argyris found that both of these attitudes *increase* over time. The longer subordinates are led with Theory X values, the more immature they become. The longer subordinates are led with Theory Y values, the more mature they become.

This being true, imagine what this means if a leader applies Theory X (autocratic) values *incorrectly* for a long period of time to a peaceful, competent, skilled, and loyal group of subordinates who really need Theory Y (teamworking) leadership. The victimized subordinates would grow steadily weaker as the months passed and they'd never understand why. They would be riding the down escalator to career stagnation and would have little hope of employee maturity because it's difficult to go *up* a down escalator.

Clearly, none of this is good news. But it gets worse. Because this discovery of the immaturity-maturity cycles ties directly into our next subject. Let's shift gears once more and discuss a part of the leadership equation that we haven't fully explored yet. Let's talk in more specifics about what happens to employees if they ride the up or the down escalator for long periods of time.

Playing Follow the Leader

As children, some of us played a game called *Follow the Leader*. One child was chosen as the leader, the other children were the followers. The leader ran, climbed, or jumped and the followers did exactly what the leader did. That children's game is probably as old as history, but it holds some serious lessons that aren't obvious at first glance. In the children's game, "following" meant to exactly *imitate* the leader's behavior. If the leader led through a briar patch or a mud puddle, the children faithfully followed. That obedience by the children who were the followers gave great authority to, and placed great responsibility on, the child who was the leader.

There's a motto in the field of education and training that says, *Monkey see, monkey do.* Humans have a strong tendency to mimic the behavior of people they admire, or people who have authority over them. People tend to say and do what the movie stars, musicians, and politicians they admire say and do. And that can be good or bad—depending on what the movie stars, musicians, and politicians are saying and doing.

This tendency to mimic leaders (for better or worse) opens the door to our next subject. Next, let's talk about how leadership styles become cast in concrete with permanent effects. Let's talk about how *cultures* are formed.

What are Cultures?

There are hundreds of books on organizational cultures. (Some writers call it corporate cultures.) We don't have time for a safari into minutia, so we won't discuss all the fascinating ins and outs of corporate cultures here. Instead, let's just start with a simple and practical definition of the word *culture*.

The Definition of Culture

*The **total habits** of an individual or group, including the habits of setting clear standards, making best choices using appropriate X or Y values in situations, and focusing on **Preactive, directive,** and **offensive-minded** strategies as much as possible.*

Notice this is a positive, optimistic view of a group culture. A *Preactive* culture such as this is usually a cheerful, encouraging, uplifting culture for a group. But to be deathbed honest, some groups have cultures that are just the opposite. Some groups have *Reactive* cultures.

We know from experience that many individuals and groups have negative cultures. In Chapter 1, we said there's probably as much negative leadership in the world as there is positive leadership. In other words, there are probably as many individuals and groups with the bad habits of fuzzy standards, weak choices, wrong values, and *Reactive* strategies as there are with the opposite, which is why the theme of this book is to focus on *Preactive* leadership both individually and as a group.

Culture

*The **total habits** of an individual or group, including the habits of setting clear standards, making best choices using appropriate X or Y values in situations, and focusing on **Preactive, directive,** and **offensive-minded** strategies as much as possible.*

But to continue, in one word, "culture" means *habits*. In two words, "culture" means *total habits*. Culture is the habitual way individuals and groups dress, eat, walk, talk, laugh, write, think, hold meetings, and do their jobs.

But here's the big lesson: Culture is *socially transmitted*. Culture (good and bad) is learned from the people around us and, primarily, it's learned from our leaders. As children, our culture began with the way we were led by our families and then grew with the way we were led by early school teachers and neighborhood playmates. As adults, our cultures have continued to be molded by our adult social lives and, most importantly, they continue to be molded today by our current *leaders* on our current jobs. The good news is that, because culture is *learned*, it can be *unlearned* if necessary. The process of learning (and unlearning) cultures is called training, education, socialization, acculturation, assimilation, and similar terms. The point is, as working adults, most of our cultural growth stems largely from the *leaders* on our jobs. They're the ones we tend to model each day.

Let's take a quick example. Most of us have some idea what a military boot camp is like. Many veterans will tell you that they've seen a bus load of undisciplined young people straggle in the back gate of a boot camp, dressed in every description of weird clothes and dragging all kinds of weird luggage—only to see those same young people march out the front gate of the camp a few weeks later as a proud and polished military unit.

How do such "miracles" happen? We can call it cultural change, acculturation, and a dozen other terms. But whatever we call it, such miracles happen because of the boot camp's *leaders*—the drill instructors who trained the recruits. And that introduces another principle we need to think about: How *habits* are formed in a culture.

How Habits are Formed

Scientists say it takes a minimum of three weeks (21 days) of continuous repetition to develop the unconscious behavior we call a new habit. In other words, a new behavior must be repeated continuously for at least three consecutive weeks before it starts to harden into a new habit. (That's why boot camps last longer than three weeks.) But even after three weeks of constant repetition, a new habit is still weak and can still be broken. However, for each week that passes after the first three, the new habit strengthens until at last it's entrenched. After that, the new habit is as difficult to break as it was to form.

Ex-military people will tell you that even years after they left the military, they continue to practice some of their military habits. They may walk a certain way, wear their clothes a certain way, or shine their shoes a certain way. That's the power of habits. That's the power of *culture*.

But even though culture is as old as people, cultures are still positive or negative. They are still effective or ineffective. Just because a culture exists doesn't mean it's the *best* one for an individual or a group to have. Throughout human history, various cultures have practiced child sacrifice, cannibalism, head-hunting, ritual torture, racial genocide, and every other form of negative behavior imaginable. Some still do. This means we can't blindly accept a culture just because it's *there*. If a culture is negative, we need to recognize that. Most of all, we need to know how to *change* a negative culture, as we'll discuss in coming pages.

The point here is this. If cultures are the sum totals of our habits, then our cultures include our habitual *leadership strategies*. Said another way, one of the habits in our personal culture is the habit of leadership we've learned—either *Preactive* or *Reactive*. So let's pause to find out what *your* habitual leadership strategies are.

What are Your Habitual Leadership Strategies?

As we said, our cultures (our total habits) include the habit of our leadership strategies. Recalling the principles of action-taking that we learned in Chapter 1, we know that each of us has leadership strategies because we *do things* during the day. We *take actions* at home and on the job, and those actions fall into one of the Identification Table categories on pages 114-115.

It doesn't matter whether we're a shoemaker, coal miner, ballet dancer, engineer, or soldier. Each of us habitually uses leadership strategies, and if we analyze those strategies, they'll be predominately *Preactive* or *Reactive*. So the question we need to ask is: "What are *my* habitual strategies?" There are only three possible answers.

1. My habitual strategies are predominately *Preactive*.
2. My habitual strategies are predominately *Reactive*.
3. My habitual strategies are a 50/50 mix of *Preactive* and *Reactive*.

Many leaders find themselves in either category 2 or 3. They're either habitually *Reactive*, or they're habitually a mix of the two strategies. In either case, they're not being *Preactive* enough. That's why the theme of this book is to make *Preactive* strategies our dominant strategies both as individuals and as group leaders.

Okay, but how do we know for sure which strategies are our predominant ones? In Chapter 4, we learned that in order to be a *Preactive* leader we had to *identify* the situations we were acting on by using the two Identification Tables on pages 114-115 and then we had to focus on the Effective-Efficient situations. Quite logically, habitual strategies can be identified the same way. Like individual actions, habitual strategies also take their identities from the situations we act on the most frequently.

So to identify our habitual strategies, we simply use the two Identification Tables with an open mind and honestly identify our daily actions. We list the actions we've taken during a typical work month, and we identify them. Such a list can be developed from appointment books, time sheets, calendars, emails, project files, and whatever other sources of personal actions we have available. In fact, let's take the *habitual strategies test* now.

The Personal Habitual Strategies Test

To take the Personal Habitual Strategies Test, enter the appropriate numbers in the boxes below. In each box, enter the number of actions you took in that category during the past month. If the past month wasn't typical because of a special crisis or project, use figures from a month that was typical of your normal work.

Part 1: Actions Taken to *Direct* Tasks
Before Trouble Started

☐ Number of Working Actions taken in Normal Work situations to move work toward objectives and goals

☐ Number of Improving Actions taken to make standards better in Work Improvement situations to surprise and delight recipients

☐ Number of Blocking Actions taken to prevent Likely Cause situations from "hatching" and creating Future Trouble

☐ Total *Preactive* Actions Taken

Part 2: Actions Taken to *Correct* Tasks
After Trouble Started

☐ Number of Suppressing Actions taken to control the costs and damage of Current Trouble situations in tasks

☐ Number of Correcting Actions taken to remove True Cause situations that were causing trouble in tasks

☐ Number of Preparing Actions set up to wait to suppress the costs and damage of Future Trouble situations in tasks

☐ Total *Reactive* Actions Taken

☐ Total *Preactive* and *Reactive* Actions Taken

☐ Percentage of *Preactive* Actions Taken

☐ Percentage of *Reactive* Actions Taken

Of course, the result we're hoping for with this test is that the majority of your monthly actions will fall into the first set of boxes (the *Preactive* boxes). Naturally, all of us take a few actions in *all* the boxes during a typical work month. But we're hoping that the *Preactive* boxes will be dominant because that will show that your habitual leadership strategy is *directive* and *offensive-minded*.

Now, to think a little deeper, let's assume for a moment that you take this test and are a little confused by it. You can't remember, or can't find, a record of the actions you took in the past month, so you have trouble putting accurate numbers in the boxes. What should you do now?

If such is the case, you can make a "judgment call" about the test with the *51% Rule*. If you treat Part 1 and Part 2 of the test as two broad *packages* of actions that you took during the month, you can probably make an overall guess about which package dominated your work *51% or more* of the time. Based on instinct and knowledge of your job role and setting, you can probably estimate whether most of your actions fell into Part 1 (*Preactiveness*) or whether most of them fell into Part 2 (*Reactiveness*). This can give you a general idea of whether your personal culture tends to be mostly *Preactive* or mostly *Reactive*—and you can plan to be more specific with your tests in the future.

It's also interesting to realize that we can take a Group Habitual Strategies Test. This same test can be taken by a family, sports team, civic club, church, corporation, government agency, or any other group of people, simply by recording the totals of all the actions taken by all the members of the group. If the majority of the group's actions fall into the *Preactive* boxes, the group has a *Preactive* culture, and vice versa.

Next, to make the Personal Habitual Strategies Test even easier to understand, let's see an example of how it looks filled out. To do that, let's return to the series of diagrams we've been using in previous chapters for the brick walkway you've been laying for the Terry Johnson family. These diagrams depicted six kinds of situations and six kinds of actions that you took for the Johnsons during the month of September, so what we can do now is count the types of actions you took on the walkway, and put them in the boxes on the test. Of course, our hope is that you worked on the walkway with a *Preactive* culture. But let's see how well you did.

A Personal Habitual Strategies Test of Work on the Brick Walkway

Part 1: Actions Taken to *Direct* Tasks
Before Trouble Started

6 Number of Working Actions taken in Normal Work situations to move work toward objectives and goals. *We talked about the brick walkway in six different chapters of the book, and if we assume you were working on the walkway each time we mentioned it, you've earned a count of six in this box.*

2 Number of Improving Actions taken to make standards better in Work Improvement situations to surprise and delight recipients. *You upgraded the quality standard on the Johnson's bricks from MW grade to SW grade and upgraded the time standard on the job from 60 minutes a day to 90 minutes a day, so you earned a count of two in this box.*

5 Number of Blocking Actions taken to prevent Likely Cause situations from "hatching" and creating Future Trouble. *You took five Blocking Actions on Likely Cause situations in the brick walkway: You put plastic over the new bricks each night. You locked the tools in the garage each night.*

You sealed the mortar bag with duct tape against moisture. You put yellow caution tape around the new bricks, and you advised the family of your schedule for the next day, so you earned a count of five in this box.

[13] Total *Preactive* Actions Taken

Part 2: Actions Taken to *Correct* Tasks
After Trouble Started

[1] Number of Suppressing Actions taken to control the costs and damage of Current Trouble situations in tasks. *You took one Suppressing Action on one Current Trouble in the brick walkway: When the trainee at the building supply store shipped you off-color bricks, you had to have them replaced, so you earned a count of one in this box.*

[1] Number of Correcting Actions taken to remove True Cause situations that were causing trouble in tasks. *You took one Correcting Action on one True Cause situation in the brick walkway: When your tools were mysteriously disappearing from the shelf in the garage, you used the cause-finding process to find the True Cause (Little Pete was taking them) and had the Johnson family take a Correcting Action by having the soccer families help with the boy's secret tree house, so you earned a count of one in this box.*

1 Number of Preparing Actions set up to wait to suppress the costs and damage of Future Trouble situations in tasks. *You took one Preparing Action on one Future Trouble situation in the brick walkway: Due to the threat of a freak October snowstorm, you purchased a tarp big enough to cover the walkway and trained the family how to use it in case a storm hit, so you earned a count of one in this box.*

3 Total *Reactive* Actions Taken

16 Total *Preactive* and *Reactive* Actions Taken

81 Percentage of *Preactive* Actions Taken

19 Percentage of *Reactive* Actions Taken

Summary: In this Personal Habitual Strategies Test of your actions on the Johnson's brick walkway project, you took 13 actions in response to Effective-Efficient sits (as defined by Table 1, page 114). But you only took three actions in response to Ineffective-Inefficient sits (as defined by Table 2 on page 115).

So the test showed that 81% of your actions were *Preactive*. Or said another way, you took 300% more *Preactive* actions than you did *Reactive* actions. Clearly, your actions on the brick walkway were 51% or more *Preactive*—a dominance of *Preactiveness*. Thus, if this case had been a true life experience that showed your true daily habits, you would have been living a *Preactive* personal culture. That's what we want. We want and need a *Preactive* culture in our personal lives and jobs. And that statement leads us to our second *Preactive* Conclusion in the book to strengthen your personal leadership.

Second Conclusion to Strengthen Your Leadership

Use Preactive Strategies
Make Preactive strategies your habitual strategies, and teach your coworkers and family to do the same thing.

Of course, that's easier said than done. That's why our next chapter is about leadership tactics—about specifically how to implement the principles you've learned in this chapter. But right now, you might be asking yourself, *Okay, but what does all this mean? What should I do next?* Let's answer that as we prepare to close this chapter.

What Should I Do Next?

This chapter described several leadership principles and techniques—all of them good. But what do they actually *mean* to you in your busy everyday life? If you're like many people, you already have enough stress and confusion. You probably

---

Second Conclusion to
Strengthen Your Leadership
Use Preactive Strategies
Make Preactive strategies your habitual strategies.
Teach your coworkers and family to do the same thing.

---

need *fewer* things to think about, not more. In the opening sentences of this chapter, we said this chapter was going to show you a picture of *Preactive* leadership that was inspiring and that would give you hope for a better life and job.

So the question now becomes: *Can* the *Preactive* habitual strategies you've learned in this chapter give you hope for a better life and job? The simple answer is "yes." A *Preactive* culture *can* give you more free time, satisfaction, rewards, and benefits. The solution to a better life and job must always be to become more effective and efficient in all that we do, right? The solution to a better life and job isn't to become more ineffective and inefficient in what we do, is it?

The real danger we face is that, as the old proverb says, "Like breeds like." The more ineffective and inefficient we are, the more ineffective and inefficient we tend to become. Think about that a second. That's definitely *not* the road to more free time, satisfaction, rewards, and benefits.

The good news is that the proverb also works in reverse. The more effective and efficient we are, the more effective and efficient we tend to become. And that's how to achieve more goals, bonuses, and promotions with less trouble, effort, and brainpower.

The lesson is this. All of us need to start forming the new habit of seeking out the Effective-Efficient sits in our lives and jobs and then focusing our time, energy, and attention on *them*. Remember, the hallmark of a *Preactive* culture is living and working in the absence of trouble. Think a moment about what it would mean to live in the absence of trouble. To live *without* trouble is winning. To live *with* trouble isn't winning.

So, can we put the whole meaning of this chapter in a nut-shell? Yes. In a nutshell, here's what this chapter is asking you to *do*.

What You Should Do Next

For the next three weeks (21 days), use Theory Y values whenever possible and seek out and act on as many Normal Work sits, Work Improvement sits, and Likely Cause sits as you can find both in your life and on your job.

Do that, and you're forming a personal leadership culture of *Preaction* based on Y values. *That's* how you can double your leadership ability in one week. What could be better than that? What's a better way to spend your time and energy?

Summary of Chapter 11

1. Leadership strategy is the general, overall set of *values* and *actions* a leader uses to *direct* and *correct* personal or group work toward a goal in the most effective and efficient way.

2. There are two basic kinds of leadership strategies: *Preactive* and *Reactive*.

3. There are two parts to all strategies: *values* and *actions*.

4. There are two ways to apply strategies: as an individual leading him or herself in a personal task or as a group leader in a group task.

5. We identify strategies by using the Identification Tables on pages 114-115.

6. *Preactive* strategies are the best overall strategies because they're the most effective ways to reach a goal and because they're the only ones that prevent Future Trouble.

7. Each of us uses leadership strategies. But we may be using a predominant *Reactive* strategy or a 50/50 balance of

---

What You Should Do Next

For the next three weeks (21 days), use Theory Y values
whenever possible and seek out and act on as many
Normal Work sits, Work Improvement sits, and
Likely Cause sits as you can find both in your
life and on your job.

Preactive and *Reactive* strategies, which means we're using too much *Reactiveness* in our lives and jobs.

8. A leadership "style" is the set of *values* (ethics, standards) that are guiding a leader's decision-making in a strategy.

9. Theory X (autocratic) and Theory Y (teamworking) values are the tools we're using in this book to interpret *leadership values.* Both sets of values serve a good purpose when needed and either one can be best if a situation demands that style.

10. The big mistake some leaders make is that they use the *same* set of values (usually the Theory X autocratic values) to guide every action they take. However, since all situations don't *need* X values, leaders who do that are using the *wrong* values in some of their situations. Leaders need the patience and courage to identify which set of leadership values a situation needs and the wisdom and strength to apply the correct values to that situation.

11. Employees who are led with X values for long periods of time become increasingly more immature by riding "the down escalator." In reverse, employees who are led with Y values for long periods of time become increasingly more mature by riding "the up escalator." For this reason alone, Y leadership values are generally the best ones to use long-term.

12. Culture is the *total habits* of an individual or group, including the habits of setting clear standards, making best choices, using appropriate X or Y values in situations, and focusing on *Preactive, directive,* and *offensive-minded* strategies as much as possible.

13. It takes three weeks to form a new habit, good or bad. After that, the habit grows stronger weekly until it's fully entrenched. This is important to know because it means that the good habit of *Preactive* strategies is formed the same way.

14. All leaders use leadership strategies daily. But the key to effective and efficient leadership is to use predominantly *Preactive* strategies with predominantly Theory Y values.

15. The Personal Habitual Strategy Test is a tool for judging which strategy (*Preactive* or *Reactive*) a leader has emphasized during a work month. The *51% Rule* can be used to make a judgment call about which strategy a leader is emphasizing, if factual evidence isn't available.

In closing our chapter on strategies, let's realize that there's a learning curve in *Preactive* leadership. That's true of everything in life. Nobody becomes *Preactive* overnight. There's a transitional period, and leaders become more *Preactive* with experience and practice.

Learning curves vary with the amount of *time* invested. So in Chapter 12, we'll see a blueprint for implementing *Preactive* leadership in a time-conscious way. We'll see the specific tactics needed to implement *Preactiveness* minute-by-minute and hour-by-hour in our daily tasks, chores, and work.

CHAPTER 12

TACTICAL *PREACTIVE* LEADERSHIP

S ome years ago, I was sitting in the office of a Fortune 500 executive. Our negotiations were interrupted by a phone call, and my attention wandered as my client talked on the phone. I glanced around his office and noticed a small gilt-edged frame on his desk. In beautiful hand-lettered script it read, "*If you don't have troubles, you're not in the game.*"

I know the little frame was meant to be amusing and motivating, but to me, it betrayed once again the upside-down priorities that many leaders have. In recent chapters, we've talked at length about *suppressive-bias*, and we know from Chapter 8 that the word "troubles" refers to Current Trouble situations in our work. So in effect, this Fortune 500 executive's desk sign was saying three things: that Current Troubles are the mark of a leader; that fighting waste, confusion, and complaints are the earmark of leadership; and that coping with defects, failures, and stress are a leader's badge of honor.

But we squashed that myth in Chapters 8 and 10. In those chapters we discussed society's *suppressive-bias*, and we talked about the billions of dollars that societies spend on *Reactive, corrective, defensive-minded* systems such as fire fighters, police, hospitals, prisons, psychiatrists, repair shops, and rework departments while spending relatively little on preventive systems.

We said that responding to trouble, no matter how aggressively and heroically we do it, is not a sign of strong leadership. It's a sign of weak leadership. We said that avoiding trouble (working in the *absence* of trouble) is the true hallmark of leadership excellence.

But precisely *how* do we work without trouble? How do we avoid trouble in our tasks? It's time to talk specifics, and talking specifics means talking *tactics.* As we saw with the word "strategy" in the previous chapter, the word "tactics" is also a military word and also comes from a Greek root. In its root, the word *tactics* meant to put things in proper order or to arrange things in proper sequence for a battle. Using that military meaning, let's define *leadership tactics.*

The Definition of Preactive Leadership Tactics

*The specific **types** of actions, and the specific **sequence** of actions, that a leader uses to **direct** and **correct** personal or group work toward a goal in the most effective and efficient way.*

At the end of the previous chapter, we started moving toward tactical thinking when we suggested that for the next three weeks you should act on as many *Preactive* situations as you can find and that you should use Theory Y values on as many of them as possible. We've also agreed since Chapter 1 that there's a learning curve in *Preactive* leadership and that you'll increase in *Preactive* leadership in direct proportion to how much time you invest in practicing it.

But now you need to know exactly what to do. So the purpose of Chapter 12 is to give you a blueprint of the specific *types* of actions and the specific *sequence* of actions that it takes to be a *Preactive* leader. This chapter gives you five interlocking tactics that you can implement weekly and that can double your level of *Preactiveness* in a matter of hours. However, since many of us grew up in *suppressive-biased* societies, the first of these interlocking tactics deals with an *attitude adjustment* that many of us need.

Preactive Tactic One

Have an Offensive Attitude that
Keeps Trouble from Starting

In 1832, the military writer, Carl von Clausewitz, wrote in his classic book, *On War* that the best defense is a good *offense*. Clausewitz said that if we merely sit and defend ourselves when enemies attack, we'll soon wear down and be defeated. He wrote that defense merely delays a defeat and that the way to win a battle is to be on the *offensive*.

Today, Clausewitz's words have been used as personal inspiration by many famous sports figures, including the prizefighter Jack Dempsey and the coach of the Green Bay Packers, Vince Lombardi. Moreover, if you read between the lines, you'll realize that Clausewitz's principle is also the theme of this book. We've been saying for many pages that *defensive-mindedness* spells defeat in life and work and that *offensive-mindedness* wins our battles. We've been saying for several chapters that leaders must be *offensive-*

> **Leadership Tactics**
> *The specific **types** of actions and the specific **sequence** of actions, that a leader uses to **direct** and **correct** personal or group work toward a goal in the most effective and efficient way.*

minded to have any hope of long term success in the workplace. So let's stop here and define what we mean by the word *offensive*.

In the military, an "offensive" is when an army is attacking and gaining ground against the enemy. In sports, a team's "offense" is when its players are controlling the ball and scoring points against the opposing team. But here's what an *offensive* means in leadership.

The Definition of Offensive-Minded Leadership

Using Preactive strategies and tactics to reach goals and objectives by keeping trouble from starting that **hasn't started** *yet.*

The purpose of *offensive-minded* leadership is not simply to reach goals and objectives—although that's very important. Its purpose is to reach goals and objectives *with the least possible trouble.* Compare that to the little sign on the Fortune 500 executive's desk that said, *"If you don't have troubles, you're not in the game."*

That executive's sign seemed to exalt *defensiveness*. It seemed to praise the virtues of *Reactiveness*. It seemed to say that the end game is *correcting* trouble. Of course, there's nothing wrong with being *defensive* if you must—if it's too late and you can't do anything else. Sometimes the circumstances mandate *Reactiveness*. If a military unit is ambushed, if a sports team loses the ball, or if a competitor invents a product better than yours, the

> ## *Offensive-Minded* **Leadership**
> *Using Preactive strategies and tactics to reach goals and objectives by keeping trouble from starting that* **hasn't started** *yet.*

only option is being *defensive*. But that's not what we're talking about. In this chapter, we're talking about a special focus, a specific attitude, a particular mindset. We're talking about a brand of leadership that's *offensive* to its core.

So, let's return now to *Preactive* Tactic One. Here's specifically what to do. To implement *Preactive* Tactic One, all you do is adopt the new mental attitude that your job is to keep as much trouble as possible from ever *starting* in your life and work. Your new attitude is not to repair trouble. It's to avoid trouble. It's not to dig a deeper foxhole. It's to launch preemptive strikes against the enemy. In *Preactive* Tactic One, you adopt a new attitude of leadership that says: *My purpose is to attack the Likely Causes of Future Trouble before they have time to attack me.*

This new attitude is the underpinning for our next four tactics, and it's also the underpinning of the three new *Preactive*

Templates we'll see in this chapter. Okay, now let's continue on to *Preactive Tactic Two*.

Preactive Tactic Two

Have Clear and Agreed On Standards

As we said earlier, the five tactics in this chapter interlock and support one another. So let's assume that you've adopted your new attitude in *Preactive* Tactic One. You've accepted your new job as a preemptive leader. With that settled, let's turn to the Identification Table 1 on page 114 and start learning the deeper secrets of *Preactive* tactics.

First, notice that the title of Table 1 says the situations and actions are for the purpose of *Directing Tasks Before Trouble Starts with Preactive, Offensive-Minded Strategies and Tactics.*

But precisely how does that work? We learned in earlier chapters that the foundation of leadership is decision-making,

---

Preactive Leadership Tactic One
Have an Offensive Attitude that
Keeps Trouble from Starting

Preactive Leadership Tactic Two
Have Clear and Agreed On Standards

and that the situations listed in Table 1 are all generic Choice Situations requiring the best Decision Actions to satisfy their needs. So, to be a *Preactive* leader, you need to do two things:

1. Focus your weekly action-taking on the three situations in Table 1.

2. Choose and implement the best actions in those situations.

But—and it's a big "but"—we agreed in earlier chapters that the key to choosing best actions is to have previously *set, clear, and agreed on standards*. In fact, if we analyzed all the books, seminars, classes, DVDs, and speeches produced annually on the subject of leadership, the one principle that would shine through them all would be that leaders need previously set, clear, and agreed on standards. Glancing at Table 1 again, you can see three reasons why that's true:

1. Clear and agreed on standards make best Working Actions possible.

2. Clear and agreed on standards make best Improving Actions possible.

3. Clear and agreed on standards make best Blocking Actions possible.

In other words, *Preactive* leadership is all about clear and agreed on standards. Standards are the keys to decision-making, and clear and agreed on standards are the keys to *Preactive* decision-making. In Chapter 5, we said the word "standards" is the most important word in leadership. That's still true. Your success as a *Preactive* leader depends on your ability to set clear standards and, when necessary, to convince other people to follow them. So let's review how that's done.

How to Set Clear and Agreed On Standards

In Chapter 4, we talked about smokescreen statements. We said a smokescreen statement is one that has fuzzy fact or a missing fact in one or more of its *what-who-when-where-amount* factual categories. But here's a deeper truth. Standards are *statements,* too. Standards are *statements* of what situations need. So, *Preactive* Tactic Two requires us to clarify any smokescreen standards in our tasks at home and on the job. To get ready for that, let's define a *smokescreen standard.*

The Definition of a Smokescreen Standard

*Any standard that has a fuzzy fact or a missing fact in one or more of its five **what-who-when-where-amount** factual categories.*

The flip side of a smokescreen standard is a *clear standard.* Let's define that, too.

The Definition
of a Clear Standard

Any standard that has at least one clear fact
*in each of its five **what-who-when-where-***
***amount** factual categories.*

In Chapter 4, you learned how to clarify fuzzy words and smokescreen statements by asking special clarifying questions. But you might want to refresh your memory of those tools before we use them again here. So, please review the relevant sections of Chapter 4 now. Start with *Fuzzy Words* on page 88 and read through *What if You Don't Know the Answer* on page 109. After reviewing those parts of Chapter 4, return to this page and continue reading with the Case of Terry's Walkway Revisited.

Smokescreen Statement

*Any standard that has a fuzzy fact or a missing fact in one or more of its five **what-who-when-where-amount** factual categories.*

Clear Standard

*Any standard that has at least one clear fact in each of its five **what-who-when-where-amount** factual categories.*

The Case of
Terry's Walkway Revisited

In Chapter 5, we introduced a mythical brick walkway that you were building for the Terry Johnson family. In your first conversation with Terry Johnson before starting work, you and Terry set some clear standards and agreed on them with a handshake. Those standards are shown below. But we've arranged them in a special *what-who-when-where-amount* structure, and we've added some new categories to the structure that we'll explain as we go along. This eleven-category structure is our fourth *Preactive* Template in this book, and it's purpose is to clarify the standards for your tasks. Let's see how it looks applied to the brick walkway.

A Standards-Clarifying Structure
for the Brick Walkway

1. *Goal*: (There's no goal in this case because it takes *less* than a year to complete.)

2. *Objective*: To build a brick walkway in the Johnson family's front yard by November 1st. (If this task was taking *more* than a year to complete, and thus had a *goal*, your intermediate objectives as stepping stones to the goal would be listed here.)

3. *Situation Statement:* The Johnsons need a brick walkway six feet wide and 100 feet long laid in the middle of our front yard by November 1st.

4. *Action Statement:* I want to choose the best Working Actions to lay a brick walkway six feet wide and 100 feet long in the middle of the Johnson's front yard by November 1st with the least risk of Future Trouble.

5. *What:* Use Moderate Weather (MW) grade bricks.

6. *Who:* Work alone as a private contractor for the Johnson family.

7. *When:* Work a minimum average of one hour per day. Work a maximum average of two hours per day. Start at a time of my choice this coming weekend. Finish the walkway by November 1st.

8. *Where:* Build the walkway in the middle of the front yard. Build the walkway from the city sidewalk to the front steps.

9. *Amount:* Build the walkway six feet wide. Build the walkway 100 feet long. Build the walkway for a fee of $900.

10. *How*: Lay all the bricks flat on the ground. Lay all the bricks with quarter-inch spaces between them. Mortar, shovels, hammers, wood, tape, and all other tools and supplies will be provided by the Johnson family. (Note: Some of the data in the *how* category might also be recognized and listed under the *what* category, but duplicated data isn't necessary.)

11. *Why*: The Johnsons want to increase the value of their property.

Notice that a *Standards-Clarifying Structure* like this one is a collection of interrelated standards statements. Clear standards for a task usually aren't just one word, number, phrase, or sentence. They're a package of statements with at least one statement in each of the five *what-who-when-where-amount* factual categories.

Notice also that we've added several new categories to this structure to provide for a *goal* or *objective*, a *Situation Statement*, an *Action Statement*, a *how* category, and a *why* category. This was done to make the task standards absolutely clear to anyone who might read them.

When completed, a *Standards-Clarifying Structure* is a powerful filter that selects the best actions to take (and not to take) in any task. Said in reverse, we *can't* take any action that the structure doesn't allow. In the brick walkway story, we *can't* build a walkway four feet wide, or eight feet wide, or ten feet wide. But we *can* build a walkway six feet wide. That's because the structure screens out any size but a walkway six feet wide.

Finally, we can never forget that a *Standards-Clarifying Structure* must have the *agreement* of the superiors, coworkers, clients, family members, or other persons who are being influenced by the task. We said in Chapter 5 that the standards in a task must be agreed on by all parties before quality work can start on a task. To illustrate that, let's have some fun. Let's consider a scenario that proves how critical the need for agreed on standards really is. We'll call this the Case of the Neighborly Trap.

The Case of the Neighborly Trap

Let's imagine that both you and Terry Johnson were clueless about how to be *Preactive* leaders when you originally negotiated the brick walkway task. So now let's create a clueless version of your negotiations with Terry back in Chapter 5.

Instead of what actually happened, this time let's imagine that Terry approaches you at your mailbox and says, "Hey, I need a new brick walkway in front of my house, and I want you to build it for me. If you can build it for $900, go ahead and get started."

You're uneasy with this vague assignment, so you ask, "Okay, but how do you want me to build it?"

Terry responds, "Oh, I don't know. You're the brick expert. Just build it the way you think it ought to be built."

Thus, wanting to be a friendly, loving, and helpful neighbor, you accept the assignment and get started. When you're finished, you invite the family outside to see what you've created. What do you think the family would say as they viewed the new walkway?

Well, they might say, "Whoa, this is beautiful. We love it!"

But there's also a chance they might *not* say that. Instead, they might squint their eyes and say, "Well, it's okay, I guess. But it's sort of narrow, isn't it? And aren't those bricks over there a little crooked? In fact, the whole thing's a funny shape, isn't it? I thought you knew what we wanted."

Can you see where the conversation is heading? You're in the neighborly trap. The rule is that if the person or persons assigning you a task don't provide you a *Standards-Clarifying Structure* for the task, it's your responsibility to help them create one. If you don't, you're heading for the neighborly trap.

In the most simple terms, if you don't have a structure of clear standards for a Normal Work situation, you don't understand the task, and you can't choose the best Working Actions to satisfy the needs of the task. Even worse, you probably don't have two specialized standards that we haven't discussed yet but that are vital in every structure of clear standards. One or both of these two special standards are requirements in every *Standards-Clarifying Structure.*

Have Clear
Goals and Objectives

Some leaders don't realize it (and some textbooks don't teach it), but *goals* and *objectives* are special types of standards. We saw these two words for the first time back in Chapter 5 on our list of 24 synonyms for standards. So let's say it again: *goals* and *objectives* are standards, too.

The difference between goals and objectives and regular standards is that goals and objectives are standards that are *specialized in time.* Let's explain that. We know from Chapter 5 that standards are words, numbers, and phrases that describe what situations need and that measure the quality of actions taken in those situations, right? Okay, but don't goals and objectives do the same thing?

Think a moment to our tales of the two physicians in the previous chapter. In our first tale, we said that Dr. Patterson's *goal* was to write his memoirs. But in our second tale, we said that Dr. Watson's *objective* was to catch the thief in his clinic.

Why did we use two different words in the tales? Why didn't we say that both characters had a goal or that both characters had an objective? The answer is that goals and objectives *measure two different lengths of time*, and the tales of the physicians happened in two different lengths of time.

To explain that, the word *goal* came from a root meaning to reach a boundary or to reach the end of an activity. For example, if a sports team today makes a *goal*, that play ends and a new play starts. So a goal is a specialized standard that measures the *end* of tasks.

Moreover, since many organizations close their books every 12 months to compute costs, income, and taxes for the year, many leaders use the word *goal* to indicate a time period of 12 months or more in the future. And since we were assuming in Dr. Patterson's tale that it would take him more than a year to write his memoirs, we called his purpose a *goal*.

On the other hand, the word *objective* came from a root meaning a target to be captured. For example, in the military today an objective is a bridge or hill to be captured. Thus, an objective is a specialized standard that measures a *target* within a task that's a stepping stone to the goal.

However, many people can't visualize a target more than a few weeks away; so many leaders use the word objective to indicate a time of less than 12 months in the future. For example, many organizations set weekly, monthly, quarterly, or semi-annual objectives in their tasks. And since we were assuming in Dr. Watson's tale that it would take him *less* than a year to catch the thief in his clinic, we called his purpose an *objective*.

Using these definitions, the word *objective* is also the correct word for our brick walkway story. You had an agreement with the Johnsons to build their walkway in 60 days. So in the *Standards-Clarifying Structure* above, we called your purpose in the walkway task an *objective.*

To close the loop, regular standards measure work in a *current* or *continuous* timeframe. For example, regulation signs such as No Parking, Keep Off the Grass, Quiet Zone, and Speed Limit 45 are regular standards. They measure work continuously. Regular standards measure performance, behavior, and work immediately—instead of monthly, quarterly, semi-annually, and annually.

Last of all, goals, objectives, and standards always link together in a chain and should be compatible with each other in that chain. This means that if we read a chain of standards from the top down, it reads like this: Goals are linked to compatible objectives, and objectives are linked to compatible standards. In reverse, if we read a chain of standards from the bottom up, it reads like this: Standards are linked to compatible objectives, and objectives are linked to compatible goals. This is good news because if your daily actions are satisfying your regular standards, you'll eventually reach your objectives, and in time you'll reach your goal.

To illustrate how a linkage of standards works, let's talk about the Johnson's brick walkway again. But this time, let's imagine the Johnson family gives you a new assignment. Now they want you to build a walkway 1,000 feet long, and they give you a year to build it. Using the *amount* factual category as an illustration, the linkage of standards in this new task would look as follows.

1. The goal: Lay a 1,000-foot brick walkway in one year
2. The objectives: Lay 250 feet of bricks per quarter
3. The standard: Lay four feet of bricks per afternoon

Note that if you satisfy your regular (continuous) standard of laying four feet of bricks per day, you'll reach your objectives of laying 250 feet of bricks a quarter, and in a year you'll achieve your goal of laying 1,000 feet of bricks. Also, note that the chain makes perfect sense reading from the top down or the bottom up.

Now, since bookstore shelves sag with books on goal-setting, we'll stop our discussion of annual goals, intermediate objectives, and regular standards here. Instead, it's time to put into *practice* what you've learned. Here's your assignment.

Clear Standards for Your Major Tasks

Here's where the rubber meets the road. We've already said several times that you'll be successful in *Preactive* leadership in direct proportion to how much time you invest practicing it. There's a big difference between just reading about *Preaction* and actually implementing it. So here's what to do next. On your computer, smart phone, yellow pad, or whatever you use, do the following.

- Depending on what leadership role you're going to clarify, make a list of the *five* most important family or job tasks you're currently working on. These are the five most important Normal Work situations you're taking action on in that role.

- Fill out the eleven categories of the *Standards-Clarifying Structure* below for each of the tasks you've listed. (This may take several days of thought and research and, remember, your superiors or the other people involved in the task must *agree* with what you've written.)

There can be no fuzzy words in your statements, and there might be several statements per category. But remember, there must be at least one statement per category. Refer to the brick walkway example above to remember how to fill out the categories. Now, here's your *clarifying structure* for your clear and agreed on standards.

Writing Clear and Agreed On Standards With the Standards-Clarifying Structure

Using the following eleven-category template as a guide, and discussing the categories with superiors, coworkers, and family members as needed, write clear and agreed on standards statements for the five most important family or job tasks assigned to you. Do necessary research by phone, files, interviews, appointment books, computer files, the Internet, and so on as needed. Create the following categories for each of your five major tasks.

1. *Goal:* (Use this category if the task will take *more* than a year to finish. Skip this level and start at category two if the task will take *less* than a year to finish and thus has no goal.)

2. *Objective:* (Use this category if the task will take *less* than a year to finish, or if the task will take *more* than a year to finish and has a goal but needs intermediate objectives as stepping stones to the goal.)

3. *Situation Statement:* (The statement of the task as it was assigned to you.)

4. Action *Statement:* (Your statement of the way you will perform the task.)

5. *What:* (What needs to be done—fully described.)

6. *Who:* (Who needs to do the task—you and/or the other people involved in the work or influenced by the work.)

7. *When:* (When the task needs to be done—all times, days, and dates.)

8. *Where:* (Where the task needs to be done—all locations.)

9. *How much / many:* (Amount of the task that needs to be done—all amounts.)

10. *How:* (How the task needs to be done—any items not already listed under the *what* category. Duplication isn't necessary.)

11. *Why:* (Why the task needs to be done—other people's motives or purposes, if relevant.)

Now, be brave. Take heart. This template may look intimidating at first glance. But as someone once said, "If not now, when?" These exercises must be done at some point in your career if you're going to be a *Preactive* leader. Filling out this eleven-category structure is where assertive, courageous, and preemptive leadership begins. This is where your leadership abilities can double or triple in a matter of days. Thus, even if this exercise takes you several hours to complete, your leadership skills will permanently rise to a newer and higher level by doing it. That's worth any investment of time, thought, and effort.

More, this exercise is also the basis of the third *Preactive* Conclusion in this book for strengthening your personal leadership.

Third Conclusion to Strengthen Your Leadership

Clarify Your Standards

Using the Standards-Clarifying Structure, review all the standards in all your major tasks each week, and be certain all of them are set, clear, and agreed on.

Next, let's continue our study of tactical *Preactive* leadership by turning our attention to *Tactic Three*.

Preactive Tactic Three

Use Theory Y Values in Every Appropriate Situation

In Chapter 11, we said that we should constantly use Theory Y values in our action-taking whenever they're appropriate. That rule was even the subject of our first *Preactive* Conclusion in the book for strengthening your personal leadership. As you'll recall back in Chapter 11, your first Conclusion went like this:

Recognize which values your situations need and apply the correct X or Y styles, emphasizing Y values and using X values only when absolutely necessary.

This Conclusion is saying that we should *only* use Theory X values when we *can't* do anything else. That is, unless the situation mandates the use of X values, we should always use Theory Y values as our default tactic.

Theory Y values, as you recall, are team oriented, relationship oriented, people centered, creative, and empowering. They're values founded on open communications, listening to what others have to say, using team decision-making, and instilling confidence, courage, and independence in followers. We said Y values are rooted in the assumption that people want to work, enjoy work, and *will work* if treated with respect and if motivated with trust, training, and clear standards.

With these principles in mind, the question then becomes: Why wouldn't *all* leaders use Y values in every possible situa-

---

Third Conclusion to Strengthen Your Leadership

Clarify Your Standards
Using the Standards-Clarifying Structure, review all the standards in all your major tasks each week, and be certain all of them are set, clear, and agreed on.

tion? They should. But they don't. Why not? The answer may hurt. Research shows that many leaders don't use Y values at home or on the job because they're *too* impatient and self-centered to do so. That's a shocker, but true.

So what we're asking you to do in *Preactive* Tactic Three is to take a personal vow that, from this moment forward, you'll use Y values in every situation where they're appropriate. As we said, Y values should be your default value system. However, there's still another reason why X values shouldn't be used unless absolutely necessary.

Don't Ride the Down Escalator

In the previous chapter, we talked at length about the immaturity-maturity cycles that Dr. Chris Argyris of Yale discovered. He found that the *longer* employees are led with Theory X (autocratic) values, the *less* confident and creative they become as employees, as if they were on a downward spiral into immaturity. I named that principle *the down escalator* in the previous chapter. But if employees *are* riding the down escalator, whose fault is it? Let's talk honestly once again about the down escalator and about some additional research that links to it.

We talked about the children's game *Follow the Leader* in the previous chapter, and we said that the obedience of the children who were the followers gave great authority to, and put great responsibility on, the child who was the leader. After all, if the children playing the game got their shoes wet or tore their clothes, whose fault was it? Was it the fault of the followers? Or was it the fault of the leader who led them through the puddles and briars?

Dr. William Edwards Deming of Yale was probably America's most famous guru on quality management. He's the person who taught quality management to the Japanese in the 1950s giving them their competitive edge for decades. In 1986, he wrote the best-selling book, *Out of the Crisis* launching the total quality management movement internationally. The Deming Institute and the Deming Prize are both named after him, and in 1987 President Ronald Reagan awarded him the prestigious National Medal of Technology.

So if anyone knew anything about how leadership effects followers, it was probably Deming. The trouble was that Deming made executives angry when he gave speeches. Fortune 500 executives were scandalized when Deming taught audiences that if things weren't going well in a company, it wasn't the fault of the followers. It was the fault of the *leaders*.

When the followers in an organization (the clerks, secretaries, assembly line workers, supervisors, and so forth) are producing poor quality, making bad decisions, and showing low morale, the leaders usually blame the *followers*. The leaders huddle behind the coffee machine and mutter in their mugs things like, "They're just lazy. Workers aren't loyal any more. Employees just don't work today the way their parents and grandparents did."

But Deming taught that if the leaders really want to know why their followers lack confidence, enthusiasm, and courage, the leaders should *look in a mirror to see who's at fault.* Think about it. Deming's research verified what Chris Argyris discovered. If workers are confused, discouraged, and inefficient on the job, why would it be *their* fault? Even children playing *Follow the Leader* know better than that. After all, who decides what products and services to produce in an organization? Who sets the budgets, forecasts, and schedules? Who arranges the financing, the lines of credit, and the stock offerings? Who sets the global strategies, goals, objectives, standards, and tactics for the organization?

Not the followers.

So let's drive a nail in the blame-game coffin, and agree here that if a group of followers is struggling (they could be in a college, civic club, church, family, or corporation), most of the blame—if not all the blame—rests with the leaders. Who else would be responsible? And that brings us to our fourth *Preactive* Conclusion for strengthening your personal leadership. Here it is.

Fourth Conclusion
to Strengthen Your Leadership

Accept Leadership Responsibility
If a person or group you're leading is on the down escalator,
that person or group isn't to blame. You're to blame.
Put them on the up escalator immediately.

If, perchance, you've been thoughtlessly using X values inappropriately and your followers are riding the down escalator in an immaturity spiral, hit the kill switch. Throw the escalator into full emergency stop. Start conditioning yourself this very minute to use Y values in every possible situation.

As a friend used to say, "No group can rise any higher than its leader." That's probably true. No matter what kind of group you're leading, your followers probably will never be more *Preactive* than you are yourself. So start today. Start holding more group meetings. Start truly listening to others. Make notes of what they say. Act on the notes. Ask others what they think should be done. Then take their advice. Lead group decision-making meetings. Start instilling confidence, courage, competence, clarity, and choice in your followers. You'll see a difference in a matter of days.

But now let's shift gears again. There's still something else you should also do. You should constantly raise the bar in your work.

Preactive Tactic Four

Constantly Raise the Bar

We've agreed that to be a *Preactive* leader, you must assertively seek out and act on the three situations listed in Table 1 on page 114. So let's continue our discussion of leadership tactics now by returning to Table 1.

Look at Row 2 where we list Work Improvement situations and the Improving Actions we take on them. We discussed WI sits and IAs in Chapter 6. As we saw in that chapter, Improving Actions are easy. They piggyback naturally on our lesson in Tactic Two about how to write clear and agreed on standards using the *Standards-Clarifying Structure.* All you need to do to take Improving Actions is to *replace* the old standards in that structure with new and *better* ones and then start meeting those new and better standards with your actions. That surprises superiors, coworkers, customers, family members, or whoever else is influenced by your actions, and they appreciate your unexpected efforts.

Textbooks call this upgrading, improving, innovating, or enriching your work. We're calling it Standards-Betterment—the habit of meeting a better standard than what you're already meeting and than what your recipient is already accepting.

In our chapter on Work Improvement, we used the analogy of a "bar" in a track meet—the long rod between two poles

---

Fourth Conclusion to
Strengthen Your Leadership

Accept Leadership Responsibility
If a person or group you're leading is on the down escalator,
that person or group isn't to blame. You're to blame.
Put them on the up escalator immediately.

---

that athletes try to jump over. We talked about how the judges raise the bar higher and higher, forcing the athletes to jump higher and higher until a winner emerges. To put it in different words, by constantly raising the bar, the judges are pushing the athletes to higher and higher levels of quality and that's what *Preactive* Tactic Four is all about—pushing yourself and others to higher and higher levels of quality.

Thus, the secret of Work Improvement is to constantly raise the bar for yourself and your followers. To make this principle clearer, ask yourself a question: What would happen in a track meet if the judges *stopped* raising the bar but continued to force the athletes to jump it? Two things would probably happen. First, the athletes would become demotivated and complacent and would jump without enthusiasm. Second, there would be no winner.

That's exactly what happens in the workplace when we keep meeting the *same old standards* in our work, month after month, year after year. We never jump any higher. We work without enthusiasm. And we never win. A client of mine used to jokingly say, "If ya' keep on doin' what you've always done, you'll keep on gettin' what you always got."

So to get ready for *Preactive* Tactic Four, stop here and re-read the summary of Chapter 6 on pages 188-190. By now you probably need to be refreshed on the principles of Work Improvement and rereading that summary will help. When you've finished the summary, return to this page and continue with the Case of the Abnormal New Cars.

The Case of the Abnormal New Cars

The word *abnormal* came from a root meaning not typical or beyond what's usual. So, the word refers to something that goes beyond what other people expect. To be *abnormal* is to do something above and beyond what people are accustomed to

---

Preactive Leadership Tactic Three
Use Theory Y Values in Every
Appropriate Situation

Preactive Leadership Tactic Four
Constantly Raise the Bar

---

seeing you do, and that's exactly what Improving Actions are. They're abnormal in the sense that they go beyond what superiors, coworkers, customers, family members, and others expect of you.

As an example of this principle, let's consider a real life illustration of how a normal standard became abnormal, and how that abnormal standard then became a new normal. I call this the Case of the Abnormal New Cars.

Years ago when you bought a new car, there was just enough gas in the tank to get you off the lot and to the nearest gas station. When you arrived at the dealership to take possession of your new car, it was parked on the outdoor lot and was often dusty inside and out. The first thing you often did before you showed your new car to friends was wash and polish it. A few weeks later, after you returned the car to the dealer for its first service, you had to bum a ride home or take a bus or cab because you had no other transportation. When the car was ready for pick up after servicing, you needed to bum another ride back to the dealer because there was no other way to get there.

Happily, that kind of customer service is gone with the wind. Today, that level of service would cause a riot. Buying a new car today is *abnormal* compared to those old standards of service. Nowadays, the gas tank is full. The car is waiting outside the showroom—and its spotless, shiny, and has that new-car smell. Today you receive gifts when you take possession of your new car such as a golf umbrella with the car company's logo on it, a leather-bound owner's manual, coupons for free service, free coffee and donuts, and plenty of smiling and hand-shaking by the staff. Later, when you return to the dealer for your car's first service, you're given a loaner to drive, your car gets free vacuuming and washing, and you get more free coffee, donuts, smiles, and handshaking.

Here's why all that happens today. Over the years, the old standards for service in new car buying gradually became *ab-normal* (untypical) as dealers raised the bar, surpassing old lev-els of service. Then, as the years slid by, this abnormal level of service gradually became the new *normal*, and everyone began to expect it in new car buying. The result was that what car buy-ers accept as normal today was actually yesterday's abnormal that gradually became the new normal. That's how raising the bar works.

But here's an interesting question. What will the next *ab-normal* level of service be in new car buying? And how soon will that next abnormal become the new normal in the car buy-ing of the future? In other words, what Improving Actions are new car dealers taking today that will gradually become new normals for car buyers in the future?

The principle is this. Improving Actions may seem abnor-mal at first and might surprise and delight people. But before long they become new normals, and the cycle repeats itself. Normal becomes abnormal, abnormal becomes normal, and

the cycle rolls on to better and higher levels of recipient satisfaction.

Here's the point. You need to start your *own* improvement
cycle rolling as soon as possible. That'll be easy because you
already know how to take Improving Actions. You learned that
in Chapter 6. So all you need to do now is get started. Next is
a *Standards-Improving Framework* you can use to start being
abnormal in your tasks. This six-category structure is the fifth
Preactive Template in the book, and it's purpose is to *improve
the standards* in your tasks. First, let's see how it applies to our
brick walkway story.

How to Do More
Than Other People Expect

Earlier in *Preactive* Tactic Two, you developed five *Standards-Clarifying Structures* for your five most important tasks.
That means you have set, clear, and agreed on standards for
each of the five major tasks in your life or job at this point in
time. Your next step is to retrieve these structures and start analyzing them for old *normals* that can be increased, decreased, or
changed in new ways to create added value for your recipients.

To see this process being applied, let's return for a moment
to the brick walkway standards set by you and Terry Johnson in
a previous chapter. But this time, let's look for ways to *improve*

the old standards that you and Terry originally sealed with a handshake.

Following is a summary or composite of the 13 original standards that you and Terry Johnson agreed on. However, now we're going to treat them as potential Work Improvement situations. (Special note: Unlike the *Standards-Clarifying Structure* we used in Tactic Two, we're not going to include the *Goal, Objective, Situation Statement, Choice Statement,* and *Why* categories in this framework because they describe the original assignment that Terry gave you. If we changed them, we'd be creating a new assignment, not improving the old one.)

In this new analysis of the standards you and Terry set, we've regrouped them under the six *what-who-where-where-amount-how* factual categories in the *Standards-Improving Framework,* and in order to answer the who category in the framework, we've added you and the Johnson family as the people involved in the task.

Next, all we need to do is decide whether any of the 13 old standards arranged under our framework can be *improved* and, if so, how. Be aware of the fact that Terry wouldn't *want* some of his standards changed. For example, he doesn't want the walkway to be wider than six feet. So we're skipping any of the 13 standards that Terry wouldn't want changed. Our thoughts for Improving Actions are italicized in parentheses following each standard.

A Standards-Improving Framework
for the Brick Walkway

1. *What:* Use MW grade bricks. (Is there a better grade? *Yes, there is the SW grade, and you ordered that grade for Terry.*)

2. *Who:* Work alone as a private contractor for the Johnson family.

3. *When:* Work a minimum of one hour a day. (Can you work longer? *Yes, and you did increase your work schedule to 1.5 hours a day for Terry.*)
   Work a maximum of two hours a day.
   Start this coming weekend.
   Finish by sundown on November 1st. (Can you finish earlier? *Yes, and by increasing your hours to 1.5 a day, you will finish earlier.*)

4. *Where:* Build the walkway in the middle of the front yard. Build the walkway from the city sidewalk to the front steps.

5. *Amount:* Build the walkway six feet wide.

   Build the walkway 100 feet long.

   Build the walkway for a fee of $900. (Can you do the task for less money? *Perhaps you could consider going back to Terry and offering to finish the walkway for $875.*)

6. *How:* Lay all the bricks flat on the ground.

   Lay all the bricks with quarter-inch spaces between them.

   Mortar, shovels, hammers, wood, tape, and all other tools and supplies will be provided by the Johnson family. (Can you or someone else provide the tools for the project? *Perhaps you could consider suggesting to Terry that you use your own tools to finish the walkway.*)

Okay, what did we discover doing this exercise? We discovered that at least *five* (36%) of the 13 original standards agreed on with Terry Johnson and regrouped under the six categories of the *Standards-Improving Framework* can be improved. And that's not unusual. It's common for between 30% and 50% of the original standards in tasks and projects to be open to improvement. Think about the potential for recipient satisfaction in that. Now, here's a blank copy of the *Standards-Improving Framework* for your personal use. Apply it to each of your five major tasks as discussed earlier.

Improving Your Own Standards
With the Standards-Improving Framework

1. *What:* (Can anything be increased, decreased, or otherwise changed in your *materials, procedures,* or *process* standards to create added value for your recipients?)

2. *Who:* (Can anything be increased, decreased, or changed in your *personnel* standards to create added value for your recipients?)

3. *When:* (Can anything be increased, decreased, or changed in your *schedule* or *timeframe* standards to create added value for your recipients?)

4. Where: (Can anything be increased, decreased, or changed in your location, *storage,* or *destination* standards to create added value for your recipients?)

5. *Amount:* (Can anything be increased, decreased, or changed your *numbers, inventory,* or *quantity* standards to create added value for your recipients?)

6. *How:* (Can anything be increased, decreased, or changed in your *techniques, technology, equipment,* or *tool* stand-

ards to create added value for your recipients? Special note: There may be some overlap between the *how* category and the *what* category—the same idea for improvement might be visible in both categories. The important thing is that the ideas become visible somewhere in the structure, but duplication is unnecessary.)

This framework shows how easy it is to improve the work on tasks and projects. The bad news is that people often *don't*. Sadly, many employees simply coast during the day. They get out of bed and go to work each morning merely to keep meeting the old standards in their tasks. As a seminar participant once said, "They're retired, but they've stayed on to draw the salary." This tendency of people to coast on the job leads to our fifth *Preactive* Conclusion in the book for strengthening your personal leadership.

Fifth Conclusion to Strengthen Your Leadership

Improve Your Standards

Using the Standards-Improving Framework, review all the standards in all your major tasks each week, and make at least one improvement in at least one standard.

This new habit means that you'll probably take at least 50 new Improving Actions in the coming year—and you might take 100 or more once the habit gets entrenched. Think about the positive impact that'll have on your life, your career, and your self-esteem.

Now, let's close our discussion of *Preactive* Tactic Four with the same statement that we made at the end Chapter 6: Every day in every way, look for a standard in a product, service, task, or behavior that can be raised, lowered, or altered to make things faster, quieter, cleaner, safer, longer-lasting, cheaper, easier, lighter, thinner, more simple, more colorful, more readable, more interesting, more modern, more convenient, more flexible, more complete, more accurate, more useful, more fun, or more profitable for your recipient, whoever he or she is, at no cost or obligation to him or her.

Next, our fifth and final tactic for *offensive-minded* leadership deals with those scary ol' *alligator eggs* again.

Preactive Tactic Five

Have Constant Alligator Egg Hunts

We talked earlier about the little sign on the Fortune 500 executive's desk that read, *"If you don't have troubles, you're not in the game."* We said that sign showed that many leaders have upside-down priorities. They have the habit of *suppressive-bias* to a greater or lesser extent. They think leadership is a process of heroically fighting trouble in work. It never occurs to them that leadership is a process of heroically *avoiding* trouble in work.

We've said repeatedly that the best way to be effective and efficient is not to have trouble. We said that's done by launching preemptive strikes against the Likely Causes of trouble. I jokingly call these preemptive strikes "alligator egg hunts." *Preactive* Tactic Five is about how to find and neutralize alligator eggs before they can "hatch" and create trouble. Turn to page 114 again. Table 1, Row 3 describes the last of our *Preactive* situations: Likely Cause sits (alligator eggs) and the Blocking Actions (the preemptive strikes) we take to neutralize them.

But before continuing, let's pause again for a refresher. It's time to reread another summary of an earlier chapter. Please turn back to pages 218-220 in Chapter 7 and reread the summary of that chapter. When finished, return to this page and continue with the Case of the Fearful Bricklayer.

The Case of the Fearful Bricklayer

Heroes and heroines in movies are often portrayed as fearless and that fearlessness often inspires their audiences. That's good. But it can also be bad because movies can teach us from childhood that *leaders* are fearless. And that's not true. The best leaders *do* have fear and they *should*. Here's why.

Fifth Conclusion to
Strengthen Your Leadership

Improve Your Standards

Using the Standards-Improving Framework, review all the standards in all your major tasks each week, and make at least one improvement in at least one standard.

The word *fear* came from a root that meant the threat of danger or exposure to danger. In its original meaning, the word simply meant to expect danger. But, being raised on heroic movies as many of us were, we think of fear as something non-heroic—it's a wimpy condition of being frightened, terrified, and panicked.

So there are really two kinds of fear. One is bad for leaders. One is good for leaders. The bad kind is the *frightened* kind. That's what we feel when we hear footsteps behind us in a dark alley. The good kind is a healthy *expectation* of trouble. That's what an army general feels while studying a map of the enemy's positions.

It's this second definition of fear that we need as *Preactive* leaders. We need to have fear in the good way. We need to have it in the form of a healthy expectation of trouble, and a healthy determination to launch preemptive strikes against the Likely Causes of that trouble. So, using this interpretation of the type of fear that *Preactive* leaders should have, let's look at the Case of the Fearful Bricklayer now—except that it's not a case. It's a test.

Back in Chapter 7, during your work as a bricklayer for the Johnson family, each afternoon at quitting time after you stopped laying bricks, you did several odd things at the jobsite. You spread a piece of plastic over your newly laid bricks. You gathered up the Johnson's tools and locked them in the garage. You sealed the top of your mortar bag tightly with duct tape. You roped off your newly laid bricks with yellow caution tape. You rang the Johnson's doorbell and told them of your work schedule the following day.

The question is, why did you do these odd things at the jobsite? That's our *test.* Circle the correct answer here:

a) You took these actions because you were *frightened.*

b) You took these actions because you had a healthy *expectation* of trouble.

Did you circle answer "b"? Good, because "b" is the correct answer. You didn't do those odd things because the jobsite was frightening you. You did them because as a *Preactive* leader you had the wisdom and experience to expect troubles on the jobsite, and you were preempting those troubles by the actions you took.

Preactive Leadership Tactic Five
Have Constant Alligator Egg Hunts

To be *Preactive* leaders, we need a strong dose of this healthy kind of fear. We need an *I-anticipate-trouble-at-this-point-in-my-work* type of fear. We said earlier that the launching pad of prevention is negative thinking for a constructive purpose. That's still true. So *Preactive* Tactic Five requires us to cultivate the healthy type of fear that knows trouble can happen, and that we must preempt it before it does. Here's how to do that.

The Trouble-Preventing Formula

In Chapter 7, we learned that Likely Causes are alligator eggs that are hidden in our tasks and that are threatening to "hatch" and create Future Troubles. For example, as an experienced bricklayer working on the Johnson's walkway, you know there are some common Likely Causes threatening the success of your bricklaying.

1. Newly laid bricks can get wet and be weakened.
2. Thieves can steal bricklaying tools.
3. Mortar bags can absorb moisture and harden.
4. Playing children can unseat newly laid bricks.
5. Bricklaying work can intrude on a family's private life.

Since you've experienced these troubles in the past, you expect them again on the Johnson's walkway. So you took Blocking Actions (preemptive actions) to keep them from occurring. You neutralized the alligator eggs before they could "hatch." Using the Johnson's walkway as a backdrop, let's walk through the Blocking Actions that you took. Here's a *Trouble-Preventing Formula* for having alligator egg hunts the same way you did on the Johnson's brick walkway. It's built on four key questions.

The Four Questions

Here's our easy-to-remember formula for Trouble-Prevention. It's structured with four interlocking questions. As usual in our structures, there can be several answers in any of the questions.

1. What *Standard* will probably be broken?
2. What *Future Trouble* will probably result?
3. What *Likely Cause* will probably trigger this trouble?
4. What *Blocking Action* can probably neutralize this Likely Cause?

Next, we arrange these four questions under seven *what-who-when-where-amount-how-why* factual categories of the task we're working on and abbreviate all terms for simplicity. For example, here's how the abbreviated questions appear in the *what* category.

WHAT
1. SD: (What *Standard* will probably be broken?)
2. FT: (What *Future Trouble* will probably result?)

3. LC: (What *Likely Cause* will probably trigger this trouble?)

4. BA: (What *Blocking Action* can probably neutralize this Likely Cause?)

Now, you can use this blank copy of the *Standards-Improving Framework* for your own use simply by repeating this identical four-question structure for each of the *who-when-where-amount-how-why* categories in your own major tasks, as discussed earlier. Special note: Remember that you're using this *Trouble-Preventing Formula* on the same task standards in your personal work that you've already tweaked twice before in *Preactive* Tactic Two and *Preactive* Tactic Four. As we said, all the tactics in this chapter interlock and support one another, and the standards you're protecting here with *Preactive* Tactic Five are the same standards you *clarified* in *Preactive* Tactic Two and *improved* in *Preactive* Tactic Four.

Okay, let's see the rest of the *Trouble-Preventing Formula* being implemented. Notice again that there can be multiple answers for any of the questions.

The Hunt for Likely Causes in the Brick Walkway

Here's how the *Trouble-Preventing Formula* looks for the Johnson's brick walkway project. Notice that it isn't necessary to protect *all* the standards in the task. It's only necessary to protect the ones that seem the most likely to be *broken*—the ones with the most dangerous weaknesses in them. For this reason we've skipped the *who* and *why* factual categories in this example since they don't seem to have any serious Likely Causes menacing them.

Finally, you'll recognize some of the Blocking Actions in this formula because you saw them in earlier chapters. But others are new in this chapter. Okay, here's the *Trouble-Preventing Formula* for your Likely Cause hunt in the brick walkway project.

WHAT
1. SD: *Use Moderate Weather (MW) grade bricks.*
2. FT: The supply store might deliver the wrong grade of bricks.
3. LC: Human error in the store's truck loading system
4. BA: Talk to store manager, explain the need for the correct bricks, and get guarantees.

WHO (Skip this category because there are no serious Likely Causes.)

WHEN
1. SD: *Work a minimum average of one hour per day.*
2. FT: I might be asked to work late on my job and miss my Johnson's work.
3. LC: Late afternoon rush assignments from my superior.

4. BA: Talk to superior; ask for late assignments to be given to coworkers.

1. SD: *Work a maximum average of two hours per day.*
2. FT: My work might intrude on the Johnson's family life.
3. LC: The Johnson's don't know my work schedule; I don't know their family plans.
4. BA: Talk to the Johnson's each afternoon about possible schedule conflicts.

WHERE

1. SD: *Build the walkway in the middle of the front yard.*
2. FT: The walkway might not be in the exact place the Johnsons want it.
3. LC: The Johnsons have their own idea about where the "middle" of the yard is.
4. BA: Have the Johnsons stake out the exact location before starting to dig.

AMOUNT

1. SD: *Build the walkway for a fee of $900.*
2. FT: The Johnsons might have trouble paying my fee.
3. LC: Unexpected family bills, medical emergency, or bad financial planning.
4. BA: Ask for three payments: 1/3 in advance, 1/3 at half completion, and 1/3 at finish.

HOW

1. SD: *Lay all the bricks flat on the ground.*
2. FT: The newly laid bricks might get wet and weaken before they set.
3. LC: Rain showers, the Johnsons may turn on lawn sprinkler, or extra heavy dew.
4. BA: Cover newly laid bricks with plastic each night.

1. SD: *Lay all the bricks flat on the ground.*
2. FT: Something might unseat the newly bricks before they set.
3. LC: Children running and playing.
4. BA: Put yellow caution tape around new bricks; remind the family to be careful.

1. SD: *Mortar, shovels, hammers, wood, tape, and other supplies provided by Johnsons.*
2. FT: Someone might steal some of the tools or other supplies.
3. LC: Human greed, vandalism, pranks, jealousy, etc.
4. BA: Lock the tools in the garage each evening.

1. SD: *Mortar, shovels, hammers, wood, tape, and other supplies provided by the Johnsons.*
2. FT: The mortar bag might absorb moisture and harden.
3. LC: Unusually high humidity overnight.

4. BA: Seal bag tightly with duct tape, store in garage each evening.

WHY (Skip this category because there are no serious Likely Causes.)

See how simple the logic of prevention is? The *Trouble-Preventing Formula* is practical, easy, and straight forward. It gives you everything you need to perform alligator egg hunts in each of your own tasks. As we've said, *Preactive* leadership is simple and practical and can revolutionize your leadership ability in a few days. But for that to happen, you need to make this formula a weekly habit. That leads to our sixth *Preactive* Conclusion in the book for strengthening your personal leadership.

Sixth Conclusion
to Strengthen Your Leadership

Prevent Future Trouble

Using the Trouble-Preventing Formula, review all the standards in all your major tasks each week and block all the major Likely Causes threatening them.

Summary of Chapter 12

1. Leadership Tactics are the specific *types* of actions and the specific *sequence* of actions that a leader uses to *direct* and *correct* personal or group work toward a goal in the most effective and efficient way.

2. *Offensive-Minded* Leadership is using *Preactive* strategies and tactics to reach goals and objectives by keeping trouble from starting that *hasn't started yet*.

3. To be a *Preactive* leader, you need to do two things: Focus your weekly action-taking on the three situations in Table 1 on page 114, and choose and implement the best actions in those situations.

4. Your success as a *Preactive* leader depends on your ability to set clear standards and, where necessary, to convince other people to follow them.

5. A smokescreen standard is any standard that has a fuzzy fact or a missing fact in one or more of its five *what-who-when-where-amount* factual categories.

6. A clear standard is any standard that has at least one clear fact in each of its five *what-who-when-where-amount* factual categories.

7. The *Standards-Clarifying Structure* is our fourth *Preactive* Template in the book, and the purpose of its eleven-category structure is to *clarify the standards* in your tasks.

8. Goals and objectives are special types of standards and are two of the synonyms for the word *standards*. The differences between goals, objectives, and standards are that goals and objectives are standards that are *specialized in time*. Goals measure the *end* of tasks and usually have timeframes of one year or more in the future. Objectives are intermediate targets within tasks that serve as stepping stones to the goal, and they usually have timeframes of *less* than a year in the future. Regular standards measure work in real time and usually have immediate timeframes that are continuously obeyed. Goals, objectives, and standards link together in chains and should be compatible with one another in those chains.

9. If the followers in an organization are producing poor quality, making bad decisions, and showing low morale, the leaders often blame the *followers*. But the fault actually rests with the *leaders* because they're the role models for everything that happens in the organization, and "no group can rise any higher any than its leader." The leaders hold the power and control in a group, and they set the tone for everything that happens in the group.

10. The *Standards-Improving Framework* is our fifth *Preactive* Template and the purpose of its six-category structure is to *improve the standards* in your tasks. It's typical for between 30% and 50% of the original standards in tasks to be open to improvement.

Sixth Conclusion to Strengthen Your Leadership

Prevent Future Trouble

Using the Trouble-Preventing Formula, review all the standards in all your major tasks each week and block all the major Likely Causes threatening them.

---

11. The *Trouble-Preventing Formula* is our sixth and final *Preactive* Template of the book, and the purpose of its seven-category structure is to launch preemptive strikes in your tasks—that is, to hold "alligator egg hunts" in your work. The structure is built on four questions arranged under seven *what-who-when-where-amount-how-why* factual categories.

Chapter 12, our tactical chapter, is one of the most practical and specific chapters in the book. It's therefore one of the chapters of the book that you'll want to reread, rethink, and practice the most. Special note about references: The five *Preac-tive* Tactics and the six *Preactive* Conclusions are included here for handy reference. They are also included in the Appendix.

As a final thought for Chapter 12, it's important to remember that all life involves transition. The word *transition* comes from a root that meant to go across. In this case, our transition is going across from an old habit to a new habit. We're going across from the old habit of *Reactive* leadership to the new habit of *Preactive* leadership. This is necessary because, if you're like many people who were raised in *suppressively-biased* societies, you might unconsciously lean toward *Reactiveness* in your life and job and might not think about prevention as much as you should or could.

It's common to unconsciously slip into a lifestyle of suppressing troubles, removing the causes of troubles, and preparing for new troubles in an endless *cycle of Reactive leadership*. And if that's true of you to any extent, you're ready for a transition to *Preactive* leadership. That transition starts in the next chapter.

Preactive **Leadership Tactics**

Preactive Tactic One: *Have an Offensive Attitude that Keeps Trouble from Starting*

Preactive Tactic Two: *Have Clear and Agreed On Standards*

Preactive Tactic Three: *Use Theory Y Values in Every Appropriate Situation*

Preactive Tactic Four: *Constantly Raise the Bar*

Preactive Tactic Five: *Have Constant Alligator Egg Hunts*

The Six Conclusions to Strengthen Your Leadership

1. ***Use Theory Y Values.*** *Recognize which values your situations need and apply the correct X or Y styles, emphasizing Y values and using X values only when absolutely necessary.*

2. ***Use Preactive Strategies.*** *Make Preactive strategies your habitual strategies, and teach your coworkers and family to do the same thing.*

3. ***Clarify Your Standards.*** *Using the Standards-Clarifying Structure, review all the standards in all your major tasks each week, and be certain all of them are set, clear, and agreed on.*

4. ***Accept Leadership Responsibility.*** *If a person or group you're leading is on the down escalator, that person or group isn't to blame. You're to blame. Put them on the up escalator immediately.*

5. ***Improve Your Standards.*** *Using the Standards-Improving Framework, review all the standards in all your major tasks each week, and make at least one improvement in at least one standard.*

6. ***Prevent Future Trouble.*** *Using the Trouble-Preventing Formula, review all the standards in all your major tasks each week, and block all the major Likely Causes threatening them.*

CHAPTER 13

TRANSITIONING TO *PREACTIVE* LEADERSHIP

We said at the end of Chapter 12 that the word *transition* means a crossing over, a passing from one place to another. That's what we're going to do in this chapter. We're going to help you cross over from *Reactive* leadership to *Preactive* leadership—or at least help you cross over to a higher level of *Preactive* leadership than you've ever known before.

One thing about transitions is that they always start with a conscious decision. We said it earlier: *As we decide, so we become.* Thus, the purpose of Chapter 13 is to help you consciously choose how much *Preactiveness* you want in your personal leadership behavior.

We've said that *Preactive* leadership is easy, simple, and practical. We've said it achieves more goals with less waste and creates more production with less trouble. Most of us would like those things if we could get them. So, to motivate you in choosing your own level of *Preactiveness*, let's reveal some of its deeper benefits—things we haven't yet discussed. Let's start by talking about how *Preactiveness* gives you more *accurate priorities*.

Preactive Leaders Have Better Priorities

The word *priority* comes from a root meaning first, in the sense of doing first things first. Priority setting means we're supposed to pause long enough as we start to work each morning to ask ourselves, "Okay, what should I do *first* today?"

Textbooks teach priority setting as a technique for assigning numbers or codes to our tasks to rank order them by importance. Some books teach how to put A-B-C codes on tasks, from Most Important to Least Important, and then how to work on the "A" tasks first. Other books teach how to use Pareto analysis, the 20-80 rule that says 20% of our tasks produce 80% of our results, and then how to work on the 20% tasks first. Still other books teach how to use the quadrant system with four boxes labeled from important-urgent to not important-not urgent and then how to work on the important-urgent tasks first.

All these techniques are good. Except they have two weaknesses. First, they're time consuming and require continuous updating. It's common for the leaders who use these techniques to have a wall covered with sticky notes and a binder full of checklists. In fact, these techniques sometimes consume more time than they save.

The second weakness is worse. The priority setting techniques don't mention strategies and tactics and don't show leaders how to focus on action-taking before trouble starts. Think about it this way. Let's say a leader is a skilled priority-setter and has plenty of sticky notes and binders. But let's also say he or she is a *Reactive* leader. That means his or her priority setting is being used to prioritize a list of *inefficient* actions. If that kind of leader pauses to ask the question, "Okay, what should I do *first* today?" he or she will be mentally asking, *Should I suppress the trouble in project ABC first? Or should I remove the cause of failure in task LMO first? Or should I prepare for a crash in the XYZ program first?*

Here's the principle. No matter how faithfully a leader sets priorities, if he or she is a *Reactive* leader, all he or she is doing is prioritizing inefficiency. As an uncle of mine used to say, that's like rearranging the deck chairs on the *Titanic*. It's a forlorn hope.

Instead, the real answer to accurate priorities starts with *Preactive* strategies and tactics. Even if your daily priority skills aren't the greatest—even if your wall doesn't have sticky notes on it—if you implement *Preactive* strategies and tactics, you're implementing a powerful prioritizing system in its own right. By definition, a *Preactive* leader is one who's being assertive, creative, and focused on effective and efficient action-taking.

Thus, when a *Preactive* leader pauses to ask the question, "Okay, what do I need to do *first* today?" he or she will be mentally asking, *Should I take accurate actions in the ABC project first? Or should I improve the standards in the LMO task first? Or should I block the Likely Causes of trouble in the XYZ program first?*

These are very different questions from the ones *Reactive* leaders ask. *Preactiveness* is itself a form of priority setting. So the quickest and easiest way to have more accurate priorities is to transitionalize to more *Preactive* leadership. After that, leaders can fine-tune their daily actions as much as they want with the classic tools of priority setting.

Next, let's reveal the second deeper benefit of *Preactiveness* that we haven't yet discussed. Let's talk about how *Preactiveness* gives you more accurate *time management.*

Preactive Leaders Have Better Time Management

Textbooks usually teach time management and priority setting as being two halves of the same discipline. Time management is usually taught as half of priority setting, and priority setting is usually taught as half of time management. For instance, one of the principles of time management is that there's never enough time to do everything, but there's always enough time to do what's important. But that leads to a discussion of what's important, and that leads to priority setting. In reverse, any discussion of how to implement a prioritized list of tasks always circles back to time management.

The point is that all the motivational slogans, scheduling charts, to-do lists, and planning tables that time management courses teach are designed to help leaders get the most bang for their buck. That is, the purpose of time management is to help leaders achieve more goals with less waste and to create more production with less trouble. But that's also the description of *Preactive* leadership. If a leader is using *Preactive*, *directive*, and *offensive-minded* strategies and tactics, he or she already has better time management than many people and is already getting more bang for the buck than many people.

As a result, the first thing leaders ought to do is transitionalize to more *Preactive* leadership. Following that, they can fine-tune their daily actions as much as desired with the classic tools of time management.

Next, let's turn to the third deeper benefit of *Preactiveness*. Let's talk about how it gives you more accurate *linkage management.*

Preactive Leaders
Have Better Linkage Management

We haven't talked about this subject much (we touched on it in Chapter 2), but it's important to realize that the law of cause and effect—sometimes called the law of causality—applies to *leadership* in the same way that it applies to the fields of medicine, engineering, accounting, and all the other fields of human endeavor. In the simplest terms, the law of cause and effect says that situations form connected linkages, and that the later situations in a chain are shaped by the earlier situations in the chain. Said another way, situations don't happen in a vacuum. As a friend used to say, "All situations are coming from somewhere, and all situations are going somewhere."

This is a well-documented phenomenon. For example, many textbooks teach *decision trees* in which linkages of choices shape one another in a chain reaction. Thus, you can't decide which new car to buy until you've decided to buy a new car and until you've decided you can afford a new car, etc.

In a like manner, many textbooks teach *fishbone diagrams* in which linkages of causes shape one another in a chain reaction. For instance, a machine is running too slowly because the operator wasn't trained because the training budget was slashed because the sales were down, etc.

Finally, many textbooks teach *daisy chains* in which linkages of troubles shape one another in a chain reaction. For example, the doctor prescribed the wrong medicine and increased the patient's illness and hastened the patient's death and made the family angry and the family filed a malpractice suit, etc.

The lesson in all this is that *Preactive* leaders understand linkages better than other people do. They realize that leadership is actually taking chains of actions to *direct* and *correct* flows of work. In fact, the Identification Tables on pages 114-115 can be seen as a list of the kinds of linkages that leaders face. Working Actions are chains of actions to reach the goals and objectives of Normal Work situations. Improving Actions are chains of actions to constantly improve standards in work. Blocking Actions are chains of actions to prevent trouble in work. Suppressing Actions are chains of actions to control trouble in work, and so on.

The message is that *Preactive* leaders are better equipped than many people to interpret linkages. *Preactive* leaders know that the six kinds of situations they confront weekly in the workplace form a tapestry of linkages that are coming out of the past, moving through the present, and going into the future. So let's pause here a moment to talk about the best way to *handle* linkages.

Act as Far Back on a Linkage as Possible

The rule for dealing with a linkage is to always act as far *back* on its links in time and space as possible: all the way back to the root, if possible. For example, in Chapter 7, in the Case of Laura Mitchell's MX Machine, the plant superintendent, William James, took a Blocking Action by having two other machine operators help Laura handle the flood of new orders. By doing that, James neutralized the root of a potential Likely Cause linkage, preventing the linkage from ever "hatching." Laura never produced bad gitwidgets, the plant never shipped bad gitwidgets, and the plant's new customer never received bad gitwidgets. Being a *Preactive* leader, William James acted as far back on the linkage as possible—he blocked its root.

Likewise, in Chapter 9, in the Disappearing Tools Caper, you took a Correcting Action by investigating back on a True Cause linkage to remove the cause of the disappearing tools. You found that the tools were being taken by Little Pete to build a tree house for his soccer team's new club, and Little Pete wouldn't admit it because of the secrecy vow the boys took. You removed the root cause of this chain by having the soccer parents loan their own tools for the building of the tree house. Being a *Preactive* leader, you acted as far *back* on the linkage as possible—you removed its root.

Let's pause and retrench. What we're talking about in this chapter are the reasons why you're transitionalizing to a higher level of *Preactiveness*. So let's summarize everything we've said in a table comparing the relative strengths of *Preactiveness* versus *Reactiveness*.

The Reasons for Transitioning

#	The Strengths of *Preactiveness*	The Weaknesses of *Reactiveness*
1	More accurate priority-setting	Less accurate priority-setting
2	Better time management	Weaker time management
3	Better linkage management	Weaker linkage management
4	Achieves more goals	Achieves fewer goals
5	Has less waste	Has more waste
6	Creates less stress	Creates more stress
7	Creates more production	Creates less production
8	More "bang for the buck"	Less "bang for the buck"

This comparison table shows that *Preactiveness* is more powerful than *Reactiveness* in every respect. But despite the obvious strengths of *Preactiveness,* many leaders still cling to their upside-down priorities. They cling to their *Reactive* leadership, experiencing the culture of *suppressive-bias* that they learned while growing up. But you're different. You've made a conscious choice to turn your priorities right-side up and to make the transition to predominately *Preactive* leadership.

But let's drill deeper. Is there a magic key to your transition? Is there any one technique that'll make your transition easier? Yes, there is. There's one trick that'll make your crossing easier, and it's something we've already discussed several times.

Words Matter

We said several times that "Words *Matter*." To be a *Preactive* leader, it's vital to use the proper terms to talk about situations and actions. Consider these facts. Likely Causes are *different* from True Causes. Work Improvements are *different* from Current Troubles. Blocking Actions are *different* from Suppressing Actions. Correcting Actions are *different* from Preparing Actions.

Because all these actions are different from each other, you can't cross over to predominately *Preactive* leadership without calling situations and actions by their proper names. Regardless of whether you're in the military, a factory, bank, church, university, or a farm, the terminology of *Preactive* leadership is the same. Only the subject matter is different.

Thus, to help you quickly form the habit of using *Preactive* terminology properly, make a photocopy of the tables on pages 114-115 and tape them to your desk. Carry a copy in your wallet or purse. Scan a copy into your smartphone. Frame a copy for your wall. Scan a copy into your computer and make it your desktop background. Most of all, don't be timid about using the proper words with family members and coworkers. Remember, *Preaction* revolves around speaking the proper leadership words to yourself and others. Words *do matter*.

Now, let's package everything we've talked about in this book in one final diagram that we'll call Figure 8 on page 446. It represents the entire leadership process and includes all the principles and terms we've talked about. Leadership is about taking action in response to one of the six situations at Level 6. Our responses start with our personal cultures at Level 1 and become more tailored and focused as they move down the chain toward the specific situation to which we're responding. Now let's look at the diagram by levels.

Leadership Level 1: To read Figure 8, start at Level 1 with the box titled *Your Culture*. Your culture includes your total habits—how you walk, talk, sleep, eat, dress, drive, work, make decisions and also your habitual leadership strategies.

Leadership Level 2: Your total habits include your habitual leadership strategies, so the box at Level 2 represents *Your Leadership Strategies* as part of your total culture.

Leadership Level 3: At Level 3, the figure separates into the two basic *types* of strategies that you implement at home and on the job. The left side of the figure represents your *Offensive-Minded Leadership Strategies*: Your *Preactive* strategies that *direct* tasks and prevent trouble. The right side of the figure represents your *Defensive-Minded Leadership Strategies*: Your *Reactive* strategies that *correct* tasks and suppress trouble.

FIGURE 8
A Diagram of the Full Leadership Process

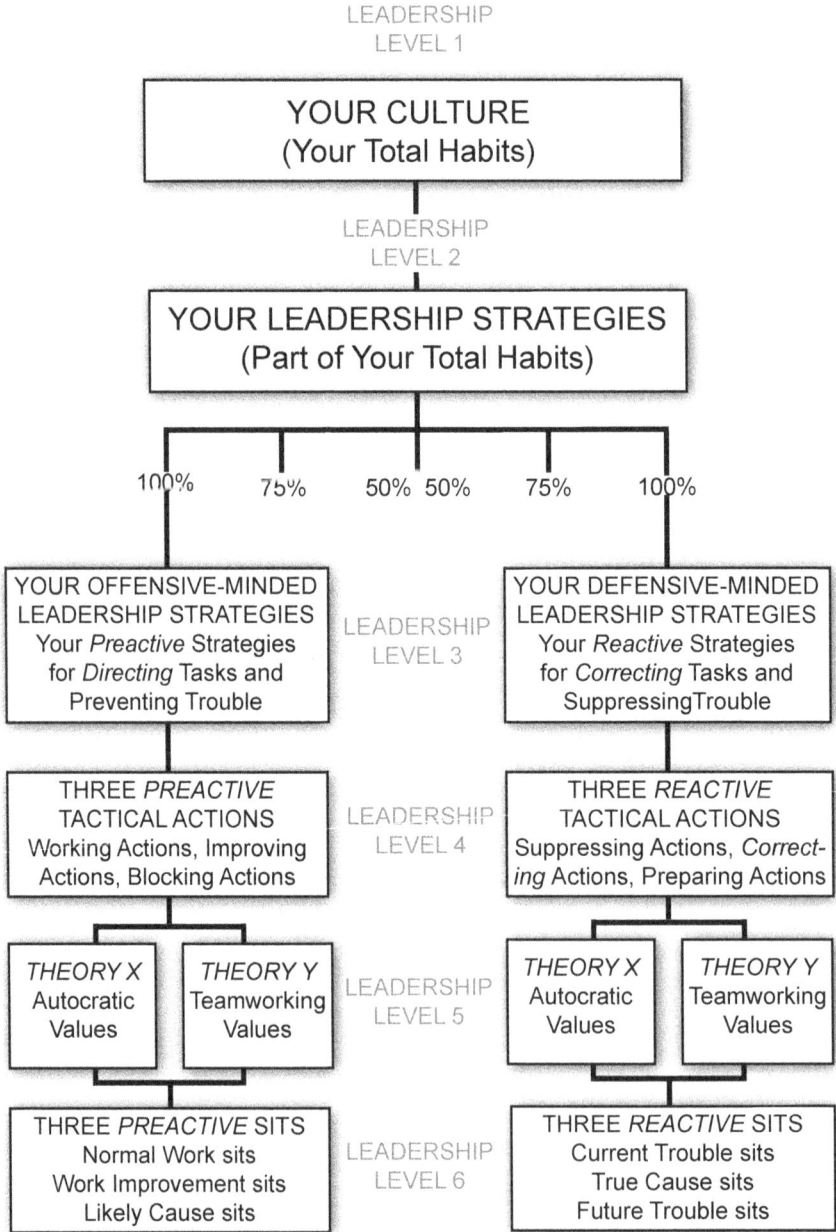

LEADERSHIP
LEVEL 1

YOUR CULTURE
(Your Total Habits)

LEADERSHIP
LEVEL 2

YOUR LEADERSHIP STRATEGIES
(Part of Your Total Habits)

100%   75%   50% 50%   75%   100%

YOUR OFFENSIVE-MINDED
LEADERSHIP STRATEGIES
Your *Preactive* Strategies
for *Directing* Tasks and
Preventing Trouble

LEADERSHIP
LEVEL 3

YOUR DEFENSIVE-MINDED
LEADERSHIP STRATEGIES
Your *Reactive* Strategies
for *Correcting* Tasks and
SuppressingTrouble

THREE *PREACTIVE*
TACTICAL ACTIONS
Working Actions, Improving
Actions, Blocking Actions

LEADERSHIP
LEVEL 4

THREE *REACTIVE*
TACTICAL ACTIONS
Suppressing Actions, *Correcting* Actions, Preparing Actions

THEORY X
Autocratic
Values

THEORY Y
Teamworking
Values

LEADERSHIP
LEVEL 5

THEORY X
Autocratic
Values

THEORY Y
Teamworking
Values

THREE *PREACTIVE* SITS
Normal Work sits
Work Improvement sits
Likely Cause sits

LEADERSHIP
LEVEL 6

THREE *REACTIVE* SITS
Current Trouble sits
True Cause sits
Future Trouble sits

Leadership Levels 2 and 3—The Measuring Line: Notice *between* Levels 2 and 3 a *percentage measuring line* connects the two types of strategies displayed on the left and the right of the diagram. In Chapter 11, we discussed the *51% Rule* and agreed that no one can be 100 percent *offensive* all the time. But we said everyone should try to be *offensive* most of the time. That's what the marks on this percentage line are measuring. They're measuring the degree to which you're being *offensive-minded* (the left side of the figure) versus the degree to which you're being *defensive-minded* (the right side of the figure).

The measurement line starts at a center position marked by the percentages 50/50. If your actions happened to score in that position, you'd be half *offensive* and half *defensive* in your actions. Then, as you transitioned to more *offensive-mindedness*, your score would move toward the left, becoming more *offensive* and less *defensive* at the same time. In other words, as your *offensive-minded* percentage increases on the left, your *defensive-minded* percentage decreases on the right. With the limited time and brainpower we have on the job, the *more offensive* we are, the *less defensive* we will be during the same hours on the job. For example, if you were at a score of 75% *Preactive* to the left, at the same time you'd only be 25% *Reactive* on the right.

Okay, but how do you know your score? How do you find out where you are on the line? Often you can tell by pure instinct. If you instinctively sense that you're spending most of your time suppressing trouble, removing the causes of trouble, and preparing to handle new trouble, you know you're somewhere on the right side on the line.

Conversely, if you instinctively sense that you're spending most of your time working accurately toward goals, improving your work standards, and taking preemptive actions against the Likely Causes of trouble in the future, you know you're somewhere on the left side of the line.

But to compute a more accurate score for Figure 8's measurement line, you can simply use your scores from the Personal Habitual Strategies Test on page 366 of Chapter 11. To do that, take your percentages on that test and apply them to Figure 8's line. To illustrate, in the sample test we presented in Chapter 11, you took 16 actions on the brick walkway for the Johnson family and 81% of them were *Preactive*. So you would bring this percentage forward to Figure 8, and it would become a score of 81 on the left side of the measurement line. (Your total score would be 81% *offensive* and 19% *defensive*.)

Leadership Level 4: The boxes at this leadership level represent the two types of tactical actions in your strategies. The left side of the figure represents your *Preactive Tactical Actions:* Working Actions, Improving Actions, and Blocking Actions. The right side of the figure represents your *Reactive Tactical Actions:* Suppressing Actions, Correcting Actions, and Preparing Actions.

Leadership Level 5: The boxes at Level 5 represent the two types of *values* in your strategies. Your values are the same on both sides of the figure. The diagram is indicating here that you must *choose* the appropriate set of values for every action you take. For example, on the left side of the figure, you can implement Working Actions with either *Theory X* or *Theory Y* values depending on what the situation needs. That's also true on the right side of the figure. Thus, regardless of whether your actions are *offensive* or *defensive*, you must choose the appropriate set of values with which to implement them. Remember that Theory X is a set of autocratic, control oriented, micromanaging values based largely on the threat of punishment, and that Theory Y is a set of creative, team oriented, relationship oriented values based largely on instilling confidence in subordinates.

Leadership Level 6: The boxes at the bottom of Figure 8 represent the foundations of all actions: the *situations* to which actions respond and that give actions their names. On the left side of the figure are the three *Preactive* situations—Normal Work sits, Work Improvement sits, and Likely Cause sits. On the right side of the figure are the three *Reactive* situations—Current Trouble sits, True Cause sits, and Future Trouble sits.

Now, stepping back and observing the full leadership process displayed in this diagram, you can see that your personal culture (the top box) dictates how you respond to the situations that you face at home and on the job (the bottom boxes). That can be good or it can be bad. If your habits are focused on the right side of the figure, it's bad. If your habits are focused on the left side of the figure, it's good. The best news is that since cultures are learned, they can be unlearned as we said in Chapter 11. That's why we're talking about transitioning from the right of the figure to the left of the figure as soon as possible and as much as possible.

Three big lessons stand out when you study Figure 8. First, we all have the ability and responsibility to choose how much we'll use *Preactive* strategies and tactics. Second, it's our ethical and economic obligation to use them as much as we can. Third, we'll reap more honors and more satisfaction if we maximize *Preactiveness* and minimize *Reactiveness*. That is, if we focus on *directing* work instead of *correcting* it and focus on *preventing* trouble instead of *suppressing* it, we'll reap more respect, rewards, and recognition.

The Alligator Farm

"But," you might say, "it's too late. I'm already so deep in the *Reactive* quicksand that nothing shows but my eyes. I'm in so much trouble now that I don't have the time or courage to transition to *Preactiveness*."

Yes, I know. I've heard that hundreds of times in seminars and, to some extent, it's true in some people's lives. But if you're having that thought, let me throw you a lifeline. Let me show you a way out by telling one last story. I've used this analogy for many years to illustrate how people can escape from the quagmires of daily trouble. Again, this analogy comes from my youth in Florida when alligator farms dotted the highways to attract tourists.

Every time someone tells me, "I'm drowning in alligators!" I ask them to stop and visualize the following scene. Imagine a large alligator farm somewhere in Florida with huge pools of hungry, vicious alligators. Imagine the farm also has sandbars and patches of reeds where the alligators can sun themselves and, during the summer, where the females can lay their eggs. Then imagine that the owners of the farm hear the news that alligator eggs are being purchased at a premium on a certain foreign market.

So each night, while the alligators are fast asleep in the pools, the owners of the farm tiptoe in with flashlights and buckets and quietly steal every egg they can find. Then at daybreak, a mysterious black limo with foreign license plates creeps into the parking lot of the farm, and the owners sell all the eggs they've collected at exorbitant prices.

Now, assume the owners did this every night for a number of years. What would eventually happen? One night, they would tiptoe into the farm with their flashlights and buckets, and the pools would be empty. The sand bars would be deserted. The reeds would be desolate. There would be no alligators. Why not? Because all of them would have died of old age. And since no new alligators were being born because the owners were stealing all the unhatched eggs each night, when the last alligator died of old age, the pools would be empty.

What's the message in this story? As we know from earlier pages, the word "alligator" is a synonym for a *Current Trouble*, and the phrase "alligator egg" is a synonym for a *Likely Cause*. Thus, this story is an analogy of a leader's life and job that's filled with *Current Troubles*. But over a period of time, as the leader patiently found and neutralized the *Likely Causes* of more trouble arising in the future, he or she woke up one sunny morning to find all the troubles *gone*.

Yes, we all contend with trouble daily. But while we're contending with it, we must also *make* the time to identify and block the Likely Causes of more trouble occurring in the future. If we do, our preventive actions will gradually overwhelm our troubles, and one happy day our alligator pools will be empty. The message is: No matter how much trouble you have at the moment, *prevention* will gradually erase it if you do a little every day. It's a law of nature.

Transitioning with the Preactive Templates

In the introduction, we said that reading this book would be an adventure. I hope that has been true for you. I hope these pages have been an unusual experience and that they've given you a completely new perspective on the mysteries of individual and group leadership.

We opened the book by saying that *Preactive* leadership is easy, fun, and pays well. We said that the *three actions* of *Preactive* leadership (Working Actions, Improving Actions, and Blocking Actions) can double your leadership ability in one week, whether you're leading a corporation, civic club, church, government agency, family, or yourself. Best of all, we said you'll be rewarded if you use the techniques because great contributions deserve great rewards.

In earlier pages, we defined *Preactive* leadership as *accomplishing as much as possible in your job and life without seeing trouble in your tasks.* That means that even if nobody else realizes you're being a *Preactive* leader, you'll still reap the private rewards of greater satisfaction, less stress, less expense, less waste, and a happier life. That makes it worth the effort whether anyone else understands or not.

We've talked about many skills and techniques in these chapters such as clarifying fuzzy words, identifying situations, taking best actions, and finding causes. But skills are only good when they're *used.* Dormant skills are valueless. That's why we said the big catch in this book is *practice.* We said you'll be successful in *Preactive* leadership in direct proportion to how much time you invest using it. If you use the skills and techniques in this book for even a few minutes a week, you'll grow impressively in *Preactiveness.*

Of course, at first that might take special effort and sacrifice. As an example, many years ago when I was completing one of my college degrees, I was also working full time and had a busy, young family—and this was before the days of accelerated courses and online degrees. So each night I set my alarm clock, got up early, ate breakfast before daybreak, and drove to my office in downtown St. Louis two hours before the company opened. Then I sipped coffee and did my reading and homework assignments for two hours, and when the rest of the employees began arriving for work, I put my schoolbooks away and started my corporate duties. Several months later, I completed that degree with honors.

My point is this. To get started, you might need to set a special time schedule or make other special arrangements to use the Six *Preactive* Templates in this book. But regardless of what it takes, you *must* use them because they're your operational weapons as a *Preactive* leader. The six templates are your weekly tools for growth and experience in *Preactiveness*. And they get easier as you gain experience using them, so that the more you use them the easier they become.

Yes, you may need to get up earlier for a few weeks. Or you may need to work later for a few weeks. Or you may need to practice during lunch and coffee breaks, or holidays and weekends. But whatever it takes—at whatever cost, price, and sacrifice—make the time to use the *Preactive* Templates, and to integrate them as a natural part of your daily life and job. Do that, and you won't be sorry. For the record again, here's a list of the *Preactive* Templates you need to use as your operational weapons. Remember that blank copies are in the Appendix.

No.	Template Name	Chapter	Appendix
1	*Mental-Verbal Format* for Decision-Making	Chapter 3 Page 71	Page 465
2	*Hard-Copy Format* for Decision-Making	Chapter 3 Page 73	Page 466
3	*Simple-Pattern Format* for Decision-Making	Chapter 3 Page 80	Page 467
4	*Standards-Clarifying Structure*	Chapter 12 Page 389	Page 471
5	*Standards-Improving Framework*	Chapter 12 Page 414	Page 473
6	*Trouble-Preventing Formula*	Chapter 12 Page 422	Page 475

A True Story of Transition

Let's close with a true story of transition that had historical significance. Sir Winston Churchill, the famous prime minister of England during World War II, is acknowledged as one of the world greatest leaders. But he wasn't elected by the English people until World War II had started. In fact, as Churchill was being sworn in, the Germans were invading Holland, Belgium, Luxembourg, and France, and a few days after his ceremony the Germans defeated the British Army at Dunkirk.

So Churchill began his new job as a predominately *Reactive* leader. That's what the situation required. The English people elected him to be a *defensive-minded, corrective, suppressive* leader. And he was. Five months later, he won the Battle of

Britain, and the Germans were unable to invade England. But as soon as he could, Churchill transitioned to a predominately *Preactive* leader. He became an *offensive-minded, directive, preventive* leader. He developed daring new types of spy and commando units, special secret code breaking units, unique floating breakwaters for beach landings, strange amphibious tanks, and a series of James Bond-type creative weapons that his soldiers called "the funnies." But as a result, history records that Churchill's *Preactive* leadership played a major role in the winning of World War II.

In the 2003 book, *Never Give In*, Winston's grandson published a collection of Churchill's wartime speeches. In one of these speeches, presented to Parliament as the tides of war were turning in England's favor, Churchill told the members of Parliament, "This is not the end. It is not even the beginning of the end. But it is, perhaps, the end of the beginning."

Let's paraphrase Churchill's words this way: This is not the end of your adventure in *Preactive* leadership. It's not even the beginning of the end of your adventure. But it is, because this book is over, the end of your beginning. From this day on, you will continue to learn and grow and develop in *Preactiveness* for many fruitful years to come.

One last word. Churchill said something else to the English people during World War II. As the bombs fell on England, as its buildings burned and its men, women, and children died in the attacks, Churchill told the English people, "Never give in, never give in, never, never, never, never give in."

As *Preactive* leaders, let's claim Churchill's words as our own challenge, mandate, and inspiration for the years of leadership we have yet ahead of us. Let's never give in as we take the three actions that can double our leadership ability in one week: accurate *Working Actions*, creative *Improving Actions*, and assertive *Blocking Actions*.

Let's never give in because we know that regardless of who we are or what we do—today or in the future—there's no better way to live and work with less stress, more satisfaction, greater peace of mind, and faster bonuses, promotions, and pay raises.

Churchill references are from Winston S. Churchill, *Never Give In* (New York: Hyperion, 2003) 306, 342.

Appendix

List of Cases

List of Figures

The Five *Preactive* Tactics

The Six *Preactive* Conclusions

1. *Use Theory Y Values:* Recognize which values your situations need and apply the correct X or Y styles, emphasizing Y values and using X values only when absolutely necessary.

2. *Use Preactive Strategies:* Make *Preactive* strategies your habitual strategies, and teach your co-workers and family to do the same thing.

3. *Clarify Your Standards:* Using the Standards-Clarifying Structure, review all the standards in all your major tasks each week, and be certain all of them are set, clear, and agreed on.

4. *Accept Leadership Responsibility:* If a person or group you're leading is on the down escalator, that person or group isn't to blame. You're to blame. Put them on the up escalator immediately.

5. *Improve Your Standards:* Using the Standards-Improving Framework, review all the standards in all your major tasks each week, and make at least one improvement in at least one standard.

6. *Prevent Future Trouble:* Using the Trouble-Preventing Formula, review all the standards in all your major tasks each week and block all the major Likely Causes threatening them.

The Six *Preactive* Templates

Preactive Template 1
Mental-Verbal Format for Decision-Making

This format is for simple decisions that can be made without visual aids. A choice is made by asking four questions mentally and/or verbally with others. The format obeys the steps of decision-making taught in Chapter 2, and the questions must be in sequence. The format starts after a simple situation has been encountered requiring the choice of a thing, person, time, place, or amount that best satisfies its needs with the least risk of trouble. A clear action statement is mentally developed and then the following questions are asked in sequence.

1 *Needs*   "What are this situation's most serious *needs*?"

2 *Alternatives*   "Do we have three or more *alternatives*?"

3 *Tentative Choice*   "Which alternative seems to *best* satisfy the needs?"

4 *Future Troubles*   "If this tentative choice is implemented, what could go *wrong*?

If no serious Future Troubles are probable with the tentative choice, the decision is made. But if serious Future Troubles *are* probable with the tentative choice, return to the *second* best alternative, and if it has *less* Future Troubles than the tentative choice, the second best alternative is the final decision.

Preactive Template 2
Hard-Copy Format for Decision-Making

Hard-Copy Format Decision-Making

(Note: See a Full Explanation of this Format in Chapter 3, Figure 1, The Case of the New Car Puzzle)

Action Statement: "*I (or we) want to choose the best* _____ "

Columns: 1	2	3	4	5	6	7	8	9	10	11	12	13	14	15
			Alternative One:			Alternative Two:			Alternative Three:			Alternative Four:		
NEEDS OF THE SITUATION	IMPORTANCE OF EACH NEED	WEIGHT OF EACH NEED	(Notes)	NEED RANK	SCORE $(3\times5=)$	(Notes)	NEED RANK	SCORE $(3\times8=)$	(Notes)	NEED RANK	SCORE $(3\times11=)$	(Notes)	NEED RANK	SCORE $(3\times14=)$
#														
1	Most Important	Weight of 6												
2	Next Most Import	Weight of 5												
3	Next Most Import	Weight of 4												
4	Next Most Import	Weight of 3												
5	Next Most Import	Weight of 2												
6	Least Important	Weight of 1												
NEEDS SCORE:			Alt #1			Alt #2			Alt #3			Alt #4		
RANK OF ALTERNATIVES IN NEEDS SATISFACTION:			[ ]			[ ]			[ ]			[ ]		

Instructions: Column 3. To create "weights," count needs in Column 1 (there are six in this example), and number them backwards by importance. These numbers become the "weights" in Columns 5, 8, 11, 14. To create "ranks," count alternatives (there are four in this example), and number backwards by degree of need satisfaction. These numbers become the "ranks" in Columns 6, 9, 12, 15. To create "scores," multiply "weights" (Column 3) times the "ranks" (Columns 5, 8, 11, 14). Answers are the "scores" to be totaled for each alternative. (Special note: Follow the same process to compute the Future Trouble scores below.)

#	FUTURE TROUBLES	SERIOUSNESS	WEIGHT	ALT #1 (Notes)	RANK	SCORE	ALT #2 (Notes)	RANK	SCORE	ALT #3 (Notes)	RANK	SCORE	ALT #4 (Notes)	RANK	SCORE
1		Most Serious	Weight of 4												
2		Next Most Serious	Weight of 3												
3		Next Most Serious	Weight of 2												
4		Least Serious	Weight of 1												
TROUBLES SCORE:				Alt #1			Alt #2			Alt #3			Alt #4		
RANK OF ALTERNATIVES IN FUTURE TROUBLE:				Needs Trouble		[ ]	Needs Trouble		[ ]	Needs Trouble		[ ]	Needs Trouble		[ ]
RANK OF ALTERNATIVES IN TOTAL SATISFACTION	*Alt #1*			*Alt #2*			*Alt #3*			*Alt #4*					

Final Instructions: The best choice is the alternative that has the best ratio of maximum Needs Satisfaction to minimum Future Trouble.

Preactive Template 3
Simple-Pattern Format for Decision-Making

This format is for decisions that are too complex to be made mentally, but not complex enough to require a statistical spreadsheet. This format is a combination of the mental and statistical approaches, and follows the eight steps of decision-making taught in Chapter 2. It can be used as a visual aid in meetings, and can be used by email, Skype, hand-held PDA devices, or any other medium. The following steps must be taken in sequence.

1. *Recognize a Choice Situation.* Recognize a situation requiring the choice of a thing, person, time, place, or amount that best satisfies its needs with the least risk of trouble.

2. *Develop a Clear Action Statement.* With all fuzzy words and the *what-who-when-where-amount* facual categories clarified, write a clear action statement starting with "*I (or we) want to choose the best* _____."
(Write *what* is being chosen, *who* is effected, the *deadline*, the *place* of implementation, and the *amount* being chosen.)

3. *Develop the Needs.* With all fuzzy words and the *what-who-when-where-amount* factual categories clarified, list a minimum of four things the situation needs. Rank the needs by importance, giving the highest number (4) to the most important need, and the lowest number (1) to the least important need. "Needs" are things the situation is "asking for," such as

most quality, production, morale, experience, and profit, etc.; and *least* cost, waste, maintenance, storage, damage, and raw materials, etc.

❑ We need _____

_____.

❑ We need _____

_____.

❑ We need _____

_____.

❑ We need _____

_____.

4. *Develop the Alternatives.* With all fuzzy words and the *what-who-when-where-amount* factual categories clarified, list a minimum of three alternatives that might satisfy the situation's needs. "Alternatives" are possible methods, ideas, people, options, places, amounts, times, plans, products, etc., that might satisfy the situation's needs. List all of the relevant facts about each alternative.

a) _____

_____.

b) _____

_____.

c) _____

_____.

5. *Make a Tentative Choice.* Compare the alternatives (Step 4) to the needs (Step 3) and make a tentative choice by asking which of the alternatives seems to *best* satisfy the situation's most important needs.

The tentative choice is _____

_____.

6. *Consider Future Troubles.* List the serious probable Future Troubles (if any) in the tentative choice if it is implemented. "Future Troubles" are serious probable mistakes, accidents, waste, bad quality, failures, misunderstandings, delays, and low morale, etc. _____

_____.

7. *Make a Final Choice.* If the tentative choice has no serious probable Future Troubles, it is the *final choice.* But if the tentative choice *does* have serious probable Future Troubles, continue to optional Step 8 of the format.

8. *Optional—Evaluate the Second Best Alternative.* To use this optional step, return to the remaining alternatives (Step 4), compare them to the needs again (Step 3), and choose the *second* best alternative in the format.

The second best alternative is _____

_____.

List the serious probable Future Troubles (if any) in the second best alternative. _____

_____.

If the second best alternative has fewer serious probable Future Troubles than the tentative choice, the second best alternative becomes the *final choice*. In the rare event that both the first and second alternatives have serious probable Future Troubles, a list of better alternatives should be developed before a choice can be made.

Preactive Template 4
The Standards-Clarifying Structure

This template is for clarifying smokescreen standards (needs) in tasks and projects, as taught in Tactic Two, Chapter 12. All accuracy comes from previously set, clear, and agreed on standards, and this template is a powerful filter for selecting the best actions to take (and not to take) in any situation. There must be at least one statement per category, but there can be several. There can be no fuzzy words in the statements, and the statements must have the agreement of any superiors, coworkers, clients, family members, or other persons being affected by the task. Necessary research for the statements can be done by phone, files, interviews, appointment books, computer files, the Internet, etc., as needed.

1. *Goal*: (Use this category if the task will take *more* than a year to complete. Start at category two if the task will take *less* than a year to complete.)

2. *Objective*: (Use this category if the task will take *less* than a year to complete— or if the task will take *more* than a year to complete and has a goal, but needs intermediate objectives as stepping stones toward the goal.)

3. *Situation Statement:* (A statement of the task as it was assigned to you.)

4. *Action Statement:* (Your statement of the way you intend to perform the task.)

5. *What:* (What needs to be done—fully described.)

6. *Who:* (Who needs to do the task—you and/or the other people involved in the work or influenced by the work.)

7. *When:* (When the task needs to be done—all times, days, and dates.)

8. *Where:* (Where the task needs to be done—all locations.)

9. *How much / many:* (Amount of the task that needs to be done—all amounts.)

10. *How:* (How the task needs to be done—any items not already listed under the *what* category. Duplicated items are not necessary.)

11. *Why:* (Why the task needs to be done—other people's motives or purposes—if they are relevant.)

Preactive Template 5
The Standards-Improving Structure
The *Standards-Improving Framework*

This template is for improving the previously set, clear, and agreed on standards (needs) in tasks and projects, as taught in Tactic Four, Chapter 12. It is common for between 30% and 50% of the original standards on tasks to be open to improvement, but many people mistakenly continue to meet the original standards in their tasks year after year. Creative answers to the six questions in this framework can be developed through brainstorming sessions, discussions with experts, Internet searches, etc., as needed.

1. *What*: (Can anything be increased, decreased, or otherwise changed in the *materials, procedures,* or *process* standards of the task that would create added value for recipients?)

2. *Who*: (Can anything be increased, decreased, or changed in the *personnel, skills, experience*, or *educational* standards of the task that would create added value for recipients?)

3. *When*: (Can anything be increased, decreased, or changed in the *schedule* or *timeframe* standards of the task that would create added value for the recipients?)

4. *Where*: (Can anything be increased, decreased, or changed in the *location, storage,* or *destination* standards of the task that would create added value for recipients?)

5. *Amount*: (Can anything be increased, decreased, or changed the *numbers, inventory,* or *quantity* standards of the task that would create added value for recipients?)

6. *How*: (Can anything be increased, decreased, or changed in the *techniques, technology, equipment,* or *tool* standards of the task that would create added value for recipients? Special note: There may be overlap between the *how* category and the *what* category—the same improvement idea may occur in both categories. The important thing is that new ideas occur somewhere in the structure, but duplication is not necessary.)

7. *Why*: (Can anything be increased, decreased, or changed in the *motivation, ethics, loyalty,* or *consistency* standards of the task that would create added value for recipients?)

Preactive Template 6
The Trouble-Preventing Formula

This template is for blocking the Likely Causes of Future Trouble in tasks and projects as taught in Tactic Five, Chapter 12. All tasks have "alligator eggs" (Likely Causes) in them, and the purpose of this template is to identify and neutralize LCs before they "hatch" and create trouble. This template is built on four questions in seven categories. Some categories will have no answer, while other categories will have several answers. Likely Causes can be identified through discussions with experts, Internet searches, interviews with employees who work in the task daily, files and computer records of past troubles in the same task or project, etc. The abbreviation "SD" stands for Standards (needs), "FT" stands for Future Troubles, "LC" stands for Likely Causes, and "BA" stands for Blocking Actions.

1. *What:*
   a) SD: (What *Standard* will probably be broken?)
   b) FT: (What *Future Trouble* will probably result?)
   c) LC: (What *Likely Cause* will probably trigger this trouble?)
   d) BA: (What *Blocking Action* can probably neutralize this Likely Cause?)

2. *Who:*

    a) SD: (What *Standard* will probably be broken?)

    b) FT: (What *Future Trouble* will probably result?)

    c) LC: (What *Likely Cause* will probably trigger this trouble?)

    d) BA: (What *Blocking Action* can probably neutralize this Likely Cause?)

3. *When:*

    a) SD: (What *Standard* will probably be broken?)

    b) FT: (What *Future Trouble* will probably result?)

    c) LC: (What *Likely Cause* will probably trigger this trouble?)

    d) BA: (What *Blocking Action* can probably neutralize this Likely Cause?)

4. *Where:*

    a) SD: (What *Standard* will probably be broken?)

    b) FT: (What *Future Trouble* will probably result?)

    c) LC: (What *Likely Cause* will probably trigger this trouble?)

    d) BA: (What *Blocking Action* can probably neutralize this Likely Cause?)

5. *Amount:*

    a) SD: (What *Standard* will probably be broken?)

    b) FT: (What *Future Trouble* will probably result?)

    c) LC: (What *Likely Cause* will probably trigger this trouble?)

    d) BA: (What *Blocking Action* can probably neutralize this Likely Cause?)

6. *How:*

    a) SD: (What *Standard* will probably be broken?)

    b) FT: (What *Future Trouble* will probably result?)

    c) LC: (What *Likely Cause* will probably trigger this trouble?)

    d) BA: (What *Blocking Action* can probably neutralize this Likely Cause?)

7. *Why:*

    a) SD: (What *Standard* will probably be broken?)

    b) FT: (What *Future Trouble* will probably result?)

    c) LC: (What *Likely Cause* will probably trigger this trouble?)

    d) BA: (What *Blocking Action* can probably neutralize this Likely Cause?)

The Personal/Group Habitual Strategies Test

To take the Personal/Group Habitual Strategies Test, enter the appropriate numbers in the boxes below. In each box, enter the number of actions you took in that category during the past work month. If the past month wasn't typical because of a special crisis or project, use figures from a month that was typical of your normal work.

Part 1: Actions Taken to
Direct Tasks *Before* Trouble Started

☐ Number of Working Actions taken in Normal Work situations to move work toward objectives and goals

☐ Number of Improving Actions taken to make standards better in Work Improvement situations to surprise and delight recipients

☐ Number of Blocking Actions taken to prevent Likely Cause situations from "hatching" and creating Future Trouble

☐ Total *Preactive* Actions Taken

Part 2: Actions Taken to
Correct Tasks *After* Trouble Started

☐ Number of Suppressing Actions taken to control the costs and damage of Current Trouble situations in tasks

☐ Number of Correcting Actions taken to remove True Cause situations that were causing trouble in tasks

☐ Number of Preparing Actions set up to wait to suppress the costs and damage of Future Trouble situations in tasks

☐ Total *Reactive* Actions Taken

☐ Total *Preactive* and *Reactive* Actions Taken

☐ Percentage of *Preactive* Actions Taken

☐ Percentage of *Reactive* Actions Taken

Glossary

51% Rule. The rule that says *51% or more* of one situation or action gives an *identity* to a mixture of situations or actions. For example, if a leader takes *Preactive* actions 60% of the time and *Reactive* actions 40% of the time, that leader can be identified as a *Preactive* leader because he or she is taking *Preactive* actions more than 51% of the time.

Action. Anything that you *do* at some time, in some place, to some extent.

Action Statement. A written or verbal statement describing the action a person or group intends to take to resolve a situation. Action statements are based on situation statements, and "mirror" the needs of situations. See "Situation Statement."

Alligator. A synonym for trouble. See "Current Trouble Situation."

Alligator Egg. A synonym for a future cause of trouble. See "Likely Cause Situation."

Alligator Farm. An analogy in Chapter 13 of a leader with many daily troubles but who with patient daily prevention gradually overcomes them all.

Alligator Training. An analogy for the inefficiency of Suppressing Action. See "Suppressing Action."

Applications of Strategies. *Preactive* strategies can be applied in two ways: as an individual leading him or herself in a personal task, or as a group leader in a group task.

Be Slow Right Instead of Fast Wrong (BSRIOFW). A motto for *Preactive* leaders. Careful thought on the front-end of actions is better than hours of repair work on the back-end of actions. See "Distorted Sense of Urgency."

Best Action. The action that *best* satisfies the *needs* of the situation.

Best Decision. The choice of an alternative thing, person, time, place, or amount that *best* satisfies the *needs* of a situation with the least risk of Future Trouble.

Binary Decision. All choices during decision-making should be made from among a field of *three* or more alternatives. Binary decisions such as Yes-No and Do-Don't are false. See "Decision-Making."

Blocking Action (BA). One of the three *Preactive* actions: Taking action to neutralize Likely Cause situations connected to the work in Normal Work situations, thus preventing the weaknesses from "hatching" and creating future costs, losses, and trouble. BAs can also be called preemptive actions or preventive actions. See "Likely Cause Situation" and "Normal Work Situation."

Booby Trap. An analogy for the unintended negative consequences of Suppressing Actions. See "Suppressing Action" and "Time Bomb."

Brick Walkway. An analogy used in Figures 2 through 7 that illustrates how Normal Work situations and Working Actions are assigned and performed.

Cause-Finding. A process within the leadership technique of Cause-Removal to find, verify, and remove True Causes. See "True Cause Situation" and "Correcting Action."

Cause-Removal Technique. One of the three *Reactive* leadership techniques: Taking Correcting Actions to remove True Causes. See "Correcting Action" and "True Cause Situation."

Chains. See "Linkages."

Choice. See "Decision."

Choice Situation. The generic situation on which Decision Actions are taken to form the decision-making process. This process is the foundation of leadership. Choice Situations wear six different "masks," and appear in life and on jobs as the six situations taught in this book. See "Decision Action" and "Identification of Situations."

Clear Standard. A standard with at least one clear fact in each of its five *what-who-when-where-amount* factual categories.

Clear Statement. A situation statement or an action statement that has at least one clear fact in each of its five *what-who-when-where-amount* factual categories.

Continuous Improvement. An improvement movement launched by Masaaki Imai of Japan with his best-selling book, *Kaizen* in 1986. See "Improving Action" and "Work Improvement Situation."

Correcting Action (CA). One of the three *Reactive* actions. Taking action to remove the True Causes of Current Trouble situations in work. See "Current Trouble Situation."

Correcting Work. Correcting work is one of the two main roles of a leader. It is the process of *Reactive* and *defensive-minded* responses to trouble in work. The other main role of a leader is *directing* work. See "*Directing* Work."

Critical Change. A person or event that is new, moving, different, or unusual in one (or more) of the five *what-who-when-where-amount* factual categories of a Current Trouble. The critical change is the person/event through which the True Cause was able to strike. See "Cause-Finding."

Culture. The total habits of a person or group, including a person's or group's leadership habits, which tend to be either dominately *Preactive* or dominately *Reactive*.

Current Trouble (CT) Situation. One of the three *Reactive* situations: A performance or behavior of a person, thing, or system that is breaking a task standard in an unwanted way that it was previously satisfying. Current Troubles are controlled by Suppressing Actions. See "Suppressing Action."

Decision Action. Any action taken on a Choice Situation. Choice Situations are the generic situation that are the foundations of leadership. The six actions in this book are all generic Decision Actions wearing six different "masks." See "Choice Situation" and "Identification of Situations."

Decision. In one word, a choice. In two words, a best choice. More fully, the choice of an alternative thing, person, time, place, or amount that best satisfies the needs of a situation with the least risk of Future Trouble.

Decision-making. The process of making best choices. More fully, the process of choosing alternative things, persons, times, places, or amounts that best satisfy the needs of situations with the least risk of Future Trouble. Decision-making is taught in Chapter 3, and three different *Preactive* Templates for decision-making are provided in that chapter. See "*Preactive* Templates."

Defensive-Minded Leadership. Using *Reactive* strategies, values, and tactics to *correct* and suppress trouble. *Defensive-minded* leadership deals with (or prepares to deal with) trouble *after* it has started. See "*Reactive* Leadership."

Directing Work. Directing work is one of the two main roles of a leader. It is the process of *Preactive* and *offensive-minded* responses to work that guide it toward goals. The other main role of leaders is *correcting* work. See "*Correcting* Work."

Distorted Sense of Urgency. A false and unnecessary emphasis on haste by leaders. It creates stress and inefficiency in organizations. See "Be Slow Right Instead of Fast Wrong."

Down escalator. When employees are led with Theory X values for a long period of time, they become increasingly immature as if riding a down escalator. Leaders should avoid using *Theory X* values unless absolutely necessary, and should make *Theory Y* values their default leadership values. See "Theory X and Theory Y" and "Up Escalator."

Effective. The degree to which goals are achieved in work. See "Efficiency."

Effective-Efficient Actions. The three *Preactive* leadership actions that are taken *before* trouble starts in work. The three Effective-Efficient actions are: Working Actions, Improving Actions, and Blocking Actions. These are the *three actions* referred to in the title of this book and that can double a person's leadership abilities in one week. See "Ineffecient-Ineffective Actions."

Effective-Efficient Situations. The three *Preactive* leadership situations that exist *before* trouble starts in work. The three Effective-Efficient situations are: Normal Work situations, Work Improvement situations, and Likely Cause situations. See "Inefficient-Ineffective Situations."

Efficient. The degree to which waste is avoided in work. See "Effective."

Eight Steps of Decision-Making. There are eight specific steps to an effective and efficient decision, as taught in Chapter 2, pages 45-53. They include: 1. recognize a Choice Situation; 2. write an action statement; 3. list needs; 4. list alternatives; 5. list a tentative choice; 6. list Future Troubles; 7. if the future troubles do not overwhelm the tentative choice it becomes the final choice; 8. but if they do, the second-best alternative is analyzed as the final choice.

False Correcting Action. An action taken against a possible cause of a Current Trouble instead of against the verified True Cause of the trouble. See "Possible Cause" and "True Cause Situation."

Five Factual Categories. All situations have five factual categories by which they can be analyzed: the *what-who-when-where-amount* categories. The *how* and *why* categories are optional. See "Situation."

Five *Preactive* Tactics. Five tactical rules for the kinds of actions and sequence of actions that leaders take. If followed, these tactical rules make leaders predominately *Preactive*. Leaders should strive to make these five rules a personal habit. They are listed in the Contents and in the Appendix. See "Leadership Tactics."

Follow the Leader. A game played by children that illustrates how followers tend to mimic the behavior of their leaders.

Future Trouble (FT) Situation. One of the three *Reactive* situations: A performance or behavior of a person, thing, or system that is not breaking a task standard in an unwanted way at this time but could break one in the future. Preparing Actions are arranged in advance to wait to suppress the damage of Future Troubles if they occur. See "Preparing Action."

Fuzzy Words. Facts, words, and phrases in statements that can refer to two or more different situations, or that can imply two or more different actions.

Goal. A standard with a special timeframe that measures the *end* of a task, usually a task that takes more than a year to complete. See "Objective" and "Standard."

Group Habitual Strategies Test. A test in Chapter 11 showing the degree to which a group's predominate actions are *Preactive* or *Reactive* during a work month.

Habit. An unconscious behavior learned by repetition. It takes a minimum of three weeks (21 days) of continuous repetition to form a new habit. Habits are important because the culture of a person or group is composed of that person's or group's total habits, and this includes their leadership habits. See "*Preactive* Leadership" and "*Reactive* Leadership."

Habitual Leadership Strategies. Leaders have habitual strategies of leadership, and these can be identified using the Identification Tables on pages 114-115 in this book or by taking the "Personal Habitual Strategy Test" in Chapter 11.

Hard-Copy Format Decision-Making. A *Preactive* Template taught in Chapter 3 for making complex or technical decisions. See "Decision-Making" and "*Preactive* Templates."

Identification of Actions. A technique that uses the characteristics of the six actions described in the Identification Tables on pages 114-115 to recognize an action's type. Actions take their identifications from the situations to which they respond. Skill in identification increases with practice and experience. See "Identification Tables."

Identification of Situations. A technique that uses the characteristics of the six *situations* described in the Identification Tables on pages 114-115 to recognize a situation's type. Situations give their identifications to the actions that respond to them. Skill in identification increases with practice and experience. See "Identification Tables."

Identification Tables. Two tables located on pages 114-115 that are used to identify the type of situation to which a leader is responding and the type of action the leader is taking. See "Identification of Situations."

Improving Action (IA). One of the three *Preactive* actions. Taking action to make the old standards in a task better, thus increasing the quality of products and services and making them exceed the expectations of recipients. See "Work Improvement Situation."

Ineffective. The degree to which goals are *not* achieved in work. See "Effective."

Ineffective-Inefficient Actions. The three *Reactive* leadership actions that are taken *after* trouble starts in work. The three Ineffective-Inefficient actions are: Suppressing Actions, Correcting Actions, and Preparing Actions. See "Effective-Efficient Actions" and "*Preactive* Actions."

Ineffective-Inefficient Situations. The three *Reactive* leadership situations that exist *after* trouble starts in work. The three Ineffective-Inefficient Situations are: Current Trouble situations, True Cause situations, and Future Trouble Situations. See "Effective-Efficient Situations."

Inefficient. The degree to which waste is *not* avoided in work. See "Efficient."

Jumping to Cause. The mistake of assuming that one of the many possible causes of a trouble is its True Cause and taking a false correcting action against that possible cause. See "Cause-Finding," "False Correcting Action," and "Possible Cause."

KISS. An acronym for the phrase, Keep It Simple, Stupid. Some leaders tend to complicate leadership by generating too much irrelevant data. *Preactive* leaders focus only on the facts necessary to be effective and efficient in action-taking.

Law of Bestness. The Law of Bestness states that leaders should take the one best action in every situation they face. That one best action is defined as the action that best meets the needs of the situation at that time and in that place. See "Master Principle."

Leader. A leader is an action-taker: a person who takes action in the presence of others and influences them enough to cause a positive change in their behavior. See "Leadership."

Leadership. Leadership is action-taking: taking best Decision Actions in Choice Situations to positively influence the behavior of others while *directing* and *correcting* tasks. See "Leader."

Leadership Strategies. The general, overall set of values and actions a leader uses to *direct* and *correct* personal or group work toward a goal in the most effective and efficient way. See "Leadership" and "Strategy."

Leadership Style. The set of values (ethics, standards) that are guiding a leader's decision-making in a strategy. See "Strategy" and "Values."

Leadership Tactics. The specific types of actions and the specific sequence of actions that a leader uses to *direct* and *correct* personal or group work toward a goal in the most effective and efficient way. See "Tactics."

Leadership Types. There are two basic types of leadership: *Preactive, directive,* and *offensive-minded* leadership; and *Reactive, corrective,* and *defensive-minded* leadership.

Likely Cause (LC) Situation. One of the three *Preactive* situations: A weakness connected to the work in a Normal Work situation that is not causing trouble now but is threatening to cause it in the future. Likely Causes are prevented (neutralized) with Blocking Actions. See "Blocking Actions" and "Normal Work Situations."

Linkages. Textbooks call linkages of choices "decision trees," linkages of causes "fishbone diagrams," and linkages of trouble "daisy chains." The earlier situations in a linkage shape the later situations. Thus, the rule for leaders is to always to act as far *back* on a linkage in time and space as possible.

Masks. All of the situations in life and on the job are Choice Situations requiring a best decision. But they look different from one another becuase they can wear one of six different "masks." They can mask as either one of the three efficient situations or as one of the three inefficient situations. Situations can be identified by using the Identification Tables on pages 114-115. See "Situation" and "Identification Tables."

Master Principle of Satisfying Needs. The key to successful *Preactive* leadership. The Master Principle is satisfying the needs of situations and dictates that leaders should not take action by guesses or opinions, but by supplying situations with what they need. See "Law of Bestness."

Mental-Verbal Format Decision-Making. A *Preactive* Template for decision-making taught in Chapter 3. If a decision is simple and non-technical, a best choice can be made by discussing it with other people, thinking about it, and making a few notes. However, the mental process must still follow the eight logical steps taught in Chapter 3. See "Decision-Making."

Milestone Report. An audible and/or visual signal that measures (either continuously or at intervals) performance on a task and records the degree to which that performance meets the standards of the task.

Negative Leadership. Influencing other people enough to change their behavior in *negative* ways. This is done by taking ineffective, inefficient, or unethical actions in their presence. Changing people in either positive or negative ways are both forms of leadership, and there is probably as much negative leadership in the world as there is positive leadership.

Negative Thinking. Some leaders are afraid of negative thinking and avoid it. But a degree of professional negative thinking is required to use the technique of Trouble-Prevention. The launching pad of Trouble-Prevention is negative thinking for a constructive purpose. See "Trouble-Prevention."

Normal. The word *normal* comes from a root meaning a carpenter's square, a tool for measuring how square things are. Thus, *normal* work is work that is regular, routine, correct, and meeting all of its standards with no errors.

Normal Work (NW) Situation. One of the three *Preactive* situations. A routine, repetitive situation (task, assignment) undertaken with previously set, clear, and agreed on standards, and requiring a series of Working Actions that best satisfy its standards with the least risk of Future Trouble. See "Working Actions."

Objective. A standard with a special timeframe that measures the intermediate *targets* or stepping stones toward a goal in work, usually with a timeframe of less than a year such as monthly or quarterly. See "Goal" and "Standard."

Offensive-Minded Leadership. The use of *Preactive* strategies and tactics to *direct* tasks toward goals and objectives. The purpose of *offensive-minded* leadership is to keep trouble from starting that hasn't started yet. See "*Preactive* Strategies" and "*Preactive* Tactics."

Parts of Strategies. Strategies break into two parts: the type of values leaders use, and the type of actions leaders use.

Personal Habitual Strategies Test. A test in Chapter 11 showing the degree to which a leader's predominate actions are *Preactive* or *Reactive* during a work month.

Possible Cause. There are always several possible causes for Current Trouble, but only one True Cause. Leaders never assume without verification that a possible cause of trouble is the True Cause, and never take false correcting actions against possible causes. See "Current Trouble Situation," "True Cause," "Verification," and "False Correcting Action."

Preactive. The process of taking actions *before* trouble starts in work, and of *directing* work toward goals and objectives in a preventive way. Being *Preactive* means to accomplish as much work as possible without seeing trouble, mistakes, or errors in it. See "*Reactive.*"

Preactive **Actions.** Actions taken *before* trouble starts in work. The three *Preactive* actions are: Working Actions, Improving Action, and Blocking Action. See "*Reactive* Actions."

Preactive **Culture.** The leadership habit of taking action *before* trouble starts in work, and of focusing daily on the Effective-Efficient Situations in work. See "Habit" and "Effective-Efficient Situations."

Preactive Leadership. Action-taking by a process of focusing on the three Effective-Efficient Situations in work, while avoiding being forced to act on the three Inefficient-Ineffective Situations. *Preactive* leadership accomplishes as much as possible without seeing trouble, mistakes, and errors in work. A motto of *Preactive* leadership is: *Leading in the absence of trouble.* See "*Reactive* Leadership."

Preactive Situations. *Preactive* situations are the three Effective-Efficient Situations: The Normal Work situation, the Work Improvement situation, and the Likely Cause Situation. See "*Reactive* Situations."

Preactive Strategies. The general, overall set of leadership values and actions a leader uses to *direct* work toward goals by focusing on the three Effective-Efficient Situations in the workplace, and by action-taking *before* trouble starts in tasks and projects. See "Effective-Efficient Situations."

Preactive Tactics. The specific types of actions and the specific sequence of actions a leader uses to *direct* work toward goals using the three Effective-Efficient situations. See "Effective-Efficient Situations" and "Tactics."

Preactive Templates. See "Six *Preactive* Templates."

Preparing Action (PA). One of the three *Reactive* actions: Taking action by arranging people, things, and systems to wait to suppress the damage of Future Troubles if they happen, and to keep the damage from spreading if they do. A Preparing Action is a delayed Suppressing Action. See "Suppressive Action."

Prevention. See "Blocking Action."

Preventive Action. See "Blocking Action."

Preemptive Action. See "Blocking Action."

Pre- Words. The prefix *pre-* means before, and many words bearing this prefix indicate *Preactive* and preventive actions—ones that are taken before trouble starts.

Priorities. The word *priority* comes from a root meaning first and thus refers to doing first things first. Leaders should rank order tasks and do their most important tasks first. One way for leaders to have good priorities is to be strategically *Preactive*: to focus on the three Effective-Efficient situations in the workplace with *directive* and *offensive-minded* strategies and tactics. See "Right-Side up Priorities," "Time Management," and "Upside-Down Priorities."

Priority Setting. See "Priorities."

Probable Cause. A possible causes of a Current Trouble that has been identified through cause-finding as being the cause that probably created the trouble. A verification test is performed to prove that the probable cause is the True Cause before Correcting Action is taken. See "Cause-Finding," "Correcting Action," "Current Trouble Situation," and "Verification Test."

"Problem." One of the many synonyms for a Current Trouble situation. The word "problem" should be avoided because it is so fuzzy and so widely abused that it has become *meaningless* to leaders. See "Current Trouble Situation," "Fuzzy Words," and "Synonyms."

"Problem-Solving." A fuzzy phrase with so many meanings that it has become *meaningless* to leaders. The fuzzy phrase "problem-solving" can imply any (or all) of the seven leadership techniques taught in this book, making it too confusing to use. See "Fuzzy Words."

Process of Elimination. A phrase referring to the cause-finding process in the leadership technique of Cause-Removal. The process of elimination is the funnel effect that eliminates the possible causes of a Current Trouble and reveals the one True Cause of it.

Raising the Bar. See "Improving Action" and "Work Improvement Situation."

Reactive. The process of taking actions *after* trouble starts in work, and of *correcting* trouble in a suppressive way. *Reactive* leadership is the process of coping with trouble, mistakes, and errors that have already occurred in work. See "*Preactive.*"

Reactive **Actions.** Actions taken *after* trouble starts in work. The three *Reactive* actions are: Suppressing Action, Correcting Action, and Preparing Action. See "*Preactive* Actions."

Reactive **Culture.** The habit of taking action *after* trouble starts in tasks. See "Habits."

Reactive **Leadership.** Action-taking by focusing on the three Ineffective-Inefficient situations in work and forgetting to act on the three Effective-Efficient situations. *Reac-*

tive leadership spends its time fighting trouble in work. A motto of *Reactive* leadership is: "*Leading in the presence of trouble.*" See "*Preactive* Leadership."

Reactive Situations. The *Reactive* situations are the three Ineffective-Inefficient situations: the Current Trouble situation, the True Cause situation, and the Future Trouble situation. See "*Preactive* Situations."

Reactive Strategies. The general, overall set of leadership values and actions that a leader uses to *correct* trouble in work by focusing on the three Ineffective-Inefficient situations in the workplace and by focusing on action-taking *after* trouble starts in tasks. See "Ineffective-Inefficient Situations" and "Strategy."

Reactive Tactics. The specific types of actions and the specific sequence of actions that a leader uses to *correct* trouble in work with the three Ineffective-Inefficient situations. See "Ineffective-Inefficient Situations" and "Tactics."

Reconciling Standards. The word *reconciling* comes from a root meaning to make things compatible; thus, reconciling standards means to negotiate with superiors and coworkers to establish set, clear, and agreed on standards for tasks. See "Standard."

Re- Words. The prefix *re-* means to do over, and many words bearing this prefix indicate *Reactive* and suppressive actions that are taken after trouble starts in work.

Right-Side Up Priorities. These are the main priorities of *Preactive* leaders. They are assertive, creative, and focused on the three Effective-Efficient situations in work using *Preactive*, *directive*, and *offensive-minded* strategies and tactics. See "Upside-Down Priorities."

Simple-Pattern Format Decision-Making. A *Preactive* Template for decision-making taught in Chapter 3. It combines the features of the *Mental-Verbal Format* and the *Hard-Copy Format* Templates, and uses the best techniques of each. See "*Preactive* Templates."

Sine Waves. The peaks and valleys that Working Actions create as they progress through time and space toward goals. *Sine* is the Latin word for "curve," as in a curved wave. Thus, scientists call the sharp oscillations in work "sine waves." See "Normal Work Situations" and "Working Actions."

Situation. Anything requiring you to take some *action*, at some time, in some place, to some extent. Often abbreviated "sit" for short. All situations are generic Choice Situations and appear in life and on the job wearing six different "masks" or identities. See "Identification Tables."

Situation Statement. A written or verbal statement describing a *task* (an assignment or duty) that a person or a group has been asked to perform. Situation statements are the foundations of choice statements. See "Action Statement."

Six *Preactive* Conclusions. Six rules or guidelines for leaders which, if followed, make them predominately *Preactive* leaders. Leaders should strive to make these six Conclusions a personal habit. They are listed in the Contents, Chapters 11 and 12, and in the Appendix.

Six *Preactive* Templates. The six *Preactive* Templates give leaders six specific structures to use as operational weapons or tools to implement *Preactive* strategies and tactics. The six *Preactive* Templates are: The *Mental-Verbal Format*, *Hard-Copy Format*, and *Simple-Pattern Format* for decision-making in Chapter 3, and the *Standards-Clarifying Structure*, *Standards-Improving Framework*, and *Trouble-Preventing Formula* in Chapter 12. These templates are listed in the Contents, at the end of Chapter 13, and in the Appendix.

Smokescreen Standard. A standard that has a fuzzy fact or missing fact in one or more of its five *what-who-when-where-amount* factual categories. See "Clear Standard."

Smokescreen Statement. A situation statement or a choice statement that has a fuzzy fact or missing fact in one or more of its *what-who-when-where-amount* factual categories.

Standard. A word, phrase, or number that describes what a task needs and that measures the degree to which actions taken in that task satisfy those needs. There are three kinds of standards: goals, objectives, and current standards. The word *standards* is the most important word in leadership, and the development of previously set, clear, and agreed on standards is the most important process in leadership.

Standards-Betterment Technique. One of the three *Preactive* leadership techniques. This technique is taking Improving Actions to improve old standards in work and make them more recipient-oriented. See "Improving Action" and "Work Improvement Situation."

Standards-Clarifying Structure. A *Preactive* Template taught in Chapter 12 for setting clear and agreed on standards for a task. This is one of the most important templates a *Preactive* leader can learn and use. See "Standard," "Clear Standard," and "Smokescreen Standard."

Standards-Improving Framework. A *Preactive* Template taught in Chapter 12 for improving old standards in work. See "Improving Actions" and "Work Improvement Situation."

Strategy. The word *strategy* was originally a Greek military word referring to a general in the army, and thus refers to the general, overall set of values and overall kinds of actions a leader uses to *direct* and *correct* work toward a goal in the most effective and efficient way.

Strategic Leadership. See "Leadership Strategies" and "Strategy."

Suppressing Action (SA). One of the three *Reactive* actions. Taking action to control the damage of a Current Trouble situation and to keep the damage from spreading. See "Current Trouble Situation," "Suppressing Action," and "*Suppressive-Bias.*"

Suppressive-Bias. The tendency by leaders, organizations, and societies to design, develop, and support *suppressive* systems and actions instead of *preventive* systems and actions. It is easier to respond to trouble than it is to creatively think of ways to prevent trouble. See "Blocking Action" and "Suppressing Action."

Synonyms. Each one of the situations and actions in this book has many synonyms (other interchangeable words that means approximately the same thing). Thus, it confuses followers if leaders use synonyms. Only the terms for situations and actions that are described in the Identification Tables on pages 114-115 should be used by leaders.

Tactical Leadership. See "Leadership Tactics."

Tactics. The word *tactics* was originally a Greek military word meaning to arrange things in the proper sequence for a battle. Thus, the word tactics refers to the specific types of actions and the specific sequence of actions that a leader uses to *direct* and *correct* personal or group work toward a goal in the most effective and efficient way. See "Leadership Tactics."

Theory X and Theory Y. A set of leadership values first described by Dr. Douglas McGregor. McGregor found that all leaders tend to use one or the other of two opposing sets of values—either *Theory X* values, which are autocratic and control-oriented, or *Theory Y* values, which are democratic and team-oriented. Both sets of values are effective if a specific situation needs them. But a common mistake leaders make is applying *Theory X* (autocratic) values to every situation they face, regardless of its needs. Instead, leaders should apply *Theory Y* (teamworking) values as their default values whenever appropriate. See "Values."

Time Bomb. An analogy for the unintended negative consequences of Suppressing Actions. See "Booby Trap" and "Suppressing Action."

Time Management. Closely related to priority setting, time management says that leaders should allot their most and best time at work doing their most important things. However, many of the time management systems taught in textbooks are too complicated. An easier way for leaders to have good time management is to be strategically *Preactive*: to be assertive, creative, and focused on the three Effective-Efficient situations in the workplace. This in itself is better time management. After that, leaders can use the classic tools of time management as much as desired. See "Priorities," "Right-Side up Priorities," and "Upside-Down Priorities."

Total Quality Management. A quality control movement launched by Dr. William Edwards Deming of Yale with his best-selling book, *Out of the Crisis* in 1986.

Transitioning. A technique taught in Chapter 13 for purposefully becoming more *Preactive* and less *Reactive*. This is done by developing the habit of using the six *Preactive* Templates every week. See "*Preactive* Templates."

Trigger Report. An audible and/or visual signal that waits to be triggered by a Current Trouble situation and that activates a Suppressing Action to control the damage of that trouble. See "Milestone Report" and "Suppressing Action."

Trouble-Control Technique. One of the three *Reactive* leadership techniques. This is the technique of taking Suppressing Actions to control the damage of troubles and to keep the damage from spreading and growing worse. See "Suppressing Action" and "Current Trouble Situation."

Trouble-Prevention Technique. One of the three *Preactive* leadership techniques. This is the technique of taking Blocking Actions to preventively neutralize and preempt the Likely Causes of trouble in work. See "Blocking Action" and "Likely Cause Situation."

Trouble-Prevention Formula. A *Preactive* template taught in Chapter 12 for taking Blocking Actions in a task or project. See "Blocking Action."

Trouble-Readiness Technique. One of the three *Reactive* leadership techniques. This is the technique of developing Preparing Actions that wait to control the damage of Future Troubles if they occur and to keep the damages from spreading and growing worse. See "Preparing Action" and "Future Trouble Situation."

True Cause (TC) Situation. One of the three *Inefficient-Ineffective* situations: A verified trigger event that caused a person, thing, or system to break a previously set, clear, and agreed on standard it had previously been meeting. True Cause situations are removed with Correcting Actions. See "Correcting Action."

Types of Strategies. There are two basic types of strategies: those that are *Preactive, directive,* and *offensive-minded* and those that are *Reactive, corrective,* and *defensive-minded.*

Two Communication Traps. See "Fuzzy Words" and "Smokescreen Statements."

Up Escalator. When employees are led with *Theory Y* values for long periods of time, they become increasingly mature as if riding an up escalator. Leaders should therefore make *Theory Y* values their default leadership values and should only use *Theory X* values when absolutely necessary. See "Theory X and Theory Y" and "Down Escalator."

Upside-Down Priorities. These are the main priorities of *Reactive* leaders. This is a passive and shortsighted focus on the three *Ineffective-Inefficient* Situations in work with *Reactive, corrective,* and *defensive-minded* strategies and tactics. See "Right-Side Up Priorities."

Values. The set of ethics and standards a leader is using to guide his or her action-taking as an individual or as the leader of a group. A leader's default values should be *Theory Y* values. See "Theory X and Theory Y."

Verification Test. A step in the cause-finding process during the Cause-Removal Technique. After the probable cause of a trouble has been found, it must be verified before a

Corrective Action can be taken. See "Cause-Finding" and "Corrective Action."

Weakness. A synonym for a Likely Cause Situation. See "Likely Cause Situation."

"What If" Game. A *Preactive* technique that helps control the tendency to have *suppressive-bias*. When faced with a Likely Cause situation that appears unpreventable, leaders should ask: "But, *what if* it *could* be prevented?" Then they brainstorm for creative Blocking Actions that might be used. See "Blocking Action," "Likely Cause Situation," and "*Suppressive-Bias.*"

Words *Matter*. It is very important to use the proper terminology when talking about situations and actions in leadership. Each of the six situations and actions in the workplace is different from all the others and thus, no one can be a *Preactive* leader without calling situations and actions by their proper names.

Work-Accuracy Technique. One of the three *Preactive* leadership techniques. This is the technique of taking Working Actions to satisfy the clear and agreed on standards of tasks and moving tasks toward goals and objectives with the least risk of Future Trouble. See "Working Actions."

Work Improvement (WI) Situation. One of the three *Preactive* situations: An old standard in a task that is currently being met but that can be increased, decreased, or changed in a way that creates added value for recipients and that exceeds recipient expectations in a surprising new way. Work Improvements are made with Improving Actions. See "Improving Action."

Working Actions (WAs). One of the three *Preactive* actions. Working Actions taken to satisfy the previously set, clear, and agreed on standards in Normal Work situations and to move work toward goals and objectives with the least risk of Future Trouble. WAs are always spoken of in the plural because they are always multiple actions taken in a linkage. WAs are the foundational behavior of all employees in all organizations. See "Normal Work Situation."

Index

Bibliography
of Leadership Classics

Alderfer, Clayton P. *Existence, Relatedness, and Growth; Human Needs in Organizational Settings.* New York, NY: Free Press, 1972.

Argyris, Christopher (Chris). *Personality and Organization.* New York, NY: Harper & Row publishers, 1957.

Churchill, Winston S. *Never Give In! The Best of Winston Churchill's Speeches.* New York, NY: Hyperion, 2003.

Clausewitz, Carl von. *On War.* Princeton, NJ: Princeton University Press, 1976

Crosby, Philip B. *Quality is Free.* New York, NY: McGraw-Hill, 1979.

Deming, W. Edwards. *Out of the Crisis.* Cambridge, MA: MIT Press, 1986.

Fiedler, Fred E. *A Theory of Leadership Effectiveness.* New York, NY: McGraw-Hill, 1967.

Hersey, Paul and Kenneth H. Blanchard. *Management of Organizational Behavior: Utilizing Human Resources.* Englewood Cliffs, NJ: Prentice-Hall, Inc. 1977.

Herzberg, Frederick I. *The Motivation to Work.* New York, NY: John Wiley & Sons, 1959.

Homans, George C. *The Human Group.* New York, NY: Harcourt, Brace & World, 1950.

Imai, Masaaki. *Kaizen: The Key to Japan's Competitive Success.* New York, NY: McGraw-Hill, 1986

Juran, Joseph M. *Managerial Breakthrough.* New York, NY: McGraw-Hill, 1964.

Lawler, Edward E. *Motivation in Work Organizations.* Monterey, CA: Brooks/Cole Publishing Co., 1973.

Machiavelli, Niccolo. *The Prince.* New York, NY: New American Library, 1952.

Maslow, Abraham H. *Motivation and Personality.* New York, NY: Harper & Brothers, 1954.

McGregor, Douglas M. *The Human Side of Enterprise.* New York, NY: McGraw-Hill, 1960.

Porter, Lyman W. *Motivation and Work Behavior.* New York, NY: McGraw-Hill, 1975.

Shewhart, Walter A. *Economic Control of Quality of Manufactured Products.* New York, NY: D. Van Nostrand Company, 1931.

Stogdill, Ralph M. "Personal Factors Associated With Leadership: A Survey of the Literature." *The Journal of Psychology* 25 (1) (January, 1948), pp. 35-71.

Vroom, Victor H. *Work and Motivation.* New York, NY: John Wiley & Sons, 1964.

About the Author

DR. J. OWEN ALLEN is executive vice president of Laurel University in High Point, NC and dean of the School of Management where he also teaches as a full professor of management.

He holds AS and BS degrees with concentrations in science, business, literature, and history from the University of the State of New York at Albany; an LLB degree in American law and procedure from the LaSalle Law School at Chicago; an MA in philosophy from the California State University at Los Angeles, and a PHD in business administration and management with a concentration in organizational behavior from the Union University at Cincinnati. He did post-doctoral work in history at Oxford University, Oxford, England, and holds several professional certifications including Certified Management Consultant and Certified Speaking Professional.

Allen has taught many college courses at the bachelor's and master's degree levels, including classes in goals and objectives, communications, personal ethics, management principles, marketing, leadership, teambuilding, corporate strategy, work processes, and entrepreneurship.

Before entering the academic world, he was president of a private practice international management training and consulting business leading corporate seminars in such subjects as situation control, trouble solving, decision making, trouble prevention, stress reduction, teambuilding, personality profiling, motivation, and job matching.

Allen's successes as a management consultant include working with nine different state governors during the War on Poverty, and working with Wernher von Braun's NASA staff to help pave the way for the moon landings. In another consulting case, when an emergency task force of fifteen textile experts could not find the cause of a nationwide textile failure in five weeks of around-the-clock searching, Allen solved the case in one day.

Dr. Allen has traveled, trained, taught, and researched in over fifty countries, and more than 30,000 supervisors, managers, and executives have participated in his seminars from such clients as General Electric, General Motors, Hilton Hotels, John Deere, Kraft Foods/Sealtest, the U.S. Navy, Westinghouse, and many local, state, and federal government agencies. A full list of his clientele is in this Appendix.

In addition to receiving corporate, civic, and government honors and awards, Allen has also been included in *Who's Who in the South and Southwest*, *Who's Who in America*, and *Who's Who in the World*. This book is his eighth book. You may reach him at: OAllen@LaurelUniversity.edu.

Client List

American Business Women's Association

American Institute of Management Services

American Meter Company

American Society of Training & Development

Appalachian State University,
    Center for Continuing Education

Armtex, Inc.

Arsenal Digital Solutions USA

Badische Corporation, Division of BASF

Barclays-American Corporation

Bowman Gray School of Medicine

Burlington Industries, Inc., Domestics Division

Capital-Mercury Shirt Corporation

Centex Homes

Cone Mills Corporation—All Divisions and Plants

Continental Can Company, Inc.

Cutler-Hammer, Inc.—All Divisions and Plants

D.A.B. Industries, Inc.

Data Processing Management Association

Duke Energy, Duke Power Division

Eaton Corporation, Controls Division

ECA International, Inc.,
    Belize City, Belize; Guatemala City, Guatemala; Mexico
    City, Mexico; San Salvador, El Salvador; Tegucigalpa,
    Honduras

Fairchild Industries, Inc.

Foster-Sturdivant Company

Gellman Management Company

General Electric Corporation,
GE Capital, GE Data & Information,
GE Semiconductor, GE Space Systems,
GE Railcar Services

General Instruments, Inc.,
Guadalajara, Mexico

General Motors, GM Training Center

General Public Utilities Corporation,
Pennsylvania Electric Company

Graphic Systems International, Inc.

Gravely International Corporation

Hanes Corporation,
Hosiery and Knitwear Divisions

Hanes Dye & Finishing Company

Hilton Hotels Corporation

Hoover Universal,
Furniture Components and Hardware
Systems Divisions

Hughes Enterprises International

Hunt Manufacturing Company

Hyatt House Hotels

Ingersoll-Rand Company

John Deere Company, Consumer Products Div.

Kraftco Corporation,
    Sealtest Foods Division
Laurel University
Leggett & Platt, Incorporated
Leroy Springs Company
Lincoln Financial Group/Jefferson Pilot Financial
Low-Income Housing Development Corporation
Marion L. Eakes Company
Marsh Furniture Company
MRC Bearings / SKF Aerospace Industries, Inc.
NASA/ Jet Propulsion Laboratory
National Association of Accountants
National Association of Bank Women
Northwest Child Development Council
OMS International, Inc.,
        Beijing, China; Hong Kong;
        Seoul, South Korea
Resource Systems Corporation
RJR Archer, Inc.
R. J. Reynolds Industries, Inc.
Salem Spring Company
Sanitary Container Corporation
Singer Company—All Divisions and Plants
South Carolina Recreation & Park Society
Sprague Devices, Inc.

State Economic Opportunity Offices,
    Georgia, Iowa, Kentucky, Missouri,
    Nebraska, New Jersey, New York,
    North Carolina, South Carolina

St. Xenia's Foundation, Inc.,
    Moscow and St. Petersburg, Russia

Stewart-Warner Corporation,
    Bassick-Sack Division

Tultex Corporation

Union Institute and University

U.S. Community Services Administration

U.S. Department of Defense

U.S. Department of Energy

U.S. Department of Health, Education,
    and Welfare

U.S. Navy

Varco-Pruden, Inc.

Wachovia Bank & Trust Company

Wake Forest University, Babcock Graduate School
    of Management

Western Electric Company, Inc.

Westinghouse Electric Corporation,
    Power Generation Division

Wilmington Delaware Housing Authority

Personal Growth
as a *Preactive* Leader

So that readers of this book can experience greater personal growth as *Preactive* leaders, an online course in the techniques of *Preactive* leadership is available from the School of Management at Laurel University, High Point, North Carolina.

Participants in the course can earn either full Academic Transcript Credit of 3.0 credits toward a degree, or can earn a Certificate of Completion with 2.0 CEUs. The course uses this book as a text, and helps participants gain a personal mastery of *Preactive* leadership through online practice and application of the techniques. For more information, contact:

The School of Management
Laurel University
1215 Eastchester Drive
High Point, NC 27265-3115 USA
Phone: 336.887.3000
Fax: 336.889.2261
Toll Free: 855.528.7358
www.LaurelUniversity.edu
Contact Admissions: Admissions@LaurelUniversity.edu
Contact the Author: OAllen@LaurelUniversity.edu

527